Horrors of Slavery

subterranean lives

Chronicles of Alternative America

Bradford Verter, series editor

Subterranean Lives reprints first-person accounts from the nineteenth and twentieth centuries by members of oppositional or stigmatized subcultures; memoirs by men and women who lived, whether by circumstance, inclination, or design, outside of the bounds of normative bourgeois experience. They include tramps, sex workers, cultists, criminals, drug addicts, physically disabled people, sexual minorities, bohemians, revolutionaries, and other individuals who have survived on the margins, within the interstices, and across the boundaries of American society. Each volume presents either a book-length memoir or a selection of shorter texts in their entirety, together with an introduction and notes.

Autobiography of an Androgyne, Ralph Werther
Scott Herring, editor

The Hasheesh Eater: Being Passages from the Life of a Pythagorean,
Fitz Hugh Ludlow
Stephen Rachman, editor

Horrors of Slavery: or, The American Tars in Tripoli, William Ray
Hester Blum, editor

The Road, Jack London
Todd DePastino, editor

With the Weathermen: The Personal Journal of a Revolutionary Woman,
Susan Stern
Laura Browder, editor

Horrors of Slavery

or,

The American Tars in Tripoli

William Ray

Edited and with an Introduction by Hester Blum

Rutgers University Press
New Brunswick, New Jersey, and London

Library of Congress Cataloging-in-Publication Data

Ray, William.
Horrors of slavery, or, the American tars in Tripoli / William Ray ; edited and with an introduction by Hester Blum.
p. cm. — (Subterranean lives)
Includes bibliographical references.
ISBN 978-0-8135-4412-0 (hardcover : alk. paper) — ISBN 978-0-8135-4413-7 (pbk. : alk. paper)
1. Ray, William. 2. United States. Navy—History—Tripolitan War, 1801–1805—Personal narratives. 3. Slavery—Africa, North. 4. Philadelphia (Frigate) I. Blum, Hester. II. Title. III. Title: Horrors of slavery. IV. Title: American tars in Tripoli.
E335.R39 2008
973.4'7092—dc22
[B]

2008007763

A British Cataloging-in-Publication record for this book is available from the British Library.

Horrors of Slavery was first published by Oliver Lyon in Troy, New York in 1808.

Visit our Web site: http://rutgerspress.rutgers.edu

Manufactured in the United States of America

Contents

Acknowledgments

I wish to thank the American Antiquarian Society, particularly Joanne Chaison and Caroline Sloat; Sandy Stelts of the Penn State Special Collections Library, who secured a copy of William Ray's *Poems* for me; and the Library Company of Philadelphia, where I first read *Horrors of Slavery*. Brad Verter invited me to propose an edition of a Barbary captivity narrative, and I am grateful for his guidance in the early stages of this project. I thank Kendra Boileau as well for her initial help with the edition. I also owe thanks to my fellow speakers on a panel addressing piracy at the 2006 American Historical Association Conference: Gillian Weiss, Larry Peskin, and especially Isaac Land, the panel's organizer; this edition is the indirect result of that panel. Samantha Guss transcribed *Horrors of Slavery* in its entirety, and I am lucky to have had her invaluable assistance. The English Department at Penn State University provided research support to make this edition possible, and I thank my terrific colleagues and students.

I am very grateful to Leslie Mitchner for her expertise and insight, and thank Rutgers University Press for its willingness to publish noncanonical works of literature.

I am most thankful, as ever, to my daughter Adelaide and to Jonathan Eburne, whose own occasional rhymes have all of William Ray's wit and none of his venom.

Introduction

In *Horrors of Slavery* (1808) William Ray describes his experience as a captive American sailor in North Africa during the Tripolitan War (1801–1805), the first military encounter of the United States with the Islamic world. Ray had been a schoolteacher and a failed shopkeeper in New York State in the 1790s. In poverty and near-suicidal desperation after his hopes of securing a newspaper editorship in Philadelphia were frustrated, he enlisted on a U.S. frigate bound for the Mediterranean in 1803. Along with more than three hundred crewmates, he spent nineteen bitter months in captivity after his ship, the *Philadelphia*, ran aground in the harbor of Tripoli and was captured. Imprisoned and consigned to hard labor, Ray witnessed—and chronicled—many of the signal moments of America's military engagements with Tripoli and the other North African Barbary states. This conflict came at a late moment in the broader, centuries-long struggle between the Barbary states and Europe. His narrative describes the trauma of his enslavement, focusing on the poor conditions the American prisoners faced, as well as how their captivity registered within the broader context of the Tripolitan economy and society. But Ray's complaints are not solely with the Tripolitan Pasha, or the Bashaw, as he calls him (this introduction follows Ray's usage), or with Barbary piracy more generally. His account details the abuses inherent in the American naval system of discipline and hierarchy as well. Throughout his captivity narrative, and in his post-captivity writings, Ray decries injustice in all forms. *Horrors of Slavery* brings to light a little-known yet crucial episode in the early history of American relations with Islamic states, and provides a searing condemnation of tyranny, whether practiced by Barbary pirates, American naval officers, or societal and political institutions more broadly.

Ray came to terms with the "horrors" of his captivity by writing about his experience while still incarcerated in Tripoli, in modern Libya. He would continue to write, in a variety of media and on a variety of topics, upon his return to New York State after his redemption. *Horrors of Slavery* is unusual, both in its tone and in its content, within the context of the dozen or so Barbary accounts also published at the turn of the nineteenth century. These include captivity narratives by John Foss and James Leander Cathcart, Algerine captives; Jonathan Cowdery, a Tripolitan captive; and James Riley and Judah Paddock, Saharan captives, among others.[1] For one, while most former captives were primarily scandalized by North African society, Islam, and their own treatment, Ray finds much to condemn in Western, Christian nations as well. Another difference lies in his narrative's titular emphasis on "slavery," which is likely a gesture toward the abolition of the slave trade in the United States in 1808, the same year his narrative was published. His attention to injustice in a comparative context is not typical, and the form of his narrative similarly resists easy categorization. By turns a captivity narrative, naval memoir, ethnographic study, political and diplomatic history, reformatory class polemic, and poetry collection, his account reflects many different genres of literary production. Most notably, Ray uses a form employed by two indigenous American types of literature: the Indian captivity narrative and the slave narrative. No matter the mode, his voice is distinct: prickly, humorous, and always provocative. Ray is aware that as an ordinary sailor, rather than a captain or commodore, he was not endowed with the literary authority that was a perquisite of higher status. But he does not shy away from this fact, instead claiming his own experience as endorsement enough.

We see this most clearly in the final lines of the lengthy poetic "Exordium," or opening statement, in which Ray anticipates criticism and promptly refutes it:

> If in the following, then, you find
> Things not so pleasing to your mind,
> And think them false, why, disbelieve them;
> Errors of weakness? then forgive them;
> And let our suff'rings and abuses
> For sev'ral *facts* make some excuses;
> And when you're captur'd by a Turk,
> Sit down, and write a better work.

The closing couplet is representative of the combative yet playful tone throughout Ray's writings. These final lines stress that his experience is its own authority, one that grants him literary license. More broadly, the "Exordium" itself is representative of his remarkable literary style: it is hard to imagine another American first-person narrative of experience, for example, opening with 421 lines of verse. Such diversity and inventiveness of form is reflected in his further forays in the wider sphere of letters. His later writings include poetry, an autobiographical sketch, and a novel entitled *Sophia; or, The Girl of the Pine Woods*; he also edited three local newspapers in upstate New York and had a habit of writing long, spirited letters, partly in verse. From his humble beginnings, Ray stands as provocative figure within the early stages of nineteenth-century America's professionalization of authorship.

Ray's attention to the inequities inherent in social classes and hierarchies is central to his ethic. In addition to offering a compelling history of a little-known war whose impact, until recently, has registered mostly in military and political annals, *Horrors of Slavery* presents the valuable perspective of an ordinary seaman concerned with the rights of citizens and the injustices of the U.S. Navy. The first third of Ray's narrative makes a case for the increased application of the ideals of revolutionary liberty to the welfare of sailors and other disenfranchised Americans, alternating fervent moral appeals with sentimental and sensational tales of the tyrannical treatment of his shipmates. Early in his narrative he condemns chattel slavery in America within the context of his ongoing concern with hypocrisy, writing in the "Exordium,"

> Are you republicans?—away!
> 'Tis blasphemy the word to say—
> You talk of freedom?—out, for shame!
> Your lips contaminate the name.
> How dare you prate of public good,
> Your hands besmear'd with human blood?
> How dare you lift those hands to heav'n,
> And ask, or hope to be forgiv'n?
> How dare you breathe the wounded air,
> That wafts to heav'n the negro's pray'r? . . .
> And while you thus inflict the rod,
> How dare you say there is a God
> That will, in justice, from the skies,
> Hear and avenge his creatures' cries?

Such rhetoric is a strategic move in his broader polemic against those who pay lip service to the standard of freedom; although a lifelong Republican, he doesn't spare his own political party from criticism.

Once Ray turns to his service aboard the *Philadelphia* and his captivity, he provides fascinating parallels between the sufferings sailors endure at the hands of both their Christian officers and their Muslim captors. He equates the use of flogging by the U.S. Navy, for example, with the use of the bastinado (a form of torture involving whipping of the feet by a cudgel of the same name) by the Bashaw's men. The middle third of the book also provides an examination of daily life in Tripoli and in Ottoman North Africa that is by turns caustic and humorous; this account is revelatory with regard to the formation of American perspectives on the Muslim world. Ray's analysis is drawn both from his personal observation as a sailor and a captive, and from existing ethnographic accounts of the manners and customs of North Africa. He mixes dispassionate reports of social, political, and economic institutions with more heated descriptions of the Bashaw's regime. In one instance, he offers a critique of the Bashaw's castle. "Like the government," he writes, the castle "is built on ruins, without either taste, elegance, or grandeur; and exhibits an apposite specimen of barbarian folly" (chapter XII). Whereas other Barbary captives play to prurient curiosity in their narratives by invoking the mythical harems of Muslim men, Ray dismisses such interest by pointing out that few Tripolitan men can justify the expense of multiple wives. Furthermore, he shows sympathy for the poor treatment of Jews in Tripoli and throughout the Near East. Throughout his description of his captivity, he employs a comparative perspective; this may be seen most immediately in his extensive citation of, correction of, and commentary on the account of Tripolitan captivity provided by Jonathan Cowdery, ship's doctor on the *Philadelphia*. Cowdery's *American Captives in Tripoli* had been published in 1806, and Ray attacks the officer-class doctor for not being mindful of the extra suffering experienced by the non-officers in captivity.

The narrative's final third reprints key diplomatic correspondence of the Tripolitan War, thus supplementing Ray's impassioned personal account with an official narrative of the Barbary conflicts. These appended documents reveal both the Tripolitan Bashaw's greed and insecurity, and the American officials' accommodations and missteps. Indeed, Ray accuses the American officers of incompetence and "reprehensible conduct." His headnote to the diplomatic correspondence explains:

> What I have before asserted respecting the reprehensible conduct of many of our naval officers, will be fully substantiated, in the subsequent pages, by witnesses of the highest credibility, and from official documents—*not to be disputed.* Read the official delinquency of Commodore Morris—read his criminal abuse of David Valenzin, the unfortunate Jew—read the tardiness and pusillanimity of the voluptuous Commodore Barron—read the intriguing pacifications of Lear, sanctioned by Barron, in giving General Eaton orders to evacuate Derne five days previous to his failing from Malta to enter on his negociations with Tripoli—read the report of the committee of Congress on the claim of the Ex-Bashaw, and also that of David Valenzin, where many highly interesting facts are developed—read ten thousand other corroborating testimonies, and then say whether I have been too severe in attaching a general, though not universal censure to our naval commanders, and their subordinate myrmidons. (chapter XIV)

Ray takes up the cause of David Valenzin, a Jewish merchant in Tripoli who committed suicide while trying to recover property unfairly seized by U.S. naval forces. In doing so, Ray once again denounces American actions that seem to betray the nation's principles of justice. Throughout, his lively poetry provides an alternative narrative of the events his prose describes, and he appends to *Horrors of Slavery* a selection of his post-captivity poems.

Ray's Early Years

William Ray was born on December 9, 1771, in Salisbury, Connecticut. It was "the middle of a very hard winter," he recounts dramatically, "in order to show me, I suppose, that my birth was to be portentous of my fate—that I should have to experience the coldness of friendship, the frost of disappointment, and to struggle through the snow-drifts of adversity."[2] Around the age of nine or ten Ray heard the calling of his literary Muse, and his first production was a funeral ode on the accidental death of a playmate; his younger sister had died shortly before. The elegy seems to have been a favorite form for Ray as a juvenile. We learn from the late nineteenth-century autobiography of Thurlow Weed, the New York journalist and politician, that Ray's youthful poetry had made him a "poet of considerable temporary celebrity." Weed cites a poem "familiar to children of that generation, found in juvenile picture-books," which was "a lament on the death of a canary bird, commencing:—" 'My bird is dead," said Nancy Ray, / "My bird is dead, I cannot play." ' "[3] Ray's early poetic efforts were modeled after the religious verse of Isaac Watts and Edward Young, eighteenth-century English poets whose works would likely have been a part of his school curriculum. Occasional verse was a popular and often-practiced genre in the late eighteenth and early nineteenth centuries, and Ray's embrace of the form is not unusual; what is striking is how he continues to privilege poetry as a means of expression throughout his life, even when writing the narrative of his captivity.

When he was ten years old his father, a farmer, moved the family to a then-unsettled part of the Hudson River Valley in New York State, where Ray would live for most of his life. At the time, he writes, he felt "literally buried in the woods for several years, without much chance of gratifying my passion for classical studies" (*P* 206). The country schoolteacher he had in New York was "captious and despotic," fond of flogging the boys; it is hard not to think of Ray's later experience with despotism and flogging when reading such an account, as he surely did when composing it. Studying independently, Ray devoured *Paradise Lost* and strove to imitate the styles of Alexander Pope's "An Essay on Man" and Samuel Butler's *Hudibras*. The influence of Butler's satirical and polemical tone, in particular, can be seen throughout Ray's writings, especially in his long poetic "Exordium" in *Horrors*. Ray goes on to cite *Hudibras*, Milton, Pope, and Watts (the English hymn writer to whose work his youthful poetry had been compared) as objects of his imitation in a later comic poem. It was around this time that Ray began exercising his poetic wit to effect social change. He describes a local man who would beat his wife unmercifully, to the distress of the neighbors. Ray "had the vanity to think that [he] could raise the laugh against him, and gain some applause among the neighbors by lashing him in doggerels" (*P* 212). The resultant rhymes proposed tarring and feathering the abuser and running him out of town on a rail. This was not Ray's only "literary squabble," as he continued his habit of writing "long string[s] of bombastic rhymes" in response to "poetical challenge[s]" (*P* 213, 215–216). His "Biographical Sketch" in his collected *Poems*, in which he quotes from these youthful poetic battles at length, shows how Ray held on to the memory of past wrongs for decades afterward.

More broadly, his description of his poetical skirmishes reveals several important details about the state of the literary public sphere at the turn of the nineteenth century. While his juvenile elegies seem to have been published, there is no indication that Ray's attack poems found print in the years before he went to Tripoli. Instead, they were likely passed among individuals, achieving a kind of coterie circulation. Since his targets were local men (from the abusive husband to a "young coxcomb" whom Ray insults), we can infer that the sphere of his literary influence was likewise local. This would remain the case to a certain extent even after Ray's Barbary captivity, when his works would be frequently published within New York State and its surroundings, but less widely nationally. Such a circumstance was not principally a reflection on the popularity or quality of his literary effort. In the late eighteenth and early nineteenth centuries the print public sphere was still relatively local and intimate, as individual printers and newspaper publishers in each community usually determined what would be available to a given reader. Not until the technological, economic, and distributional advances of the post-1830s would mass publishing on a national scale become widespread. Thus, Ray's youthful forays into public writing would necessarily be directed at an audience of neighbors and community members. But it is nevertheless striking—and equally indicative of this historical moment—that he chooses literature as a means to challenge others, rather than using direct confrontation or force.

In 1790, at nineteen, Ray became a schoolteacher in Dover, New York, and tried his hand as a clerk. He survived a bout of smallpox and opened a country store in 1792, but an embargo the following year frustrated his shopkeeping venture. By his own account, he spent the next five or six years dodging creditors after his business partner fled to Canada; in these years he took "a very imprudent step" (given his financial situation) by marrying. Around this time he read Voltaire, Thomas Paine, and Volney (or Constantin François de Chassebœuf), whose Enlightenment humanism, religious skepticism, and rationalism affected him deeply. The influence of such writings strongly marks *Horrors of Slavery*. Indeed, his reflections on Voltaire's and Paine's notions of reason and humanity (as detailed in the "Biographical Sketch" in *Poems*) can stand as a digest for the views of authority that Ray expresses in the account: "the Christian religion was like all others, the instrument which power used to subdue resistance, either by force or persuasion" (*P* 219). In Ray's sense of the abuses performed in the name of Christian values of obedience to authority, we might see a comparison to the observations made by chattel slaves and abolitionists in America on the abuses of Christianity under slavery.

Other than his commercial setbacks, Ray's activities leave little trace in the historical record in the decade between his shop's failure and his naval service; he resurfaces only in 1803, the year of his fateful enlistment on the *Philadelphia*. In that lost decade, though, he must have distinguished himself in some literary or intellectual fashion, since he had the prospect of a job as the editor of a Philadelphia newspaper, for a wage of $30 a month. At the age of thirty-one, married and father to a young girl (he would eventually have three daughters), Ray traveled from New York to seek the editorial position, but was delayed by illness. When he finally arrived in Philadelphia in the spring of 1803, he found that the newspaper opportunity had been given to another, and he fell into despair: "I had been sick among strangers until I had expended the last solitary cent I was commander of, and not yet restored to health; but was in a debilitated state of convalescence," he recalled; "I tried every mean, and exerted every faculty in my power to obtain employment, but in vain" (chapter II).

This disappointment found him "exhausted by lassitude and woe, pondering with gloomy solicitude on my deleterious fate"; he confessed that his own poor decisions—his "imprudence, vice, intemperance, and prodigality"—had led him to this state (chapter II). He wandered to the banks of the Delaware River, entertaining thoughts of suicide; there, like Herman Melville's Ishmael (likewise a former schoolteacher), Ray chose to go to sea as a substitute for—or a means of—killing himself: "I enter'd, in hopes with America's foes, / Some dang'rous, warm conflict to find; / For anxious was I, at that time, to expose / A life I'd have gladly resign'd" (chapter II). On June 13, 1803, he enlisted as a marine private on the U.S. frigate *Philadelphia*, commanded by William Bainbridge. At the time, America's conflict with Tripoli and the other Barbary powers was, as Ray describes it above, "warm." Rather dramatically, he characterizes his enlistment as analogous to impressment, the reviled British policy of forcible recruitment into maritime service. He felt degraded by his enlistment, which he believed was forced upon him by circumstance. He took great offense that "a man driven from his family and friends by a ruthless hord of exorbitant, vindictive, and insatiable creditors; destitute of all pecuniary resources—of no mechanical occupation, or professional employment—unaccustomed and unable to perform manual labour—among suspicious and inhospitable strangers, more void of humanity than Turkish Barbarians, should be brought to as great an extremity of abject misery" as to join the navy (chapter II). Such rhetoric is typical of Ray, aptly described by one historian as a "professional martyr."[4] His service aboard ship and in Tripoli would bear out his bitterness; for while the forms of his literary response to captivity may have been exceptional, his experience with Barbary captivity was not unique.

The Tripolitan War

The Barbary states of North Africa, including present-day Algeria, Libya, Morocco, and Tunisia, took their name from the region's Berber natives and from the "barbarity" that Christian nations attributed to Africa's Islamic powers. The region's inhabitants were known among Ray's fellow captives as "Turks," a reference to the Ottoman Empire's centuries-long occupation of the area. (To "turn Turk" meant to convert to Islam, and several of Ray's shipmates would do just that in order to secure improved treatment and freedom from captivity—at the price of permanent residence in North Africa.) The Tripolitan War, the subject of Ray's narrative, represented an escalation of an ongoing conflict between America and the North African states that had begun in 1784. Yet the preamble to this conflict had been written centuries earlier in the first European encounters with piracy.[5] The Barbary powers had been much feared in the Mediterranean and Atlantic world for hundreds of years, based on their practice of taking captives and demanding money for their redemption and for protection from future seizure. Barbary captives of literary note include Miguel de Cervantes, John Smith, and the fictional Robinson Crusoe. Most European states paid what was known as "tribute" (in the form of cash or gifts) to the North African principalities. It is estimated that from the sixteenth to the nineteenth centuries, over one million Europeans were taken captive by Barbary pirates.

Prior to America's declaration of independence from Britain, American sailors had been included in the protections from piracy held by the British empire; afterward, American ships became vulnerable to piratical attack. The threat was especially acute to a new nation whose naval strength had been largely expended in the Revolution, and whose finances were too scant to afford to pay preemptive tribute to the Barbary states. American sailors therefore were at the mercy of the North African pirates in the years after the Revolutionary War; between 1785 and 1820 over seven hundred Americans would be taken captive. The first American ship taken was the *Betsey*, which was seized by Morocco in 1784 and redeemed in a settlement treaty, the first U.S. treaty with a non-European nation. Next, the *Maria* and the *Dauphin* were captured by Algerian (or "Algerine," the descriptor in use at the time) rovers in 1785. The crews of the *Maria* and the *Dauphin* would remain in Algiers for eleven years, the longest-held captives in Barbary. Among the Algerine captives was James Leander Cathcart, who would later become consul to Tripoli; Ray's narrative reprints several of his diplomatic letters to the secretary of state. In his posthumously published journal Cathcart expressed his fellow Algerine captives' sense that they were forgotten, indirect victims of the Revolutionary War: "Why are we left the victims of arbitrary power and barbarous despotism, in a strange land far distant from all our connections, miserable exiles from the country for which we have fought, forgotten by our contemporaries who formerly used to animate us in all our expedition with tales of liberty?"[6] In 1786, in the midst of debates about tribute payment for the release of the captives in Algiers, Thomas Jefferson wrote to John Adams that he "should prefer the obtaining of [peace] by war," explaining that "Justice" and "Honor" favored force over "buy[ing] peace."[7] Nevertheless, the Algerine captives were redeemed in 1796 for $1 million, one-sixth of the nation's budget at the time. Such payment was necessary in part because the United States had no navy to speak of after the Revolution; one result of the Algerine crisis was that Jefferson uncharacteristically urged the formation of a new navy and a marine corps to combat future piracy.

In 1801 the Tripolitan pasha, Yusuf Qaramanli (or Jusef/Joseph Caramanli/Caramanly, as Ray and his contemporaries variously rendered the Arabic name), impatient with an American government that had defaulted on its $225,000 tribute payment, captured several ships and chopped down the American flagpole in Tripoli on May 14, 1801—this, after William Bainbridge had been compelled to fly the Ottoman flag on a U.S. ship when arriving in Constantinople in 1800. In its military response, the navy sent the frigate *Philadelphia* as part of a squadron to help enforce a blockade of the port of Tripoli. Ray was a crewmember of that ship, which was captured by the Bashaw's forces after it ran aground, to U.S. embarrassment, in the harbor on October 31, 1803. Imprisoned and initially consigned to hard labor, Ray later was a witness to the chaos spawned by the most-celebrated moment of the Barbary wars: an audacious nighttime raid on the Tripolitan-occupied ship, led by Stephen Decatur in February 1804. When Decatur destroyed the enemy's prize by setting fire to the *Philadelphia*, the American sailors suffered reprisals. As Ray reports, of later retribution "the infuriate Turks, wherever we met them, would strike, spit upon, and stone us.... The Turks told us that the Americans were all drunk, or they would not have ventured as they did, and fought so furiously" (chapter X).

The squadron led by American Commodore Edward Preble continued to bombard Tripoli throughout 1804; in the meantime, American military strategists turned to a different front. Yusuf Qaramanli had become Bashaw only after deposing his brother, Hamet (or Ahmed) Qaramanli, the rightful Bashaw. American consuls William Eaton and James Cathcart proposed backing Hamet—in exile in Egypt—in a coup attempt. With a force of only eleven Americans and roughly four hundred North African and European mercenaries, Eaton marched five hundred miles across the dessert to Derna, or Derne, east of Tripoli in what is now Libya. Eaton's force was able to take Derna in April 1805. By June of that year, however—before Eaton could continue his march to Tripoli—a settlement was reached to end the war and to redeem the American captives for $60,000. William Ray was among many who felt that Eaton's initiative and success had been squandered by the settlement and by the U.S. abandonment of Hamet Qaramanli, who remained in exile in Egypt. In *Horrors of Slavery* Ray even compares Eaton to the Spartan king Leonidas, known for his daring against a superior Persian force; he writes of Eaton, "The disinterested patriotism, the enterprize, the activity and the intrepidity of this second Laonidas, cannot be too highly appreciated, or too much extolled. Had he not been basely deserted by Com. Barron [Preble's replacement as commodore], who had promised to aid his exertions, he would unavoidably have marched triumphantly to Tripoli, and saved the United States 60,000 dollars, besides a large amount of national honour" (chapter XV). Despite the Eaton controversy, this settlement ended American conflict with Barbary for several years, although there would be a flare-up of discord during the War of 1812.

Captives in Tripoli

In *Horrors of Slavery* William Ray details his own experience of captivity, and reflects on the difference between the treatment given the common seamen and that given the officers of the *Philadelphia*. He acknowledges that his readers might be familiar with the journal of Jonathan Cowdery (1806), ship's doctor aboard the *Philadelphia*, but promises that his account will greatly amplify and correct Cowdery's brief narrative. Indeed, Ray's concerns extend far beyond the conditions of his captivity. He offers his narrative, he explains, "to prove that petty despotism is not confined alone to Barbary's execrated and piratical shores; but that base and oppressive treatment may be experienced from officers of the American, as well as the British and other navies; that our countrymen, as well as those of other nations, when invested with the robe and cockade of authority, can act the insolent tyrant, inflict tortures for petty offences, and often for no offences at all, and with a contemptible pride and brutal ferocity, that would disgrace the character of a savage despot, stamp an indelible stigma on the name of an American officer" (chapter I). Yet he assures his reader that his anger is not "the vindictive effusions of invidious resentment for personal injuries; for I never received the least chastisement while I was in the service." Instead, Ray writes, his concerns "originate from a sympathetic source, and from an innate abhorrence of every species of oppression" (chapter I).

This idea of sympathy, or a shared sense of fellow-feeling, is crucial to the opening chapters of his narrative. He tells two stories of unnamed, unfortunate men he meets, one of whom contemplates suicide after a thwarted love affair; the other becomes his shipmate on the *Philadelphia* after his own misfortune in love compels him to enlist. To the latter, Ray reports, he "felt [him]self attracted, by the mysterious magnetism of congenial sympathy" (chapter III). This sympathy is based in part on Ray's identification with the man, who as a typographer shares his experience in the world of letters. The two stories of woe related at the outset of *Horrors*, both unrelated to Barbary captivity per se, show Ray's familiarity with and skillful literary invocation of a broader contemporary interest in sympathy. American literature and culture of the late eighteenth and early nineteenth centuries was pervaded by representations of sympathetic or sentimental attachment, a notion that humans are bound together by affective relationships based on feeling. Contemporary Early American fiction overwhelmingly featured such affiliations, in novels such as William Hill Brown's *The Power of Sympathy* (1789), Susanna Rowson's *Charlotte Temple* (1794), and Judith Sargent Murray's *Story of Margaretta* (serialized 1792–1794). The power of feeling would continue to wield enormous influence throughout the nineteenth century in such hugely popular novels as Susan Warner's *Wide, Wide World* (1850), Harriet Beecher Stowe's *Uncle Tom's Cabin* (1852), and Maria Cummins's *The Lamplighter* (1854). Stowe's novel, like Ray's narrative, used the power of sympathy to advocate for social change.

In showing his ability to feel sympathy for the plight of others, and not just those in shared captivity, Ray might be strategically anticipating criticism that his outrage might issue from a congenitally bitter and isolated character (which if fact might have been the case, as the story of his life could suggest). His two tales of other men's woe also help to orient a reader in the familiar, as both tales are conventional within the period's literature. He even acknowledges as much in introducing the typographer, who like many figures in romantic fiction bears "something in his physiognomy indicative of merit superiour to his station"; Ray discovers, though, "that he was no Lord or Duke in disguise, as was common in the days of chivalry and romance, but a mechanic of no ordinary abilities" (chapter III). Note here Ray's embrace of the "mechanic" profession of this man, which he esteems above high rank. This is true even of the other sentimental tale he tells in the opening chapters, that of the thwarted and suicidal lover; he offers the second story as a "digression" that, "although it does not participate of the *wonderful*, like many novel tales," nevertheless "has the merit of not being imported from the manufactories of aristocracy" (chapter IV). Even in his employment of two conventional romantic narratives, he esteems the common over the elite.

These stories set the scene for Ray's turn to his naval experience, in which he details the harsh treatment received by the enlisted men, who board ship "sober as a gallows throng" (chapter V). Many of the common seamen had joined the navy out of financial hardship or other desperation, as Ray himself had, and he laments the state that would drive men to this recourse. He particularly chafes at having to follow inconsistent orders: "One officer orders a man to do one thing; a second immediately comes and orders him to do another thing: then he is flogged by the first for leaving his work, and ordered back to it: then served in the same manner by the second. A third comes—'what are you about, you d—'d puppy,' and orders him to a new place:—'not a word!' if he attempts to parley—'a rope's-end!' if he refuses to obey his officers *tacitly*—'no jaw, you d—'d scoundrel!' if he essays to reason, or complain of exorbitant commands—'stubborn villain!' if he looks serious—'impertinent one,' if he smiles" (chapter V). Flogging, by which a seaman was whipped using a rope or cat o' nine tails, was a source of special outrage for Ray and for sailors more generally; later in the nineteenth century, anti-flogging reforms would be instituted, led by advocates such as Richard Henry Dana, Jr., author of the bestselling *Two Years before the Mast* (1840). But during Ray's time it was a common punishment for falling asleep or back-talk, as well as for more serious offenses.

In support of his arguments throughout *Horrors of Slavery*, Ray invokes the ideals of liberty promised by the American Revolution. In one example, he protests the lack of redress for two sailors flogged for failing to say "sir" to an officer:

> Are such cruelties authorized by the constitution of our country? . . . Is it a crime so atrocious—a thing so degrading, to enter voluntarily into the service of the United States, that a man must be no longer considered as a citizen of America? And are citizens of this free country to be treated with as much contempt, as great barbarity, and as villainous injustice as the sable vassals of the West-Indies? . . . Or, is a man, when he is once on board a man of war, dead to all justice, to all humanity, to all sense of feeling? and must he be treated like a slave—an out cast of society—a villain—a beast? (chapter VI)

The comparison of sailors to slaves was not an uncommon one in maritime narratives of the nineteenth century, and the argument was used to support the anti-flogging reform movement. In Dana's sea narrative, to use one example, a sailor threatened with flogging tells the captain, "I'm no negro slave."[8]

Ray's complaints of poor usage of the common sailor in the U.S. Navy at the time are verified by many sailor accounts and other sources, the most striking of which can be found in the detail of a court-martial that occurred on June 23, 1804, aboard the ship *President*, part of the U.S. squadron in the Mediterranean. The sailor in question, Robert Quinn, wrote a letter of complaint about "horrid usage" to Commodore Barron, and this letter was judged mutinous for the following line: "some of our friends in America and other parts shall know of this [treatment] shortly and in time we hope to get redress—death is always superior to slavery—we remain your *unhappy slaves*." Quinn was spared death (the usual penalty for mutiny) at a court-martial supervised by William Eaton, but received the following sentence: "to have his head and eyebrows shaved, branded in the forehead with the word *Mutiny*, to receive three hundred and twenty lashes equally apportioned along side of the different ships of the squadron: during which time he shall wear a white cap with the label *Mutiny* in large capital letters inscribed on its front, and to be drummed on shore under a gallows in a boat towed stern foremost, by a boat from each ship in the squadron, as unworthy of serving under the flag of the United States."[9] Ray writes of similar cruel treatment throughout the *Philadelphia*'s passage to the Mediterranean.

While cruising off the harbor in Tripoli on October 31, 1804, the *Philadelphia* spied a Tripolitan ship and gave chase. At this point, Ray documents, his captain William Bainbridge expressed worry about the harbor's shallowness, but was assured by Lieutenant David Porter (who would later become a hero in the Pacific theater of the War of 1812) that the harbor was navigable. The *Philadelphia* struck bottom, however, and Ray sees a remarkable difference in tone from his officers after the ship became stuck and vulnerable: "I could not but notice the striking alteration in the tone of our officers. . . . It was no time now to act the haughty tyrant—no time to punish men for snoring—no time to tell men they had '*no right to think*'" (chapter VII). The Americans tried to come off the reef by lightening the ship (throwing its guns overboard), but to no avail. Ray and the seamen were shocked when the flag of the ship was struck, signaling surrender to the enemy, before significant damage had been done. They were dismayed by what they perceived to be insufficient courage on the part of their officers, and indeed, when Ray and the enslaved crew later met the Bashaw, Qaramanli disparaged Captain Bainbridge: "He [the Bashaw] said there was no necessity for throwing our guns overboard; that we might have known she would be got off, as soon as the wind shifted, and assured is she was already afloat—that if we had not struck our flag, they would not have ventured to board us, and highly ridiculed our captain's cowardice" (chapter VIII).

Upon their capture, Ray and the common seamen were separated from the officers, who enjoyed better treatment. At this point in his own narrative, as if to underscore this distinction, Ray turns to long quotations from Dr. Cowdery's, for which he provides commentary. While he affirms Cowdery's observations on many points, Ray is more likely to refute the doctor's perspective and experience, mocking him variously for his tone, small physical stature, and writing style (an example: "That the Doctor should have seen a 'burying ground, full of graves,' is very astonishing, indeed! It is as wonderful as if he had seen a town full of houses" [chapter IX]). Taking issue with the lack of inclusivity in Cowdery's use of the word *we*, Ray tells his reader, "Although the Doctor here makes no discrimination between men and officers, it must not be understood that he includes the former when he says *we*, excepting servants. . . . You will, therefore, please to remember, that when the Doctor says *we*, it is the very same as if he had said *we officers only*; for he does not think proper to descend to the task of relating how the crew were provided for, or whether they were but half alive or all dead" (chapter VIII). Ray would continue to feel that the officers, from Captain Bainbridge down the chain of command, did not advocate for the seamen sufficiently. Tripoli was, in fact, a city teeming with consuls working on behalf of the captives, and it was the Danish consul Nicholas Nissen—not the American consul—who became a special friend to the Americans in captivity.

Ray's descriptions reveal the heavy labor and poor nutrition forced upon the enslaved men. Bread, water, and olive oil were frequently their only food. The captives' tasks were various, and included lighter chores such as running errands, and more debilitating work such as raising wrecks from the beach, repairing walls, and building batteries; those with backgrounds in carpentry or blacksmithing were recruited to put their skills in the Bashaw's service. Similar labor was compelled from the other Barbary captives in North Africa in the period. For example, Robert Adams, a shipwreck victim held in the Sahara from 1810 to 1813, was employed in "building walls, cutting down shrubs to make fences, and working in the corn lands or in the plantations of tobacco."[10] Yet Ray was ultimately spared much of the more onerous work: on May 27, 1804, he was granted an exemption from labor by the Bashaw, in part because his fine penmanship and literary experience made him useful in other ways.

These skills helped Ray act as an organizer for his fellow crewmembers. He helped write a petition to the Bashaw, reasoning that if well fed the prisoners would labor more productively for the Tripolitans. When their weekly food allowance was reduced by their captors, there was "much dissatisfaction and murmuring among the men, respecting the division of their late rations." His solution borrowed from shipboard regulations: "I classed the men into messes of eight, and made them choose their messmates; then numbered the messes, as on board the ship. The meat was then cut up by two of the petty officers, and divided into as many heaps as there were messes" (chapter X). Later, when bread shortages sorely affected them, the seamen staged a prison hunger strike. "For several days we had been without bread or money, . . . and the men were unanimously determined not to labour any more unless one or the other was allowed us," Ray reports, and the tactic was successful; they continued to engage in collective action in other ways (chapter XI).

The shared sense of community felt by the captives was necessary to keeping up their spirits. One indication of the survival of their nautical wit and habit can be seen in the nicknames they give to their captors. The chief warden, Abdullah, was called Captain Blackbeard; the playful Soliman earned the moniker Scamping-Jack. A Greek warden was known as Bandy for his bow-legs, and an old Algerine with weak eyes earned the name Blinkard (chapter XI). Because of their feelings of solidarity, the American sailors were especially disdainful of the five members of their crew who betrayed their mates by becoming renegades or turning Turk—that is, converting to Islam to earn the Bashaw's favor. When the articles of peace were signed on June 3, 1805, thus ending the Tripolitan War, the Bashaw offered the five renegades the option to return to their country and to Christianity. Four of the five didn't recognize this as a test, and when they accepted the insincere offer were sent deep into the country under heavy guard, "horror and despair depicted in their countenances" (chapter XI).

Ray and his companions were happy to reward those who had been loyal to them, however, regardless of national affiliation. One Neapolitan (whose countrymen were frequent captives of the Barbary powers) had been kind to the Americans even as he worked for the chief warden, and the sailors cobbled together $300 by subscription in order to buy his release, which led to his work aboard an American ship. Ray could not resist, though, punctuating the story with a jab at the U.S. Navy, adding, "I have been informed, however, that when he found what severity was practiced in our service, he seriously repented of his leaving Tripoli!" (chapter XI). After nineteen months of severe captivity, all but six of the more than three hundred men from the *Philadelphia* survived their enslavement in Tripoli.

Publishing *Horrors of Slavery*

William Ray returned to America in August 1806, via the *Essex*, on which he had been named "poet laureate" while serving as ship's clerk after his June 1805 release from the Tripolitans. The independence song he wrote for the occasion, which was circulated in broadsides and newspapers, celebrated freedom from North African slavery while still noting the dangers of British impressment: "And never may the Tar be *press'd*," the song concludes, "*But in his fair one's arms*" (*P* 249). The pen that had served him during his Barbary captivity did not rest upon his liberation. In the spring of 1807 he published a poem that demonstrated that his concerns with fairness and justice likewise remained active. "On Reading the Debates of Congress Respecting Gen. EATON's Gold Medal" (later included in *Horrors*) addresses the postwar investigations into the conduct of William Eaton in his march to Derna at the close of the Tripolitan War. Ray begins with his characteristically caustic tone: "And is it then a subject of debate, / With these wise solons in the house of state, / Whether should Derna's conquerer stand or fall? / Or matchless bravery meet reward at all? / . . . Or should his trophies be by all forgot, / Mix with the rubbish of the times and rot!"[11] This poem, which the *Mercury* notes was "*Written at Gibraltar, by* William Ray, *one of the captives from Tripoli*," may have been intended in part as pre-advertisement for the proposed captivity narrative.

For example, on May 18, 1807, the *Vermont Precursor* announced that "Mr. *William Ray*, has issued Proposals for publishing a volume, entitled, *Horrors of Slavery; or, The American Tars in Tripoli*"; the proposed narrative would "contain about 300 duodecimo pages, and will be neatly bound and lettered: price one Dollar, payable on delivery." In addition to an account of the fate of the *Philadelphia*, the volume promised discussion of Tripoli and its inhabitants and of General Eaton's expedition, as well as "poetry on various subjects." A stanza of verse closed the advertisement, giving a specimen of Ray's ongoing concerns with the structural effects of tyranny: "Ye lurid domes! whose tott'ring columns stand, / Marks of the despot's desolating hand; / Whose weed-grown roofs and mouldering arches show / The curse of Tyrranny, a nation's wo; / In ev'ry ruin, ev'ry pile, I find / A warning lesson to a thoughtful mind."[12] Ray continued to advertise his narrative in New York and New England papers in the spring and summer of 1807, and most of the proposals specified that the volume would be published by subscription.

The subscription method, by which a reader would financially commit to the purchase of a book before it was actually published, was common, as many printers could not afford to produce works that did not have a guaranteed audience. The advertisements for *Horrors of Slavery* promised that the work "will be put to press as soon as a sufficient number of subscribers appear to defray the expense of publication."[13] (Significantly, the redemption or ransom process by which many Barbary and Indian captives were redeemed, whether in North Africa or in North America, was also a subscription method—such as had freed the kind Neapolitan.) The invitation to subscribe to *Horrors of Slavery* was not framed disinterestedly, as Ray composed a poetic address to potential readers: "No venal motive has the writer shewn, / The Author's benefit is all your own; / Subscribe, peruse the volume, and you'll find / Both pain and pleasure thrill the pensive mind; / Mark the strange thesis, count the loss and gain, / And feast on pleasure at th' expense of pain."[14] He frames the final couplet to suggest that the reader's intellectual "pleasure" will come at the cost of the trauma the author experienced.

Even as he appealed to the public in his newspaper writing, Ray sent personal applications to political figures. One of his poems in the *Albany Register*, "Song," was a celebration of the election of Daniel Tompkins as governor of New York State. Addressing a dozen long letters to Tompkins for over a year beginning in 1811, Ray petitioned for a political appointment and complained to him of his wrongs. Eventually, in August 1812, Tompkins gratified Ray with an appointment as quartermaster of New York's Third Brigade in Plattsburg; there is no evidence, however, that Ray participated in any battles in the War of 1812 while in this position. But Tompkins was not the only politician whom Ray approached. Aiming as high as possible, he sent copies of *Horrors of Slavery* to Thomas Jefferson and James Madison when each was president, and both replied to the gift with letters of praise for the volume (which Jefferson retained in his personal library). In turn, Ray used this correspondence to promote a hoped-for second edition, never issued, of his narrative. In fact, Ray wrote to Jefferson asking, remarkably, for a loan of $100, which he claimed was necessary to rescue his "late publication," presumably *Horrors*, from a "knavish printer" who would "sacrifice" the work. Provocatively, he asks the president for money to "redeem" his writing, employing language identical to that used with reference to the redemption of the Barbary captives.[15]

Jefferson does not seem to have replied to Ray regarding this request for money. Ray next turned his attention to James Madison, writing to the president in 1812 to remind him of the copy of *Horrors* Ray had sent him (along with a poetic epistle) and to appeal for a political appointment. As with Jefferson, Ray did not shirk from asking the sitting president for money, mentioning that "a small *pecuniary* donation would not be rejected."[16] When Madison apparently did not respond, Ray did not modulate his tone. Writing to him on October 4 of that same year, Ray presumed that Madison must not have received his gift of *Horrors of Slavery*, for, as he wrote with sarcasm, "I am not willing to suspect that the *Chief Magistrate* of a free people, who owes his political existence to the suffrage of men of all ranks, would treat with silent contempt the honest effusions or well-meant offering of one who has greatly suffered in the cause of that Government over which he presides."[17] Neither Jefferson nor Madison seem to have responded to Ray's petitions (not without reason), and in their silence Ray must have experienced anew the disappointment in American leadership he had felt so keenly while in Tripoli.

Ray's Final Years

In the remaining decade and a half of his life, William Ray would intermittently continue his newspaper and poetical work, while holding several different local offices and trying his hand at being a druggist and a novelist. The second newspaper he edited, the *Onondaga Gazette* (1816), displayed somewhat less partisanship than the pro-Republican *Reveille* had shown, while still paying attention to the affairs of the day. His third and final editorship was of the *Miscellaneous Register* (1822–1823) of Geneva, New York, where Ray moved in 1822. By then Ray eschewed any political stance, reporting that "it is unnecessary to say that Party Politics will find no place in our columns," as the *Register* prominently featured a Religious Department and a Moral Department, and was strongly in favor of temperence.[18] In it, Ray serially published his only known novel, *Sophia; or, The Girl of the Pine Woods* (serialized 1822–1823; published 1823).

Sophia is a sentimental novel about a girl who is pressured to marry a cruel lawyer in order to satisfy her father's creditors; the father, like Ray himself in his pre-captivity days, had run into debt after mercantile failures involving produce. Sophia is rescued by a stranger who proves to be one of her father's unintentional creditors, but their eventual happy marriage is delayed by vicious gossip about Sophia's supposedly compromised virtue and an erroneous newspaper report of the benevolent stranger's marriage. In all ways the novel reflects the conventions of sentimental fiction in the early part of the nineteenth century in America, in which love plots were constantly under threat from false rumors, financial insolvency, misrecognition, and imposture. In keeping with the tone of the *Register* more generally, *Sophia* displays little of Ray's vicious wit. This fact demonstrates that Ray could, when he desired to, modulate his tone to produce a narrative calculated for popular appeal. And indeed, it was a success, according to William Kable (who first identified Ray as the pseudonymously published author), going through at least four editions between 1823 and 1838. One of these editions was bundled with a few of Ray's less political poems, such as "The Onondaga Indian Chief," "The Plough Boy," and "Village Greatness"; a later edition packaged *Sophia* with a novel called *Lafitte; or The Barratarian Chief.*[19]

Ray's newspaper poetry was collected in a volume called *Poems, on Various Subjects, Religious, Moral, Sentimental and Humorous* (1821), which went through two editions; the second, in 1826, appeared shortly before he died. Both editions appended an autobiography as well as a description of his "captivity and sufferings among the Turks and barbarians of Tripoli," and "a description of the country, and the manners and customs of the inhabitants." The title of the collection is a conventional one, used by dozens of British and American writers in the eighteenth and nineteenth centuries; one such precursor was Phillis Wheatley, the enslaved woman whose poetry appeared as *Poems on Various Subjects, Religious and Moral* in 1773. While there is no evidence that Ray read Wheatley's work, he may have wished to align himself with the enslaved woman, as he did discuss his own captivity or enslavement in North Africa. Yet he stresses the "sentimental" and "humorous" qualities of his poetry in his own title. In any event, the conventional titles used by Wheatley and Ray, neither members of the literary elite, signaled their desire to include their work within a broader culture of letters.

"As a poet," one newspaper notice of *Poems* read, Ray "possesses genius of no ordinary cast," and other reviews were similarly appreciative.[20] Most of these reviews were in northeastern newspapers; few literary periodicals took notice of his poetical productions. The second edition of *Poems* featured more than the first, as well as an expanded sketch of Tripoli and Ray's experiences there. Yet he cut many of his more overtly political poems, apologizing for the hostility to Christianity evidenced by the "Exordium" to *Horrors* (which is reproduced in *Poems*). But even as Ray expresses regret for getting lost in the "mazes of sophistry" invented by "infidel writers," he condemns the printer's errors—caused by sloppy "boys"—that contributed, he believes, to making his work "unintelligible where it was before plain, and contemptible where it was before tolerable" (*P* 200). Even in confessional mode, Ray always kept a target of scorn in view.

Ray died of unknown causes at the age of fifty-four on July 29 or 30, 1826, in Auburn, New York. Obituary notices, which ran in newspapers from Baltimore to Salem, Massachusetts, granted him some measure of the literary credit he had sought so hungrily in life. The death notice in the Washington, D.C., *Daily National Journal* is representative of the sentiment found in his obituaries: "The effusions of his pen have long rendered him celebrated throughout our country. . . . Some of his fugitive productions obtained for him a considerable eclat in the literary world."

Remarking, as most papers did, the troubled financial situation in which Ray left his family, the *Journal*'s notice promoted the recent edition of his *Poems:* "He has lately published a neat pocket volume of his poems, which should be owned by every American patron of genius, particularly, as we presume, in becoming possessed of it, he will contribute to the relief of his widow and daughters, who are left to struggle alone in embarrassed circumstances."[21]

Whether or not the family found their way out of financial hardship is unknown, but Ray's solid reputation as a poet endured for some decades after his death. Anthologies of American literature, and especially poetry collections, made space for his poems; in these volumes, he was often identified first and foremost as a survivor of Barbary piracy. Evert and George Duyckinck's *Cyclopædia of American Literature*, for one, inaccurately glossed Ray as "one of the 'Algerine Captives'" and gave as a sample of his work the song hailing independence that he wrote as the captain's clerk and laureate of the ship *Essex*, on which he made his way home from Tripoli.[22] Another of his poems, an ode to the navy, was reprinted in an 1842 anthology of verse on national subjects.[23] Yet "Village Greatness" was mentioned favorably in the *Lowell Offering* in January 1844, suggesting that Ray's audience was not confined to those interested in martial topics.[24] He was included in the anthology *Poets of Connecticut* in 1843; was referred to as "the celebrated Yankee poet" in the collected speeches of a New York politician in 1867; and, perhaps most provocatively, appeared in an 1847 collection of prison writing.[25]

But by the twentieth century Ray had fallen back into an obscurity that persists to this day. Other than the original 1808 edition, the only version of his Barbary narrative that has ever been reprinted was as a supplemental insert—"Extra No. 14"—to the *Magazine of History*, which in 1911 issued *Horrors of Slavery* under the title *The American Tars in Tripolitan Slavery*.[26] The title change may indicate that the word *slavery* would have needed to be more specifically modified for a post-Reconstruction audience. The is little indication, however, that the 1911 reissue attracted much notice. Ray's name has only resurfaced in recent years as historians and literary scholars, mindful of America's recent engagements in the Middle East, have turned their attention to the nation's first conflict with the Islamic world.

Horrors of Slavery presents new insights into the early national period and the aftermath of the American Revolution, and contributes to ongoing debates about citizenship, justice, and America's engagement with Islamic states. Ray's invocation of revolutionary ideals resonates beyond his own experience, as he displays a cultural relativism that condemns tyranny in whatever form. The narrative speaks to anyone interested in American history and literature, especially those curious about the pre-history of U.S. engagement with the Islamic world. As a hybrid of different literary genres, it offers compelling ways to think about narrative history and representation. And Ray's class consciousness and ongoing critique of despotism, combined with his lively writing style, make the case for his elevation within the world of early American literary history. Ray did not have an established professional career in anything but writing, and even his literary life was erratic and unstable. He lived at the very early stages of an increasing professionalization of authorship in early to mid-nineteenth-century America, when the prospect of making a living by writing first became imaginable and available. Coming in response to the extraordinary circumstance of North African captivity, Ray's first acts of public writing authorized him to enter a wider sphere of letters even though he did not find sustained success. This edition of *Horrors of Slavery* argues that William Ray earned his right to a public voice.

NOTES

1. A list of Barbary captivity narratives for further reading can be found at the back of this book. For more on the literary form of Barbary captivity narratives, see Paul Baepler, "The Barbary Captivity Narrative in American Culture," *Early American Literature* 39, no. 2 (2004): 217–246, and Baepler, *White Slaves, African Masters: An Anthology of American Barbary Captivity Narratives* (Chicago: University of Chicago Press, 1999); and Hester Blum, "Pirated Tars, Piratical Texts: Barbary Captivity and American Sea Narratives," *Early American Studies* 1, no. 2 (Fall 2003): 133–158, and Blum, *The View from the Masthead: Maritime Imagination and Antebellum American Sea Narratives* (Chapel Hill: University of North Carolina Press, 2008).

2. Ray, *Poems, on Various Subjects, Religious, Moral, Sentimental and Humorous. To which is added, a brief sketch of the author's life, and of his captivity and sufferings among the Turks and barbarians of Tripoli, on the coast of Africa—written by himself* (Auburn, N.Y.: U. F. Doubleday, 1821), 201. Further references to *Poems* will be cited parenthetically as *P.*

3. Thurlow Weed, *Autobiography of Thurlow Weed*, ed. Harriet A. Weed (Boston: Houghton, Mifflin, 1884), 35.

4. Milton W. Hamilton, *The Country Printer New York State, 1785–1830*, 2nd ed. (Port Washington, N.Y.: Ira J. Friedman, 1964), 182.

5. Information regarding the Barbary pirates, the Barbary states, and the early American response is distilled from the sources that follow. On the centuries-long history of North African piracy, see Paul W. Bamford, *The Barbary Pirates: Victims and the Scourge of Christendom* (Minneapolis: University of Minnesota Press, 1972); Stephen Clissold, *The Barbary Slaves* (London: P. Elek, 1977); and Godfrey Fisher, *Barbary Legend; War, Trade, and Piracy in North Africa, 1415–1830* (Oxford: Clarendon Press, 1957). On the American military and diplomatic response, see H. G. Barnby, *The Prisoners of Algiers: An Account of the Forgotten American-Algerian War 1785–1797* (London: Oxford University Press, 1966); James A. Carr, "John Adams and the Barbary Problem: The Myth and the Record," *The American Neptune* 26, no. 4 (October 1966): 231–257; Donald Barr Chidsey, *The Wars in Barbary: Arab Piracy and the Birth of the United States Navy* (New York: Crown Publishers, 1971); Ray W. Irwin, *The Diplomatic Relations of the United States with the Barbary Powers 1776–1816* (Chapel Hill: University of North Carolina Press, 1931); Michael L. S. Kitzen, *Tripoli and the United States at War: A History of American Relations with the Barbary States, 1785–1805* (Jefferson, N.C.: McFarland, 1993); Frank Lambert, *The Barbary Wars: American Independence in the Atlantic World* (New York: Hill and Wang, 2005); Frederick C. Leiner, *The End of Barbary Terror: America's 1815 War against the Pirates of North Africa* (Cambridge: Oxford University Press, 2006); Joshua E. London, *Victory in Tripoli: How America's War with the Barbary Pirates Established the U.S. Navy and Built a Nation* (Hoboken, N.J.: Wiley, 2005); *Naval Documents Related to the United States Wars with the Barbary Powers*, 6 vols. (Washington: U.S. Government Printing Office, 1939–1945); Richard B. Parker, *Uncle Sam in Barbary: A Diplomatic History* (Gainesville: University Press of Florida, 2004); Martha Elena Rojas, "'Insults Unpunished': Barbary Captives, American Slaves, and the Negotiation of Liberty," *Early American Studies* 1, no. 2 (Fall 2003): 159–186; A. B. C. Whipple, *To the Shores of Tripoli: The Birth of the U.S. Navy and Marines* (New York: William Morrow, 1991); and Richard Zacks, *The Pirate Coast: Thomas Jefferson, The First Marines, and the Secret Mission of 1805* (New York: Hyperion, 2005). On the American cultural

response to captivity, see Baepler, "The Barbary Captivity Narrative in American Culture"; Edward C. Carter II, "Mathew Carey, Advocate of American Naval Power 1785–1814," *The American Neptune* 23, no. 3 (July 1966): 177–188; and Gary Ebersole, *Captured by Texts: Puritan to Postmodern Images of Indian Captivity* (Charlottesville: University Press of Virginia, 1995).

6. James Leander Cathcart, *The Captives: Eleven Years a Prisoner in Algiers* (La Porte, Ind.: Herald, 1899), 144–145.

7. Thomas Jefferson, Letter, "Jefferson to Adams, July 11, 1786," in John Adams et al., *The Adams-Jefferson Letters: The Complete Correspondence between Thomas Jefferson and Abigail and John Adams* (Chapel Hill: University of North Carolina Press, 1959), 142.

8. Richard Henry Dana, *Two Years before the Mast* [1840] (New York: Library of America, 2005), 97.

9. *Tripolitan War collection, 1804–1805*, American Antiquarian Society Manuscript Division, Mss. Dept., Misc. mss. boxes "T." 1 folder, 5 items. Court Martial record for mutiny: June 23, 1804, ship *President*, accused Robert Quinn.

10. Robert Adams and S. Cock, *The Narrative of Robert Adams, an American Sailor, Who Was Wrecked on the Western Coast of Africa, in the Year 1810, Was Detained Three Years in Slavery by the Arabs of the Great Desert, and Resided Several Months in the City of Tombuctoo. With a Map, Notes and an Appendix* (Boston: Wells and Lilly, 1817), 74.

11. William Ray, "On Reading the Debates of Congress Respecting Gen. EATON's Gold Medal," *Middlebury Mercury* 6, no. 22 (May 6, 1807): 4.

12. William Ray, "Literary," *Vermont Precursor* (May 18, 1807): 4. This poem later appeared in *Horrors of Slavery* as the headnote to chapter XII, and in Ray's other published work under the title "Tripoli."

13. [William Ray], Advertisement, *Farmer's Register* 5, no. 12 (April 7, 1807): 4.

14. [William Ray], Advertisement, *Albany Register* 19, no. 1616 (July 3, 1807): 2.

15. William Ray, letter to Thomas Jefferson, March 7, 1809, in *The Papers of Thomas Jefferson, Retirement Series*, 3 vols., ed. J. Jefferson Looney (Princeton: Princeton University Press, 2004), 1:33.

16. William Ray, letter to James Madison, July 27, 1812, in The James Madison Papers, 1723–1836, Manuscript Division, Library of Congress, <http://lcweb2.loc.gov/ammem/collections/madison_papers/ > (accessed August 24, 2007).

17. Ray, letter to James Madison, October 4, 1812, in The James Madison Papers, 1723–1836, Manuscript Division, Library of Congress, <http://lcweb2.loc.gov/ammem/collections/madison_papers/ > (accessed August 24, 2007).

18. [William Ray], *Miscellaneous Register* 1, no. 1 (July 20, 1822): 5.

19. William Kable suggests that Ray may have been the author of *Lafitte* as well. For detailed bibliographic information on *Sophia*, see William S. Kable, "William Ray and Sophia; or, The Girl of the Pine Woods," *Proceedings of the American Antiquarian Society* 78 (October 1968): 313–322.

20. *New-York Spectator* 24 (August 17, 1821): 1.

21. *Daily National Journal* 2, no. 619 (August 12, 1826): 3. The same obituary appeared in the *Baltimore Patriot* and the *Salem Gazette*, and similar notices were published in the *Watch-Tower* of Albany and the *New-Bedford Mercury*. Another obituary remembered William Ray as follows: "He possessed considerable merit as a poet; he was the author of many fugitive pieces, which have been widely circulated in our public journals, and his 'Horrors of Slavery,' has been generally read. 'As a husband, he was tender and sincere; as a father, kind and affectionate; and as a neighbor, generous and hospitable. He has left a widow and three daughters, to mourn his loss.'" *Western Recorder* 3, no. 110 (August 8, 1826): 127.

22. Evert A. and George L. Duyckinck, *Cyclopædia of American Literature; Embracing personal and critical notices of authors, and selections from their writings, from the earliest period to the present day; with portraits, autographs, and other illustrations*, 2 vols. (New York: Charles Scribner, 1866), 1:609.

23. William McCarty, ed., *Songs, Odes, and Other Poems, on National Subjects, Compiled from Various Sources* (Philadelphia: Wm. McCarty, 1842), 2:377–379.

24. "Editorial," *Lowell Offering* (January 1844): 72.

25. Charles W. Everest, *Poets of Connecticut; with Biographical Sketches* (Hartford: Case, Tiffany and Burnham, 1843), 113–122; John R. Dickinson, ed., *Speeches, Correspondence, etc., of the Late Daniel S. Dickinson, of New York* (New York: G. P. Putnam & Sons, 1867), 497; and *Voices from Prison: Being a Selection of Poetry from Various Prisoners, Written within the Cell* (Boston: C. & J. M. Spear, 1847), 97–99.

26. Other extras in this magazine of historical documents included the original narrative of Israel Potter; a Dartmoor Prison memoir; and a Revolutionary War soldier's narrative.

Chronology

William Ray's Life

1771	Born December 9, 1771, in Salisbury, Connecticut
circa 1781	Writes first poem, an elegy for a playmate
1782	Ray's father moves family to New York State
1790	Becomes schoolteacher in Dover, New York
1792	Opens a shop; business fails within a year or two due to embargo
1803	Travels to Philadelphia upon promise of newspaper editorship; enlists on *Philadelphia*
1803–1805	Held captive in Tripoli for nineteen months
1805	Released from captivity; serves as ship's clerk on *Essex*
1806	Returns to America September 1
1807	Begins publishing poems in *Albany Register* and New England newspapers; advertises widely for subscribers to his Barbary captivity narrative
1808	*Horrors of Slavery* is published in Troy, New York
1809–1812	Appointed justice of the peace in Essex, New York; involved in mercantile business
1812	Edits newspaper *The Reveille*, Elizabethtown, New York; staunchly Republican paper
1814–1816	Works as druggist in Skaneateles, New York
1816	Edits newspaper *Onondaga Gazette*, Onondaga Court-House, New York
1816–1821	Appointed justice of the peace, magistrate, and commissioner of court of record, Onondaga, New York
1821	*Poems, on Various Subjects, Religious, Moral, Sentimental and Humorous* published by U. F. Doubleday, Auburn, New York

1822–1823	Edits newspaper *Miscellaneous Register*, Geneva, New York; less political, more religious than previous papers
1823	*Sophia; or, The Girl of the Pine Woods* published in book form, Geneva, New York. Ray's only known novel, it had been serialized in the *Miscellaneous Register* in 1822 and would be reprinted in 1834, 1836, and 1838
1823	Appointed justice of the peace, Geneva, New York
1826	Second edition of *Poems* published for the author, New York
1826	Ray dies July 29 or 30, Auburn, New York

Relevant Historical Events

1453	Ottomans conquer Constantinople
1492	Spain expels the Moors, or Muslims of North African descent; piratical attacks on Spanish properties begin
1500s–1900s	North African pirates attack thousands of ships and take thousands of captives from Mediterranean and northern European states, as far north as Iceland; raids would continue until the nineteenth century
1551	Ottoman empire takes control of Tripoli
1575	Miguel de Cervantes taken captive by Algerine pirates; held for five years
1711	Qaramanli family comes to power
1783	Britain recognizes U.S. independence
1784	*Betsey*, seized by Morocco, becomes first U.S. ship taken by piracy
1785	Algiers declares war on America; ships *Maria* and *Dauphin* taken; captive American sailors, including James Leander Cathcart, remain in prison for eleven years
1786	Settlement treaty with Morocco, first Muslim nation to recognize the United States
1787	Constitutional Convention held in the United States
1789–1797	George Washington president
1794	Susanna Rowson's play *Slaves in Algiers* first performed; Mathew Carey publishes *A Short Account of Algiers*
1795	Peace negotiated with Algiers
1796	Algerine captives redeemed and released
1797	Royall Tyler publishes novel *The Algerine Captive*
1797–1801	John Adams president
1798	John Foss publishes *A Journal of the Captivity and Sufferings of John Foss; Several Years a Prisoner at Algiers*
1798–1801	The United States fights Quasi-War with France; maritime rights at issue
1801–1809	Thomas Jefferson president

1801	Tripoli declares war on the United States
1803	*Philadelphia* runs aground off Tripoli and is captured
1804	Stephen Decatur leads party that sets fire to the *Philadelphia*
1805	William Eaton and mercenary force take Derna; Tobias Lear brokers peace with Tripoli; captives released
1806	Jonathan Cowdery publishes *American Captives in Tripoli*
1808	Slave trade abolished in America
1809–1817	James Madison president
1812–1815	War of 1812; U.S. tribute payments to Barbary end in 1815
1815	James Riley's ship *Commerce* wrecks on Saharan coast; his 1817 narrative of Moroccan captivity, *Authentic Narrative of the Loss of the American Brig Commerce*, would become a bestseller
1817–1825	James Monroe president; "Era of Good Feelings" sees decline in partisan politics
1830	French conquest of Algiers signals beginning of the end of European encounters with Barbary piracy

A Note on the Text

This edition of *Horrors of Slavery* has been retyped from the original 1808 edition, the full title of which is *Horrors of Slavery; or, The American Tars in Tripoli. Containing an Account of the Loss and Capture of the United States Frigate Philadelphia; Treatment and Sufferings of the Prisoners; Description of the Place; Manners, Customs, &c. of the Tripolitans; Public Transactions of the United States with That Regency, Including Gen. Eaton's Expedition; Interspersed with Interesting Remarks, Anecdotes, and Poetry, on Various Subjects. / Written During Upwards of Nineteen Months' Imprisonment and Vassalage among the Turks.* The book was published in Troy, New York, by Oliver Lyon, the printer who seems to have withheld the book's plates from Ray (see introduction); it consisted of 298 pages in 16mo or sextodecimo size, and cost $1.12 1/2. No other edition appeared in Ray's lifetime; in 1911, *The Magazine of History* reprinted the narrative as an "extra," amending the title to *The American Tars in Tripolitan Slavery* (*The Magazine of History with Notes and Queries. Extra Numbers—No. 13–16* [New York: William Abbatt, 1911]: 255–550). *Horrors of Slavery* has not otherwise been reprinted; at the time of its publication this edition presents the only scholarly edition of an unabridged Barbary captivity narrative in print.

Ray's frequent use of the long or medial *s* (*ſ*) has been modernized; with the exception of obvious printer's errors, all other irregularities or mistakes in spelling, usage, or expression are Ray's and have been preserved.

All poems included in *Horrors of Slavery* are by Ray unless otherwise noted. Those poems included in this book were all later reproduced in the first edition of *Poems, on Various Subjects, Religious, Moral, Sentimental and Humorous* with the exception of "Triumph of Principles: In the election of Governor Tompkins.—Quidism deprecated."

Horrors of Slavery;

or,

The American Tars in Tripoli

Containing an Account of the Loss and Capture of the United States Frigate Philadelphia; Treatment and Sufferings of the Prisoners; Description of the Place; Manners, Customs, &c. of the Tripolitans; Public Transactions of the United States with That Regency, Including Gen. Eaton's Expedition; Interspersed with Interesting Remarks, Anecdotes, and Poetry, on Various Subjects

WRITTEN DURING UPWARDS OF NINETEEN MONTHS' IMPRISONMENT AND VASSALAGE AMONG THE TURKS

WILLIAM RAY

"Nature ne'er meant to form a *slave;*
"Her birth-right's *liberty.*"
——*Slavery!* Thou art a bitter cup.
—STERNE[1]

Exordium

WHAT has been always customary,
Legal becomes, and necessary;
And, 'mongst ten thousand stranger things,
When wonder from a volume rings,
Is that anxiety we show,
The writer of the book to know;
Whether he ignorant or wise is—
A *knave*, or *fool* with *virtuous* vice
And hence the practice is to shew
In biographic sketch, or proem:
Here follows, then, or Truth's a liar,
Some pat remarks, if you desire,
And leisure have to halt and read
If not, skip o'er, and never heed 'em.

That he was born, you well may know,
For any fool could tell you so;
Of whom, perhaps, you wish to hear,
The day, the month, the hour, the year:
And these we very well remember;
'Twas on the ninth day of December,
In seventeen hundred seventy-one,
Before the rising of the sun,
And just, if you'll believe the story,
As chaste, and blushing, fair Aurora
Burst the clasp'd arms of negro Night,
A RAY from darkness peep'd to light.

His father, wise as most of men,
Found out that five and five made ten;
(But still he taught his docile son
That one were three, and three were one)
And prov'd of philosophic lore,
The more we know, we know the more.
That pain would pain, and pleasure please him—
That fire would burn, and frost would freeze him;
And though he could not name the causes
Of planets' motions, and the pauses,
He judg'd that *black* could not be *white*—
Of course, that *darkness* must be *night;*
Except when some eclipse befell us,
Which by ephem'ris he could tell us.
All this he knew, by perfect rule,
Although he never taught a school;
Never, with all his stock of knowledge,
Was graduated at a College,
Where thousands take their learn'd degrees,
In arts less useful far than these;
And yet the son was counted rather
More learn'd and skilful than his father.

Now busy *Fame* and staring *Wonder*
Have nearly burst their orbs asunder,
And *Curiosity* stands tip-toe,
And *Slander*'s dying, to let slip too,
And asks what dung-hill of the earth,
Was known by such a *crowing* birth?
While some, yet none but silly asses,
Will judge it to have been Parnassus.

In hopes it will not blast the fame of
America, he boasts the name of
American. "But," says the Yankee,
"If you will tell me *where*, I'll thank 'e;
"For since the *country* you have told, Sir,
"What *place*, if I may be so bold, Sir?
"For asking questions we are famous,
"And *strangers*, therefore, cannot blame us."
O, not at all—what you demand, Sir,
Prompt as a witness I shall answer.

Connecticut, to frogs once fatal,[1]
Is the same State he calls his natal;
A State which other States surpasses,
For pumpkins, jonny-cakes, molasses,
Rogues, priests, attornies, quack-physicians,
Blue laws, and black-coat politicians;
Where many a father's son, aye, plenty
Is father of a son at twenty;
And many a mother's maid has been
A mother made at seventeen;
And many more, at twenty-sev'n
Pray more for husbands than for heav'n;
Where people live, while they have breath,
And die, whene'er they meet with death.
Of Litchfield County's mud and clay,
Was form'd the flesh of WILLIAM RAY;
And Salisbury the very place
Where first he dar'd to shew his face:
A county where the feds prevail,
And Selleck Osborn[2] pin'd in jail,
To prove of *martyrdom* the fitness,
By giving to the world a *Witness*
That men may *Freedom* have, and lose her,
Court, and *wed Pow'r*, and then abuse her.

Early in life he went to school,
To gather wisdom from a fool;
Who, senseless dolt, no reason knew why
One had a black, and one a blue eye;
Why some than other men were taller,
Had longer noses, or were smaller;
Nor why so many sons of Adam
Had not *black skins*, while others had 'em;
Nor whether that complexion sable
Mark'd Cain, for killing brother Abel;
Nor could he tell us, by *Addition*,
How many quacks made one physician;
How many pettifoggers, pliant,
Made one true lawyer to his client;
How many priests, that cant and whine,
Made one good orthodox divine;
How many pray'rs there must be giv'n,
To send one hypocrite to heav'n;

How many prudes, that fancy no man,
Made one chaste, virtuous, honest woman;
Nor could he tell with *all* his brains,
Take pride from alms and what remains;
Nor yet, although he knew *Subtraction*,
Take *lust* from *love* and leave a fraction;
Nor shew us, by *Multiplication*,
How many scoundrels rule a nation,
While many good men, by *Reduction*,
Are brought to prison and destruction.

But he could shew, by *Rule of Three*,
As *warfare* is to *butchery*,
So heroes equal guilt exhibit,
To cut-throats, dangling on a gibbet;
And prove, from *Int'rest*, (which a fact is)
The just in word are knaves in *Practice:*
By *Barter*, and by *Loss* and *Gain*,
How fools *Exchange* their ease for pain.

Of Ethicks he knew not a little,
For he could tell us to a tittle,
Though the distinction very nice is,
The *names* of virtues and vices:
That *Friendship* nothing meant but *pelf*,
And *Social Love*—to *love one's Self;*
That *Truth* was made—*not to be spoken*,
And vows of Honour—*to be broken;*
That rigid *Justice* all detest,
And *Mercy*, painful to the breast;
That *Love of Country* meant the same
As *Pride*, *Ambition*, *Pomp*, and *Fame;*
That *Courage*, term it as you will,
Was nought but fear that greater ill
Would *follow*, if we took to flight,
Than *meet* us, if we brav'd the fight;
That *Honesty*, so much applauded,
Had thousands of their rights defrauded;
So hidden was, so marr'd and twisted,
He could not tell where it existed.
And to his knowledge pedagogic,
He added all the pow'rs of *Logic*;
For he could prove from reasons strong,

That *wrong* was *right*, and *right* was *wrong*;
That is, by Pope's "unerring light,"
He show'd "whatever is, is right";
And hence, by reasons full as strong,
Whatever is not, is not wrong;
And thus *probatum est* it stood,
That there is neither bad nor good.
But halt—the muse flies quite too fast,
And some important things has past.

Ere yet he reach'd septennial years,
To raise his hopes, and calm his fears,
Respecting what some zealots tell,
How span-long infants roast in hell,
Who into it were luckless hurl'd,
Before they ever saw the world;
'Twas found expedient he should know
The terms of future bliss or woe.
The first was infantile baptism,
And then to learn his catechism,
Dug from the Scriptures' deepest mines,
By Reverend Synod of Divines.
In which they taught him to believe,
The snake that courted granny Eve,
Though like a *gentleman*, so civil,
Was his "*grim majesty, the Devil*";
Who with his tongue took such a grapple,
He coax'd her to accept an apple;
Which she, like any well-bred woman,
With her lov'd husband shar'd in common;
And being left to free volition,
Brought us into our curs'd condition.
Yet God himself ordain'd the sin,
Which could not otherwise have been;
That God, from all eternity,
By his immutable decree,
Elected some of Adam's race,
The minions of his partial grace;
Inspir'd the Gospel to believe,
Compell'd his mercy to receive;
From crimes atrocious call'd, or driv'n,
And dragg'd by violence to heav'n;
While far the greater part remain

Predestin'd to eternal pain;
The objects of his wrath, created
On purpose to be reprobated;
Mock'd by an ineffectual call,
And told that grace was offer'd all;
Debar'd from ever *faith* receiving,
And damn'd at last for *not believing*.
Like one who spreads a free repast,
And calls his servants all to taste,
Admits a few to be his brothers,
And bolts his door against the others,
Then punishes, with ruthless hand,
Those who obey'd not his command.

To bring such dogmas reconcil'd,
Would puzzle any *common child;*
He, therefore, while his faith was sprouting,
Began to doubt, and still is doubting;
But here he rests, here all his trust is,
That God both merciful and just is,
And will not plunge our souls in woe,
For crimes six thousand years ago.

In childhood, plumbs, and cakes, and toys,
These constituted half his joys;
And buckles, buttons, or a knife,
Were valued dearly as his life;
The mirror pond, the gurgling rill,
Whereon he built his little mill;
The sling, whence buzz'd the pebble missile.
The jews-harp, whirligig, and whistle:
But, lest we weary your attention,
With things too trifling *now* to mention,
With sweetest joys of life we'll class them,
And so in fond remembrance pass them,
And come to tell you how he acted,
As time and years his life protracted.

In youth, the tyranny of passions,
And versatility of fashions,
Though sober call'd, by some, and steady,
Made his head whirl till it was giddy;
For pleasure led him such a caper,

He thought he could not well escape her;
And *Happiness*, *Contentment*'s daughter,
He fancied once that he had caught her;
But on a strict examination,
Lo! 'twas the termigant, *Vexation!*
That, like a Vixen, ever follow'd
Those pleasures not by temp'rance hallow'd;
That gaudy clothing, brilliant dances,
And *love*, which all the foul entrances,
That vision of a vision, which is
A phantom all the world bewitches,
To follow in a certain train
The path that often ends in pain,
Was happiness: but, ah! we find
'Tis seated only in the mind,
By reason into truth conducted,
And sound morality instructed;
Arm'd with philosophy t' oppose
Our passions, worst of all our foes.

At twenty-two he enter'd trade;
But Fortune, that capricious jade,
Soon as he mounted on her back,
Fled frisking from the beaten track,
Took to the woods, through thorn and brier,
And left him sprawling in the mire.
While creditors' voracious jaws,
Cursing insolvents and their laws,
Yawn'd, frothing like a beast that battles,
To swallow all his goods and chattels;
Each swearing he'd have what was his own,
Or end the debtor's life in prison.
In such a just and noble cause,
They had the sanction of the laws;
Which give us liberty to seize,
And murder debtors, if we please;
For when they nothing have to give,
They should not any longer live:
So erst the wisdom of the state,
Hatch'd from some Dutchman's pond'rous pate,
Ordain'd that each insolvent debtor,
To live and pay his debts the better,
Should, or might be, forthwith invested

To seize his property, while any,
And when he'd not another penny,
To take his body, sick or well,
And drag it to a *worse* than hell;
Depriv'd of all the joys of life,
Perhaps a family and wife,
Camelion-like to feed on air,
Or worse, on mis'ry and despair;
Without the means or pow'r to pay,
Much longer than the *judgment* day,
Unless the three-fourth act[3] he take,
Or make his fortune with a break;
If not, why let the rascal lie,
What is it for a man to die,
Who must discharge, sooner or later,
The debt he owes to mother nature?
And 'twill be own'd by any dunce,
He'd better pay them all at once,
For death's a debt we all must pay,
Our life's expences to defray.

Such is the sample Candour draws,
To shew the mildness of our laws,
Which force men to abscond or sly,
Turn swindlers, or in prison die;
He, therefore, to avoid the times,
Embark'd to visit foreign climes.

And by experience 'twill be found
That man is man the world around;
Whether in *England* we behold him,
Fawning round tyrants that have sold him,
Licking the hand that chains him down
To *bleed* for *honour* and the crown;
Or *Ireland*, where an opposition
To chains and halters is sedition;
(And 'tis confest that many need 'em,
Who anarchy entitle freedom;)
Or whether farther we advance,
And take a peep at reeking *France;*
Where sanguinary Robespierre
Serv'd priests as we do poultry here,

And thought no more of cutting throats
Of men and women, than of shoats;
Where Bonaparte, with flag unfurl'd,
Spreads carnage o'er the trembling world,
And conquers kingdoms, states, and nations,
Easier than lovers do their passions;
Or *Spain*, where horrid inquisition
Extorts the curse of superstition;
Or *Portugal*, where priests from heav'n,
To people are as one t' eleven;
Whether a *Russian Czar* he shines,
Or labours in Siberian mines;
Or pass to *Asia*, if you can,
Whose God's a corpulent old man;
Or *Africa*, where men are barter'd
For gewgaws, or for market quarter'd;
On *Barb'ry*'s coast, where dread Bashaws[4]
At pleasure make and break their laws;
Where tyranny, with hungry zeal,
Devours his thousands at a meal,
Yet hopes to rise to heav'n's high summit,
Through intercession of Mahomet.

Or whether back again we come,
And take a view of things at home;
At Georgia's southern point begin ye,
And travel up through Old Virginia;
What's to be seen where people boast
Of being friends to freedom most?

Behold the lordly planter stand,
The lash still reeking in his hand,
O'er the poor slave, whose only sin is
That his, alas! a sable skin is;
This gives the wretch, whose hide is white,
To slay him an undoubted right;
From country and his friends compel him,
To starve, to murder, or to sell him;
Whose treatment crueler and worse is,
Than that of cattle, swine, or horses;
And e'en they often say the slave
Has not, like them, a soul to save.

Are you republicans?—away!
'Tis blasphemy the word to say—
You talk of freedom?—out, for shame!
Your lips contaminate the name.
How dare you prate of public good,
Your hands besmear'd with human blood?
How dare you lift those hands to heav'n,
And ask, or hope to be forgiv'n?
How dare you breathe the wounded air,
That wafts to heav'n the negro's pray'r?
How dare you tread the conscious earth
That gave mankind an equal birth?
And while you thus inflict the rod,
How dare you say there is a God
That will, in justice, from the skies,
Hear and avenge his creatures' cries?
"Slaves to be sold," hark, what a sound!
Ye give America a wound,
A fear, a stigma of disgrace,
Which time nor you can e'er efface;
And prove, of nations yet unborn,
The curse, the hatred, and the scorn.

And eke, behold our legislators
Receiving bribes, and turning traitors;
Our judges, governors, and sages,
The Catalines[5] of modern ages;
Our clergy, imps of superstition,
Blowing the conk-shells of sedition;
All, all is topsy-turvy whirl'd,
And vice and folly curse the world;
You therefore may pronounce an oath,
Our author has a share of both;
And he's a knave, or lost his senses,
Who to perfection makes pretences.

Yet some there are to whom belong
The raptures of the poet's song;
Who fiery trials have withstood,
And prov'd themselves both great and good.
Amongst our worthies, count as one,
The great, the peerless JEFFERSON.
Illustrious Chief! whose wisdom shows

The fountain clear, from whence it flows;
Whose vast and philosophic mind,
Embraces all the human kind—
Holds to that faith which owns men brothers,
And twenty gods allows to others.
While Europe's threat'ning posture bore
The sword of war, the cup of gore;
Whose ships on ours made depredations,
And broke the sacred laws of nations;
At home, while discord, feuds, and treason,
Late menac'd Freedom's life to seize on,
His firmness, prudence, and his skill
Keeps peace and safety with us still;
Columbia triumphs o'er her foes,
And smiles and blossoms like the rose.

But tardy Muse, come, trudge along,
And close the prefatory song.

Reader, lay prejudice aside,
And let calm reason be your guide;
If in the following, then, you find
Things not so pleasing to your mind,
And think them false, why, disbelieve them;
Errors of weakness? then forgive them;
And let our suff'rings and abuses
For sev'ral *facts* make some excuses;
And when you're captur'd by a Turk,[6]
Sit down, and write a better work.

CHAPTER I

Introductory Remarks

In a government bottomed on the will of all, the life and liberty of every individual citizen becomes interesting to *all*. —JEFFERSON[1]

> Who search for knowledge, mental food of man,
> Roam the wide field, and gather all you can;
> Sweet's the repast where reason guides the way,
> But, ah! how bitter if from her we stray;
> Here taste the product of that barb'rous clime,
> Where truth is error—virtue is a crime.
> No venal motive has the writer shown,
> The Author's benefit is all your own.
> Attend, peruse these pages, and you'll find
> Just indignation thrill the patriot mind;
> Mark the mean rascal, curse th' infernal train,
> Who feast on pleasure at th' expence of pain.

ALTHOUGH much general, authentic and interesting information has been conveyed to the public, through the medium of many private and official communications from sundry gentlemen and officers of the United States' navy, relative to our hostile operations, our pacific transactions, or ultimate adjustment of differences with the power-humbled and recreant Regency of Tripoli; yet no one has given an accurate, full and circumstantial detail, of our capture and sufferings while under the domination of those predatory miscreants and ferocious barbarians.

The most that has been written on the subject, or the most that has met with publicity, are the extracts from Dr. Cowdery's journal,[2] at the conclusion of which, the public were promised with a larger and more particular relation, to be printed in a pamphlet, or small volume. But, as the Doctor has since relinquished the plan, and as the public anxiety is supposed to be in a measure excited by those cursory and imperfect remarks to enquire for a more full and consummate account of all that might be anticipated from those who endured the horrors of Turkish vassalage, it is thought the following will not be deemed preposterous, or prove unacceptable to such readers whose patriotic bosoms glow with the consecrated fire of American liberty, and whose sympathetic hearts and homogenial souls can participate in others' woes, and derive pleasure from the soft, but manly sensation.

In passing through the subsequent field of narrative, the writer will be guided by the undeviating footsteps of impartial, unprejudiced and undisguised truth; which will inevitably lead to the development of several unpleasing occurrences, standing as witnesses to prove that petty despotism is not confined alone to Barbary's execrated and piratical shores; but that base and oppressive treatment may be experienced from officers of the American, as well as the British and other navies; that our countrymen, as well as those of other nations, when invested with the robe and cockade of authority, can act the insolent tyrant, inflict tortures for petty offences, and often for no offences at all, and with a contemptible pride and brutal ferocity, that would disgrace the character of a savage despot, stamp an indelible stigma on the name of an American officer.

Born and educated in this unrivalled region of liberty and independence, far from the clanking of the tyrant's chain, secure from the lacerating scourges of his sanguinary myrmidons; remote from the view of slavery's pallid visage, or the sound of her grief-extorted groans; revering the constitution of our country as the conservator of liberty, which expressly declares that her invaluable blessings are the equal and unalienable right of all mankind; and holding in the highest veneration the judicious administration of our mild and benificent government, who could repress the impetuous impulse of his feelings? Who, that had an opportunity, could restrain his hand from portraying, or his tongue from uttering the indignation he has felt, at seeing a fellow-shipmate, who, perhaps, himself had suffered, fought and bled in the achievement or defence of freedom, for a very trifling unintentional trespass of, very probable, an inexplicable injunction, manacled, stripped, castigated, flayed, and mangled worse than the vilest Virginian slave, or the most atrocious felon?

Far from implicating the whole group of our navy-officers in this condign accusation, infuriate justice, while she points her fulgid sword at a great many with menacing abhorrence, acknowledges that a few deserve discrimination, and merit, by a just, generous, and humane disposition of authority, our unequivocal and unreserved applause.

It is very well known by every person of intelligence, that a more rigorous exercise of power is tolerated by the martial than the civil law; but why this is expedient, or at all admissible, the statesman and philosopher may determine; it is certain that it is made the pretext for that domineering haughtiness, unjustifiable severity and despicable superiority assumed over the resistless objects of their displeasure, by those who are possessed of ambition, power, or office of dictatorial command; while the British navy is referred to as the great and perfect paradigm of our emulous imitation.

It may appear really surprising that sailors, after so generally, and we may say universally complaining of the harsh and illiberal usage they meet with in our service, should so soon forget the smart of the lash, and enter again into a situation which they so seriously deprecate, and so solemnly promise to avoid; but the fact is, their minds, actions and passions being long under restraint, like water, obstructed by a mound, when let loose overflows its channels, they lose themselves in the torrent of dissipation and lasciviousness, and are caught like fishes when the pond is drained; and like them, impatient to return to their congenial and favourite element, they plunge again into the vortex of the ocean, and entangle themselves with perplexities, from which they are unable to extricate their mind, until the tedious routine of another cruise.

The gen'rous tar, whose dauntless spirit braves
War's blood-dy'd squadrons thund'ring on the waves,
Facing grim death in all his hideous forms,
By tempests blacken'd and array'd in storms,
Mounts the high mast and danger's host defies,
Midst billows, raging to assault the skies;
Pierc'd by the wind and palsied by the cold,
By hunger tortur'd, still his breast is bold;
Who bleeds our freedom and our fame to save,
What's his reward? the treatment of a slave.

These are not the chimerical rants of exaggerating fantasy, nor the vindictive effusions of invidious resentment for personal injuries; for I never received the least chastisement while I was in the service; but they are reflections which originate from a sympathetic source, and from an innate abhorrence of every species of oppression. No person will deny but that it is just and absolutely requisite to observe and maintain a strict discipline and proper subordination on board of a man of war; but this is no reasonable excuse for a cruel, vain and magisterial coxcomb of an officer, to display his diabolical disposition, by punishing men for frivolous faults or errors, with the austerity of a West-Indian slave-driver, and inhumanity of a Tripolitan or Algerine.

That this is the real truth, ask any seaman that has ever sailed in the States' service, and he will corroborate the assertion; or ask those tumid imps of tyranny themselves, and they cannot deny it. But if the seaman meets with unmerited insult and undeserved punition, the fate of the luckless marine is still more unpropitious, and his perturbated life far more calamitous; for, by an inveterate antipathy, an implacable animosity between a sailor and a soldier, the latter is made the miserable object of incessant contumely and querulous abuse—reprehended or corrected for the omission of duties which are out of his power to perform; and, like the hapless infant, by the infamous savage Arnold, lashed to the bone for not understanding what he has never been taught, and never had an opportunity to learn. But without fear or affection for any of them, I shall pass, for the present, over many transactions which would brand with infamy the agents of them, and come to a more regular concatenation of exemplifying circumstances and co-operative remarks.

CHAPTER II

Commencement of Service

—I am a soldier, older in practice, abler than yourself to make conditions.
—CASSIUS[1]

Our foes by earth and heav'n abhorr'd
'Tis God-like to unsheath the sword.
—PAINE[2]

Who's he that walks with such a swagger—
A cockade, uniform and dagger,
Holding this motto up to view,
"I am much better, sir, than you?"
Why, 'tis our officer—young Davy—
A smart lieutenant of the navy;
Who's challeng'd—though they call him cruel,
Twice twenty bumpers to one duel,
And fought where clubs, not cannon, rattle,
A score of watchmen in one battle;
Wounds he's receiv'd—in all his clothes,
And bled profusely——at the nose;
For which, grown bolder still and braver,
He basks in governmental favour.
And who is he with feather'd head,
A coat broad-fac'd with warlike red?
That blust'ring—tell me what it means?
Why, he's lieutenant of marines;
Whose duty 'tis to follow fashions,
To draw his pay and eat his rations;
T' enlist recruits for calls emergent,
To drill them, or to make his serjeant—
Defraud them out of half their pay,
Then flog them, if a word they say;

For all the art of war consists
In pay-rolls and provision lists,
Well fill'd which men are forc'd to sign—
This, this is martial discipline.

On the 13th of June, 1803, I was pressed[3] into the maritime service of the U. States: I say pressed, for I was compelled by an irresistible, horrific band of complicated wants, commanded by imperious necessity, more formidable, and as rapacious as a British press-gang. But that a man should be reduced to this degrading alternative in a free and prosperous country, overflowing with all the good things of this life, where every honest employment meets with liberal and prompt encouragement, and prudent industry with due reward, may excite sensations of inquisitive surprise, in the breasts of those who are unacquainted with the dispositions of mankind to oppress the unfortunate, and who have never tasted the nauseous cup of adversity: but to those who have ever experienced the freakish vicissitudes of versatile Fortune, it will not appear incredible; but as a natural and inevitable succession of consequences, that a man driven from his family and friends by a ruthless hord of exorbitant, vindictive, and insatiable creditors; destitute of all pecuniary resources—of no mechanical occupation, or professional employment—unaccustomed and unable to perform manual labour—among suspicious and inhospitable strangers, more void of humanity than Turkish Barbarians, should be brought to as great an extremity of abject misery, as to enter in a private capacity, as one of those whose "folly fights for kings, or dives for gain."[4]

I doubt not but that many a brave and patriotic veteran, who deemed it no disparagement to shoulder his musket and buckle on his knapsack, to repel the nefarious aggressions of our fell enemy, in the lowering days of our revolutionary contest, will feel a virtuous indignation pervade his war-worn breast, when he is informed that it has now become almost as ignominious for an American to serve his country as a private voluntary soldier—to embark in defence of our insulted rights, or to guard our extending commerce from surreptitious depredations, as it would be to be sent to a corrigible penitentiary for felonious misdemeanors. And unless better encouragement were given, or sufficient inducements or honors held out to inspire emulation; were it not for the fascinating influence of specious flattery, with collusive promises of preferment, added to the bewildering, reason-destroying auxiliary of spirituous liquors, our barracks would be inhabited but by rats, and our ships of war, by pigmy officers, without men to command.

When hope forsakes us, and when fear alarms,
The well-fill'd bottle hath a thousand charms;
Eager 'tis drank; but wee to him that drains;
Increasing horrors, and augmented pains,
Take full possession of the sinking heart,
Tear ev'ry wound, and rankle ev'ry smart.
And when intoxication fires the brain,

The voice of sober reason pleads in vain;
Deaf to all counsel, blind to ev'ry rule,
The man of wisdom sinks beneath a fool;
He construes evil what it meant for good,
And striks the hand out-stretch'd to give him food.

I need not tell those who are under the life-wasting, health-destroying dominion of this pestiferous beverage, that so transcient, so fallacious is the mitigation of woe the intemperate use of it promises, that,

To ardent spirits when we fly,
To seek from pain relief;
It adds a groan to ev'ry sigh,
A pang to ev'ry grief.

But we must not decry the prevalence of a custom which is found to be so necessary and effective in procuring our navy to be manned, and our army to be supplied with those living engines of vengeful carnage, and which produces a large proportion of the revenue that goes towards defraying the expences which they incur. Such is the logic made use of by those who wish to see our army and navy in a progressive state of terror and defence. And, indeed, under the existing circumstances of affairs, while such opprobrium is made the common appendage to the name of a soldier, or man of war's man; nothing but the insanity of Rum, violence, perfidy, artifice, or the most distressing penury, can draw men into a situation, where, instead of meeting with promised smiles, approbation, reward and honour, they find nothing but frowns, chastisement, contempt, and disgrace.

It is true in some important achievement of arms, when some obstinate and bloody conflict has been sustained with intrepidity, and terminated with glory and success, they often participate in the general indiscriminate plaudits bestowed on victorious valour; and sometimes the tear of humanity is shed over the war-mangled soldier and death-wounded tar; but the lambent blaze of glory soon devolves on, and is refracted by the officers, and with the breath of applause reverberating to the chief commander; the whole merit of his men having fought valiantly, is ascribed to his inspiring courage and superiour skill; and for which he shares adequate honour and reward, while nothing is left to those who "bore the burthen and heat of the day," but poverty and fears. The stratagems also made use of to allure men into the service, are as base and atrocious as their treatment is often afterwards severe and tyrannical. A marine crimp[5] serjeant or corporal is employed, who, for the sake of ingratiating himself in the favour of his officers, or for the "mighty mead of the large honours" that he is flattered will redound upon his empty head, armed with a whinyard of enormous length and huge dimensions, suspended by a leathern strap passing over the shoulder and crossing the dauntless breast of the champion, on which is a large harness buckle, polished, and glittering like the shield of Achilles; on his snow-powdered sconce a cap; on the front of which a large brass plate, with the American spread eagle, like the helmet of Hector, dazzling all eyes with the effulgence of its beams; on the summit of whose terrific brow, nods in towering panoply the blood-dyed insignia of war, the crested plumage of the martial goose; thus equipped, and taking a few others arrayed in nearly as gorgeous attire and armour as himself, assisted by the enlivening and necromantic sound of warlike music, and a few dollars in his pocket, marches forth with as much ostentation, at the head of his band of patriotic heroes, as a commander in chief of a provisional army, in times of profound peace. The first object of probable success that he meets with is, perhaps, an honest Hibernian, who has but one fault, and that is, he loves his worst enemies better than himself—he has a helpless, indigent family, who depend on his laborious industry for daily subsistence; but the sons of Erin will sometimes have a drinking frolick, and he has just awakened from a sleep of intoxication; his pockets emptied, by being a little too generous in giving to, and treating those who are the first to censure his prodigality; or, perhaps, cozened or pillaged by a dishonest pickpocket landlord—ashamed to go home and meet the dreadful frowning of his injured helpmate—shivering with the cold—sick at the stomach—burning like Tantalus with thirst, and not a friendly drop to warm or cheer his desponding bosom; he would almost sacrifice his existence for one oblivious draught of the cordial of his pangs. The perspicacious crimp, the servile, sycophantic tool of his authoritative master, observing him to be in hopeless perplexity, and not very erroneously conjecturing the situation of his mind, perceiving him to be a manly, robust looking fellow, generously invites him to share the bounties of a flowing bowl. This is an act, a favour, a proof of disinterested hospitality, that moves in his perturbed breast the soft emotions of pathetic gratitude. He reiterates the catholicon, and finds his spirits exhilerated, and his bosom glows with grateful ardor to manifest to his friendly benefactor the feelings of his soul; and overtly deposits in his breast the secrets of his condition. The happy life of a soldier is delineated in all its captivating forms and delusive, facinating colours; until the enraptured listener becomes infatuated with the phantasma, and continuing to imbibe the Lethe of his cares, he grows inebriated, and falls an easy prey to the prowling banditti. But who can describe the agonies of his mind, when he awakes to sober reason and serious reflection? when he hears the chiding voice of his wife, and sees the reproachful tears of his children? The scanty stipend of his services is scarcely sufficient to keep them from the jaws of hunger; and if he is sent to sea, he can leave them but a moiety of that; but it is too late to retract; he has taken the dreadful, irrevocable oath of fidelity to his adopted country, and three years of the most debased servitude in his unavoidable lot. In vain may the widowed wife, with tears in her eyes, and an infant at her throbbing breast, plead the deplorable wretchedness of herself and her helpless, guiltless babes; in vain may she remonstrate against the villainous advantage that was taken of her husband being in a paroxism of ebriety; in vain may she proffer the sacrifice of her household furniture and every cent that she can muster, to hire a substitute; in vain is one procured. The inflexible integrity of the commanding officer will not vouchsafe to relinquish his honourable title to a prize so valuable, and spurns with insolent threats the supplicating mediations of the friendless, heart-broken, disconsolate woman. The next, very probably, is an artless, country bumpkin, as ignorant of the ways and manners of this deceitful world, as we are of the next. He has just arrived at twenty-one, and emancipated himself from domestic slavery—the pertinacious reign of his arbitrary father; and having an insatiable curiosity to see how people live in the metropolis, he possesses himself of a little cash, and, travelling to the distant sea-port, wanders with sauntering gaze through the decorated streets of the voluptuous emporium of commercial resort. The pompous coach-and-four; the rich and splendid articles of pleasure and of use, exhibited for sale; the brilliant group of fair and charming belles; the tawdry circle of facetious beaux; the crouded theatre's enchanting scenes; the rapturous dulcet strains of choral music, and all the nameless baubles of the novel place, seize upon his giddy brains, and his disordered imagination half claims the wealth of thousands as his own. He soon finds himself drained of the most necessary ingredient to gain a passport to the temple of sensuality, and meeting with the aforesaid kidnapper, he sells himself for honour, with the specious promises of rapid promotion. But he soon, alas! wishes himself with his deserted parents and his rustic companions; and, like the prodigal son, would be glad to feed on husks, with his father's swine.

The third is a young man of a liberal and refined education; but has no profession, and is without the means to pursue the study of one, destitute of friends and support. He is not qualified for any employment, save that of school-keeping, and finds it very difficult to obtain even the unthankful situation of a country pedagogue, and more difficult, when obtained, to discharge, to general satisfaction, the critical duties required by capricious parents. He is mortified, chagrined, and discomfited; and being unskilled in the duplicity and finesse of mankind, he is easily duped, by alluring wiles, to become a candidate for a corporal or serjeant. If it should be said that "such discouraging representations ought not to be made, and that we must have sailors and soldiers"—these are the very arguments adduced by the British to justify their infernal policy in impressing so many seamen: "they must have men," is the plausible, but hellish pretext for all their diabolical press-gangs, and for the numerous insults offered to our nation, by dragging our brave tars from under their own colours, to compel them to fight under those of his most Satanic, not gracious nor sacred majesty. If we must have men, let appropriate honours, comparative emolument, and suitable gratitude be extended to those who risque their lives in the protection or defence of their country's rights, and wipe from the honourable appellation of soldier or sailor, that ungrateful tarnish of vulgar prejudice, and there would be no difficulty in finding plenty of either. Fired by a laudable ambition, or patriotic emulation, our youth would strive to rival each other in being foremost in rallying round the standard of American independence, at every emergency of danger, and would glory alike in the musket of the field, or the trident of the ocean.

At the time of my entering the service, no person could have been in more distressing circumstances. I had been sick among strangers until I had expended the last solitary cent I was commander of, and not yet restored to health; but was in a debilitated state of convalescence. I tried every mean, and exerted every faculty in my power to obtain employment, but in vain. Though often promised, and encouraged to pursue, I was as frequently disappointed. The surly, unsociable, churlish, and suspicious curmudgeons of the interior of Pennsylvania, shun an itinerant stranger in distress, as they would a rattle-snake or a viper; and you might with more hopes of success, expect friendship or relief from the Esquimaux of America, or the wandering Arabs of Asia, than from the black-Dutch Pennsylvanians; especially, if you add to the appearance of poverty, the epithet of Yankee.

The day previous to my arrival at Philadelphia, as I was walking down the Schuylkill, almost exhausted by lassitude and woe, pondering with gloomy solicitude on my deleterious fate, I came to a ferry, which I was directed to cross. It was on Sunday, and I saw no person near the place; but a small house, nearly opposite, I supposed was the residence of the ferry-man. I advanced to it, and knocked at the door; but no person answered or appeared. The sash of the window near the front door was raised, and I, very naturally concluding that some of the people must be in or about the house, innocently took a look in, to convince me; but seeing no person, I turned round, and was walking towards a public house not far distant, when I heard a smart voice, and turning obliquely, saw a man stalking firmly across a field, and making towards me with great rage, asked me "what I wanted at his house, and what business I had to peep in at the window of it." I told him, I wished to cross the river, and was looking for the ferry-man. "You lie, damn you," says he, "you was going to rob my house." I strove to convince him that I had no guilty designs; but all endeavors to reconcile, seemed only to exasperate him the more, and seizing a large club that lay in the street, began to strike me with all the exertion of his might. I was unable to make any effectual resistance, and he continued his blows with redoubled fury, until a generous Irishman sallied from the tavern, and came to my rescue. He sternly enquired the cause of the fracas, and from both our stories, judging that I was innocent of any evil intentions, in looking in at the window, perceiving that I was indisposed, and I being informed that I was a total stranger, vengeance flashed from his eyes, and giving my villainous antagonist a hearty damn or two, with a beatle-like fist he instantly levelled him to the ground, and beat, and mauled him, so unmercifully, that he bellowed like an ox, and raised the people of the Inn, who came running to know what was the matter. After a brief explanation of the affair, they joined in universal imprecations on the scoundrel that dared to use a stranger in such a manner, and advised me to take the law of him. But I told them, if he would acknowledge that he had acted like an infamous villain, and treat all of them to as much as they would drink, I would take no further notice of the fray. They swore he should do what I required, and give me a dollar in the bargain; or they would beat him twice as much, and get him indicted beside. To which harsh and humiliating decision of justice, the savage caitiff was obliged to submit; for he was surrounded by a rugged half score of the true sons of Hibernia; who are ever ready to evince their manly dispositions to see a stranger not insulted or abused. I mention this as a specimen of Pennsylvanian hospitality, and as an example of quick and commendable, if not legal punishment, for a base and dastardly action; and I shall not pretend to deny, that I felt gratified at the transaction, and went on my way rejoicing, for a moment; but soon a relapse of melancholy glooms inveloped the faint glimmerings of transcient delight; for although I had what some might term flattering visions of bettering my condition in Philadelphia, I had but indifferent hopes of success, and my portentous apprehensions of disappointment on experiment, were unfortunately realized. I now found myself in the populous, magnificent, opulent, and flourishing city of Philadelphia, without a shilling—without any friend or acquaintance—unable to labour, and too proud to become a mendicant, or fully to divulge the secrets of my situation. In this wretched and hopeless wilderness of trouble, I inadvertantly strayed to the banks of the Delaware; and,

As wand'ring, by suicide tempted to die,
A victim to horrid despair,
The flag of Columbia was hoisted on high,
And wantonly play'd in the air.

I enter'd, in hopes with America's foes,
Some dang'rous, warm conflict to find;
For anxious was I, at that time, to expose
A life I'd have gladly resign'd.

Admitting that imprudence, vice, intemperance, and prodigality, were the primary cause of my misfortunes, the miseries and horrors of a painful mancipation, and a thousand concomitant evils and sufferings, in some degree, perhaps, ought to expiate my follies, and my faults, in the benignant eyes of celestial Charity; if not, let the immaculate finger of scowling Censure, point at her own image, in the mirror of conscience, and cease to vent reproaches, while she sees a blot of guilt remaining there.

Before I enter on board the ship, to take a luckless voyage, I beg the liberty to devote a short chapter to the remembrance of a character with whom I often sympathised in adversity, and to whom I still find myself bound by the ties of mutual sufferings.

Of friendship, we can only guess,
Until we find it in distress;
And nothing but the fire of woe,
Can try the friend or prove the foe.

CHAPTER III

A Sketch of Biography

Worth makes the man, and want of it the fellow;
The rest is all but leather, or prunella.

—POPE[1]

I glory in publicly avowing my eternal enmity to tyranny.

—HANCOCK[2]

Let British novelists record
The splendid virtues of "my lord,"
And venal poetasters raise
To titled fools the spaniel-praise;
Or, let Americans, for shame,
Extol a Burr's[3] seditious name;
The man of *honesty* and *merit*,
Who holds a noble, gen'rous spirit,
Though not two cents his pockets bless,
Though plung'd in mis'ry and distress,
Though driv'n, by want, to measures which
There's no temptation for the rich;
But who, with blacker crimes and folly,
Are still denominated holy;
That man is more real worth,
Although an alms-house were his birth,
And ought, and must be counted greater,
Than all the pompous knaves of state are;
And more deserves the world's attention
Than all the Burrites in——*convention.*
Now by these presents all men know ye,
Such is the character I'll show ye.

AMONG my new companions in arms, I observed one to whom I felt myself attracted, by the mysterious magnetism of congenial sympathy. There was something in his physiognomy indicative of merit superiour to his station, and to the vacant stare of vulgar ignorance. On becoming acquainted with him, I discovered that he was no Lord or Duke in disguise, as was common in the days of chivalry and romance, but a mechanic of no ordinary abilities—a skillful typographer. And though he had never rendered his life or actions illustrious by immolating his fellow-creatures at the impious altar of bleeding war; although he never mounted the heights of power and office by the slippery and filthy step-stones of wealth and bribery, laid by mercenary parasites, or hereditary slaves; and though he had never acquired the honours and independency of riches by a penurious economy, sordid avarice, or flagitious speculation: yet, if ever that Phoenix, *honesty*, was found to tenant the human breast, he might be pronounced one of

"The noblest works of God;"

On which radical and cardinal virtue, to wit, honesty, were engrafted all the amiable ramifications of the social affections; fidelity in friendship, disinterested generosity, unbounded benevolence, and universal philanthropy. He was learned, without pedantry; intelligent, without loquacity; serious, without hypocrisy; cheerful, without levity; and communicative, without vanity. But too great a portion of sensibility frequently conducted him into follies, imprudence, indiscretions and difficulties; and sober reflections often made him miserable. He possessed no contemptible genius, and wrote several excellent things; but, like the unfortunate Chatterton,[4] was too modest to give them to the world. He informed me that he was born in the city of Dublin, although by his dialect you would not judge him to be an Irishman. His father was a reputable mechanic, and kept a shop opposite the former mansion-house of that eccentric genius, the vivacious, learned and patriotic Dean Swift.[5] He was a rigid Methodist, a class-leader among those puritans, and early instilled into the minds of his children, the principles of that Religion, to whose gloomy dogmas I have heard him frequently ascribe the origin of much unhappiness. For being taught that the least deviation from the line of perfection, either in thought, word, or action, called down the wrath of heaven upon mankind, and witnessing the frailties and imperfections of our natures, created in his mind awful apprehensions of future misery. His father, designing him for the sacerdotal functions, sent him to an eminent seminary of learning; where he continued until some divisions in the family frustrated the plan of his farther progress in his studies. The old gentleman had married his second wife, and she proved to be a Xantippe.[6] An implacable malignity towards the son, persuaded the father to take him from school, and send him fifty miles into the country, to learn the trade of a stay-maker. Here he was treated with a severity that rendered his life almost unsupportable, for three tedious years before he prevailed on his father to revoke his indentures, the ties of which, by his master's abuses, had become forfeit and nugatory. He was, therefore, called home; and after a short time had elapsed, was put to a printer; where he remained until he had perfected himself in that useful, noble, and preservative art of all arts. During which time, a heart like his was not indifferent to the charms of the fair, nor invulnerable to the Indian-like arrows of the sightless deity of love. He became enamoured of a worthy clergyman's lovely daughter. Their passion was reciprocal, and flattering hope, that supernal charmer of the world below, forestalled to their enraptured imaginations the delectable elysium of connubial joys. But death, that cruel despoiler of the fairest works of heaven, rifled from his arms the rich gem of his happiness, and tore the beloved maid from his bleeding and forlorn bosom.

The barm of discontent was now fomenting the cup of insurrection in that insulted and oppressed country, and being a warm republican, safety, as well as the hopes of accumulating property, or obtaining a livelihood with more facility, and of enjoying the inestimable blessings and privileges of peace, liberty and independence of sentiment, prompted him to seek an asylum in the transatlantic regions of the United States. He took a filial, affectionate, and final valediction of his pious father, and landed in New-York, where he wrought journeywork for a year or two; but that deletery pestilence, the yellow fever, like the destroying angel, spread the dark mantle of death over thousands of its devoted inhabitants, and to avoid which he directed his way to the city of Philadelphia. He continued here for several years; but was disappointed in both places of his expectations. Wages, it was true, were tolerable good; but when earned, difficult to be collected; and board, contingent expences, and articles of clothing were in proportion; so that the difference, in his favour, between America and Ireland was not so great in his occupation, as common report had represented. He made out, however, to maintain himself genteely: but so many of his countrymen flocking to see him, and being somewhat liberal, he could not save enough to establish a press of his own. For although he was *typically* as great a man, he was not a Franklin in economy; and I have frequently heard him censure the parsimony of that lightning-tamer, when in London, boarding with a poor widow, who supported herself and family by victuallying and selling beer, he was too avaricious to afford himself the use of that nutricious beverage, and drank, as a substitute for that and for coffee, the vapid dose of water-gruel; thereby disappointing the woman in the trifling gains which she expected from him, and which she received from other boarders. But with due deference to him and his "whistle," we return to the subject. At length he got entangled in a love-snare, and before he could extricate himself from this labyrinth of danger, he found himself involved in pecuniary embarrassments, and the idea of not being able to discharge a debt when demanded, wrought so forcibly upon the sensibility of an upright heart, that he abandoned his mind to gloomy reflections, to dispel which he had recourse to the worst of all poisons, and one day meeting with a nominal friend of his, a person with whom he had formerly boarded, and who had now become a crimp, to avenge himself of his wife's infidelity, he was prevailed on by the insidious blandishments of glazing friendship to take a little too much of this antidote of despair, and committing amnesty on his reason, subscribed to the indentures of war, and became an apprentice for the third time in his life, to the trade, art, or mystery of homicide.

The next morning, awaking from his catalepsis, he could not be convinced that he had relinquished the press for the musket, until the supercilious airs, and dogmatical orders of his imperious new masters, gave him a *type* of what would be *printed* on the *parchment* of his back, if he should refuse to *compose* and reconcile himself to the strict *letter* of their commands.

His typographic friends, hearing of his *new edition* of war tactics, came to see how he looked, *newly bound, gilt*, and *lettered* in *cowskin*. They seriously *perused* the prognostic *pages* of his fate. They advised him to decamp, provided he could not obtain an abrogation of his enlistment—offered to advance him money to discharge his debts, and for other purposes. But he frankly told them that he would not desert from under the flag of the United States to which he had sworn to be true, for the consideration of thousands. But would thank them if they would use their efforts to obtain for him an honourable discharge, by procuring another person to take his place; which was all he asked; for his creditors had been to see him, and told him if he could exonerate himself from the obligations of his recent contract, they would forgive him one half of their demands, and give as long a time to pay the rest, as he in reason would wish or ask. They therefore went to the commanding officer, and he promised to accept of a substitute and discharge him. But before one could be found, a young man, an acquaintance of his, came to see him, got intoxicated, and was warm for enlisting; but the man having a family, and a good trade, knowing the poignant remorse that would follow on his being restored to reason, he ingenuously dissuaded him from his purpose. This being promulgated by some of their pragmatical pimps, called down the dreadful vengeance, and awful fulminations of the officers, who swore they would flog him if he ever attempted to discourage another friend of his from entering the service—that they would not discharge him on any account, and that suitable precautions should be taken to prevent his deserting.

The United States frigate Philadelphia was now lying nearly opposite the barracks in the river Delaware, demanding, waiting for, and receiving repairs; of which he was shortly sent on board, with strict orders not to let him leave her, and all hopes or prospects of redemption from this ligneous hell, until the period of a cruise, were blasted and destroyed.

A few days after he was sent on board, and before the rigid laws and regulations of the ship were known, and, in fact, they are never taught but by the rope's-end, or the cat,[7] when all hammocks were piped down in the evening, he happened to be, with many others, on the birth-deck. There were no ladders shipped, and the hatchways being pretty high, and he but a short man, and not very nimble withal, found it impossible to get on deck in proper time; and seeing one of his messmates above, earnestly requested him to pass his hammock down; which he faithfully promised to perform. But by some precipitate mistake, he handed a wrong hammock, and the one intended was left on deck until the rest were all carried below. The heinous and unpardonable crime of leaving a hammock a few moments too long in the nettings, on that consecrated platform, the quarter-deck, was now to be made known and punished. The mark and number were examined and it was found to be a marine's. This was matter of great exultation amongst the cockade-gentlemen, and more so, when it was found to be the person's I am speaking of. Now was the time to wreak due vengeance for his past offences. He was called, and without being permitted to speak a word in his defence, was ordered, with the most horrid maledictions, instantly to strip off his jacket. A boatswain's mate was summoned to attend, and, with a rope of enormous size, ordered to give the "damn'd rascal" three dozen with all his might! This barbarous order was so faithfully executed, by the unfeeling ruffian, that the delinquent's back exhibited a spectacle disgraceful to human nature. From his neck to his waist it was bloody with gashes, and livid with contusions. Complaint was made to the officer of marines for this unlawful immanity, but to no effect. This is a solemn fact, and might be proved by hundreds. Heavens! thought I, is this the usage we are to expect in the service of our country? Are men to be condemned without a hearing, and punished without a cause? Tortured without mercy, and murthered with impunity?

It is obvious, that base malversation was the cause of his enlisting—his commendable generosity in persuading his friend from forsaking an indigent family, depending on his labour for support, to bring himself into a despicable bondage, the cause of his not being relinquished, according to promise; and the mean spirit of revenge in his officers, the virtual cause of his subsequent sufferings in Turkish servitude. Citizens of America! are these things too trifling to be taken notice of? Is it a matter of no consequence that an unfortunate foreigner, driven by the harpics of tyranny to seek a refuge under the shadows of the American Eagle's wings, should be hawked by the vultures of perfidious peculation, and revengeful malice, and have his flesh beat, bruised, and dilacerated for no offence at all? And because a man is a private marine, must he endure every insult, shame, and abuse? And shall it not be mentioned, because it will discourage others from becoming the dupes of strategem, and the objects of tawdry misery, derision, and ignominy? If some exalted personage, "stuck o'er with titles, and hung round with strings," meets with the least fancied wrongs, how soon does the clarion of public animadversion, filled by the breath of resentment, blow the tidings, and blast the perpetrators? And shall an honest, worthy character, though walking in the obscure paths of private life, receive from men commissioned by our Executive, who derives a measure of its power from the lowest ranks of society, such unauthorized and unmerited cruelties, and not be allowed even to complain?

Be assured, it shall be my business and delight, to expose, in the following pages, every act of cruelty, every abuse of authority, that I witnessed, during my continuance in the service of the United States. But, in justice to the character of Captain Bainbridge, it ought to be mentioned, that the foregoing was not done by his orders.

This is only one instance among a thousand; but this alone is sufficient to verify what is predicted in the antecedent part of this work, viz. that base and oppressive, unjust and tyrannical treatment marks the features, and disgraces the name of that tyranny-fostered infant, our navy.

CHAPTER IV

Suicide Attempted

Reader! your patience for a while—
'Tis granted—for I see you smile;
But, looking gravely on the text,
Ask what catastrophe comes next?
Peruse, peruse a little further,
And hear of love, and almost murther.
Love is the strangest of all creatures,
He lurks in *forms*, and kills in features—
With lips and eyes, and though so simple,
He sometimes murders with a *dimple*;
But most delights to skulk in hearts,
And other precious hidden parts;
Whence creeping slily through the veins,
He takes possession of the brains;
And when he once has enter'd there,
He's metamorphos'd to despair.
Love makes the wisest man a fool,
And reason turns to ridicule;
He wakes, some say, (and faith I know it)
A love-crack'd pedagogue, a poet—
In short, the little blind-fold boy
Is equal friend and foe to joy.

ALTHOUGH I have been mentioning what was transacted on board of the Philadelphia, this was unavoidably necessary as being connected with the relation I was giving, and I now return to the place from whence I took my departure in the latitude and career of eclat.

Nothing of any great consequence occurred, from the time I entered, until we were sent on board of the frigate, excepting the following interesting circumstance, and its sequacious peculiars; which, as it is expected that this volume will fall into the hands of the young and facetious as well as the old and serious, the warm and sensuous lover, as well as the cold and stoical philosopher, with some apology for the digression, I shall take the liberty to relate: and although it does not participate of the *wonderful*, like many novel tales, it has the merit of not being imported from the manufactories of aristocracy, and in quality and substance assimilates very nearly to strict veracity.

One Sunday, in the afternoon, as a number of us were refreshing ourselves under the refrigerant shade of a wide expanding willow, on the delightful banks of the keg-famous Delaware, we perceived a well dressed man, running with the utmost pernicity towards the banks of the river, and coming to a place where there were some remains of an old wharf, he precipitated himself headlong into the miery dock. A number of spectators followed, and with many struggles and much difficulty, dragging him out, rescued him from the abyss of death—the perpetration of suicide. With every exertion, it was a considerable time before he was resuscitated. He appeared to be a man about twenty-three or twenty-four years of age, of a genteel appearance, with a watch in his fob, and money in his pocket. On being restored to life and sanity, he gave the following account of himself, his misfortunes, and the cause of his attempting to commit the rash and horrible act of self-murder.

His father, he said, was an opulent and celebrious practitioner of physic, in the town of ———, in Massachusetts, and that he was his only surviving child. His father had given him a liberal education, at the University in Cambridge, and had designed him for the study of jurisprudence, to which profession he had early imbibed, and still retained, the greatest aversion, and was anxious only to embark in the mercantile business. His disinclination to prosecute the study of the calling appropriated by his father, was construed into a tacit disobedience of his will, want of filial affection, and morose pervicacity. His father, however, consented to establish him in commerce, provided he would espouse the daughter of a friend of his, who was very rich, and had but one child, like himself; and as he was a merchant, this would accelerate his projects of commencing and pursuing his favourite occupation. His contemplated partner for life was not the paragon of beauty, nor the prototype of juvinility; and as his inclinations were prepossessed in favour of a silver-smith's daughter, the magnifying mirror of fancy rendered the former even disgusting. He remonstrated with his father against the proposed match; but the old man was deaf and contumacious, though not apprised of his son's predilection for another lady. At length he became acquainted with the true cause of his son's repugnance to his requisitions, banished him from his house, and solemnly swore he should never have a cent of his money, nor an item of his property, unless he made suitable retractions, and acceded to his proposals of marrying the merchant's daughter. He was so sincerely attached to the silver-smith's daughter, that he found it impossible to comply with his father's wishes, and consequently rendered himself obnoxious to paternal ire, and threatened indigence and misery; for the darling object of his affections was poor indeed, as to pecuniary estimations, but rich in the lore of mental acquirements, and personal attractions. He was determined to sacrifice the good will of his father to the gratification of his passion. He had a friend in Philadelphia, with whom he had been long acquainted, on terms of the greatest intimacy, and who shared his entire confidence and esteem. He had a few years past migrated to that place, was wealthy, and well established in business; to whom he dispatched a letter, stating the sad dilemma in which he was intricated, and his resolution not to prostitute his heart to the love of lucre; requesting permission provided it met his approbation, to let him send his Venus to his charge, and that himself would follow in a short time, and be married at his house. He was positive, that if they eloped together, his father would devise means to frustrate their plan, by discovering the course of their flight. In a few weeks, he received a categorical answer, fraught with terms of the warmest friendship, assurances of his fidelity, and of his assistance in procuring him some kind of lucrative employment, to enable him to subsist without the aid of his father. He went to the young lady, told her of his plan, and arrangements, and with some difficulty prevailed on her to consent to his overtures, and, accordingly, she was sent to Philadelphia. His father soon heard of her elopement, and took every vigilant method to prevent his son from following, although he did not, as yet, know where she was lodged. He was to follow his charmer, in about four weeks; but, when he attempted to do so, was pursued and brought back, by order of his father; and closely confined in an upper story, for about three weeks; when he effected his escape, through the chamber window, which cost him the dislocation of an ancle. He had a horse and chaise at a friend's in town, previously prepared for the purpose, and with the most excruciating pangs, he made out to hobble to the place; but his father had discovered the plot, and previously bribed the man, not only to refuse him the means of, but also to anticipate his flight, by giving immediate information. When he was denied the chaise, with slight and laconic subterfuge, he instantly suspected treachery; and while the man was hastening to his father's, to give notice of his desertion, he limped to a stage-house, near by, and luckily the stage was that moment starting. He was helped into it, and whirled off twenty miles from town before they made a halt, but it was the course contrary to Philadelphia. Here he found a surgeon, who performed what was necessary to the restoration of his ancle. He hired a man, with a horse and chaise, to take him a few miles back, and then steering in a western direction, drove all day and the succeeding night, and at length put up at a tavern, in a little village, "remote from any intercourse with the town he had left." Here he dismissed his man and chaise, with strict injunctions not to divulge, should any one enquire where he was; which was affirmed in the negative. He remained two or three days, for his ancle to gain strength. Another chaise was provided, and just as he was departing from the tavern, he saw two men riding towards him with great celerity. One of them was his father, who had heard of his route by means of the stage-driver, and the person who had taken him to the place where he now was. The old gentlemen, infuriate in his wrath, struck him several times; and hired the man who was about to take him another course, to drive him to his home. On their return, his father lodged him in the common jail of the county, and he was treated with no less severity than a malefactor, until the old man received a letter from the merchant in Philadelphia, informed him of the whole intrigue; and as a proof of what he wrote, enclosed the letter of his son, and one which the young lady had written to her lover, also. The whole mystery was now unravelled, by the hand of perfidy, and he immediately wrote an answer, that if he would find a match for the young woman, who was now in his power, or be the means, in any manner, of preventing his son's intended union with her, he would give him a thousand pounds. That, for fear his son might come there, he must remove her to some other place, and if he should come, not to let him see her at all on any account. As he had now found out the secret, and had taken such effectual measures to circumvent their designs, he took his son from prison, but still kept a strict watch over his actions, till he received another letter from the base and perfidious merchant of Philadelphia, informing him that he had sent the young lady over the Schuylkill, into the country, to remain in the house of a very wealthy Frenchman, who was an old bachelor, and had a very amiable sister, that was an excellent performer on the forte-piano; and as a pretext for sending her thither, she was to be taught the polite art of that music, by the French lady. He had told the Frenchman that she was his niece, and had persuaded her to consent to the collusion; which was no great evidence of the stability of her mind, or the sincerity of her heart. That he had made her believe this measure to be absolutely necessary to prevent discovery and complete their wishes, and that as soon as her lover should appear, they would be forthwith joined in the indissoluble banns of matrimony. That he had seen the Frenchman once or twice, and he seemed to be much enamoured of the young lady, and that he thought it very probable he would proffer marriage, and did not doubt but that she might be persuaded to consent. That if his son should come, he could easily evade his enquiries, until something would transpire to cool him at once of his passion; and that he thought all would operate to ultimate satisfaction, and reciprocal felicity.

The father now grew less vigilent, but the son more sedulous to effect an escape from paternal oppression; and accordingly he found an opportunity, secretly to carry his trunk on board of a schooner, bound to New-York; and agreed with the captain to secrete him in some place, until they were out of sight of the harbour. He had availed himself of some cash by means of some property given him by his grand-father. They had not been out but a few hours when a furious storm arose, which lasted three days, dismasted the schooner, washed his trunk, which had been left on deck, overboard, and drove them into Providence, Rhode-Island. He had upwards of four hundred dollars in his trunk, and all of his most valuable clothing; besides a miniature likeness of its beloved original, set in gold. He then took the stage, with about one hundred dollars in his pocket, which was all he had left, and hastened to Philadelphia, with all possible dispatch. The schooner was left to be repaired. On his arrival in Philadelphia, he went with the most impatient expectation to see his friend and his mistress, but was greatly surprised and disappointed on being told, that she had been absent for a considerable time, on a visit at Newcastle; but that she was expected home in about a week. He could not be prevailed on to wait twenty-four hours, and a week seemed an age. The merchant finding him determined on going to Newcastle, in search of her, wrote a letter to a fancied friend he had there, containing a short account of the intrigue, and requesting him to tell the young gentleman that the object of his enquiry had been at his house, but that she was gone with a daughter of his to Baltimore; or make use of any other subterfuge he thought proper, to elude his searches. The merchant delivered this letter to the unsuspecting young gentleman, with directions where to find his friend. He immediately set out, with the fullest expectations of finding her at Newcastle; and without the smallest suspicion of his friend's perfidy or tergiversation. The letter was handed to the gentleman to whom it was addressed, who read it with visible agitation. "I never had but a slight acquaintance with the author of the letter," said he, "and yet he has taken the liberty, indirectly, to tell me I am a villain—infamous scoundrel! does he imagine that I am to take an agency in a love intrigue, and make myself at once a liar, a promoter of treachery, fraud, falsehood, and, in short, as great a rascal as himself?" The young man was petrified with astonishment. "Young man," said he, "you have been basely deceived"—and gave him the letter. He read it with violent emotions. It contained, as before observed, a brief and cursory detail of the whole plot, and of the stratagem that had been used to dupe him; but did not mention where she was. In the mean time the French gentleman had become passionately in love with his sister's pupil, and the abovementioned merchant had been to see her, and used all his rhetorick to persuade her to marry the Frenchman. Now was a fortunate and the only time to have it accomplished. He told her that her lover had been there on his way to Baltimore; that he had abandoned the idea of marrying her, and called only to tell her so, and to assist her in getting back to her parents; that on his return home he was to be married to the lady of his father's choosing, and that he had authorized him to communicate the tidings to her, and assist her in returning to her friends. He gave such an exact description of his person, dress and appearance, that the young lady entertained not a doubt of his having seen him in Philadelphia, for she knew he had not seen him elsewhere, and believing him to be her sincere friend, and not in the least suspecting his veracity, gave full credence to all he said. Her not having received a letter from her lover in a long time seemed also to confirm what he had told her. Being ashamed to return, and not knowing what to do with herself, and the Frenchman being very rich, she consented to be married to him that very night that her legitimate lover was gone to New-Castle.

The very day that the preceding melancholy attempt happened, he had returned from New-Castle. He went to the house of his insidious friend, to find out the retreat of his love, and to vent his indignation and revenge; when entering the house, the first that he saw, was his long sought paramour, in the arms of the

Frenchman. She fainted at the unexpected sight of her late amoroso, and he was madness and fury when he was informed of her marriage. They alternately recriminated, and charged each other with inconstancy and deception; while the wonder-dumb Frenchman was motionless at what he saw and heard. At length he flew in a raving passion, swore he would shoot him if he offered any father abuse to his wife, and for what he had said already, he would immediately prosecute him.

The false-hearted merchant now appeared, and told him that he had heard such a character of him from his father, that he was no longer his friend, and ordered him to leave his house instantly; for he must not come there to insult gentlemen of honour, and ladies of fortune; and that if he heard or saw any more of his abuse to the Frenchman or his wife, he would have him confined in prison.

Exiled by his father; circumvented and betrayed by his friend; rivalled in his affections; torn by the warring passions of love, hatred, jealousy and revenge; his money nearly exhausted; at a distance from any friend or acquaintance—horror and despair seized upon his lymphated senses: he ran from one public house to another, poured down the maddening cup of inebriation, and, in the paroxisms of hopeless grief, and frantic rage, attempted to leap into the pit of destruction.

He was taken to the habitation of benevolence itself—a worthy Quaker. The balmy cordial of heavenly consolation was poured into the deep wounds of his heart, by the lenient hand of divine humanity.

Since my return to America, I have seen the same person in New-York, and knew him by a certain scar in his face. He informed me that the humane Quaker above mentioned, and several other philanthropic gentlemen, wrote to his father, who immediately came to Philadelphia—informed him that the lady to whom he had wished him married was wedded to another—begged his forgiveness, with tears of remorse and renewed affection; and promised, if he would return home, never to thwart his inclinations again. That the lady, on being informed and convinced of his fidelity, and of the chicane and duplicity that had been the cause of her giving her hand to the Frenchman, wrote to him; and being assured of his undiminished attachment, and of his willingness to receive her, she had left her husband, who consented to relinquish her, when he found she did not love him, and for some trifling consideration gave her a divorce; and that they now lived and enjoyed uninterrupted felicity.

CHAPTER V

Embarkation—Celebration of Independence—Exemplary Punishment, &c.

Patriotism is ever united with humanity and compassion. This noble affection, which impels us to sacrifice every thing dear, even life itself, to our country, involves in it a common sympathy and tenderness for *every citizen*, and must ever have a *particular feeling* for one who suffers in a public cause.

—Hancock[1]

Now comes the time, and now the word,
For soldiers to repair on board;
And, sober as a gallows throng,
With knapsacks slung, we march along:
Enter the Trip'li destined frigate,
Turn sailors, and assist to rig it.
  Next morn we *chanc'd to live* to see
Our annivers'ry jubilee!
Some *slaves* might independence hail,
Or sing of *liberty* in *jail*,
With more propriety than we,
For all of *us* were *bound*—to sea.
  Pray what's the end of punishment?
To make men better, and repent?
Or is it just for those who fun wish,
To shew they have the *pow'r* to punish? . . .
How few there are, t' enslave, to kill,
Give them the *pow'r*, would lack the *will*.

In the afternoon of the third of July, those of us who were destined for the frigate, were ordered, at a moment's warning, to repair on board. All hands were employed in shipping her top-masts, taking in spars, lumber, rigging, &c. The ship was in the utmost confusion—no water nor provisions for the men, and nothing to sleep on the following night, and for many nights after, but the hard and pitchy deck. The next morning ushered in the glorious anniversary of American Independence; and such an independence as I never saw before nor since, and never wish to see again. The one which I witnessed in Tripoli, afterwards, was heaven itself, compared to this: for while the voluptuous sons of idle dissipation, throughout the union, were quaffing the delicious blood of the exotic vine, our industrious and patriotic seamen, who had just embarked to expose their lives in the defence of that commerce which procured them their luscious and exhilerating libation, had not even a refreshing draught of cooling water to sate the feverish thirst of intense labour; for nothing but the warm and sickening river-water was to be obtained. While the high-fed, rich and slothful epicureans of our sea-ports were gorging the dainty luxuries of various climes, and different oceans, our enterprising tars, on whose hazardous labours they had fattened and were feasting, had not the strengthening viands of an ordinary repast. While the enchanting sound of the dulcet lute was made to ravish the ears of our sluggish, intoxicated cits on shore, the only instrumental music that we had on board, was the thrilling pipe of the arbitrary boatswain, and his ruffian apish mates: and while the choral songs of heaven-born freedom were carolled from the halter-favoured throats of many an imported aristocrat, mingled with seditious toasts and federal blasphemy—"all hand ahoy!" vociferated from the sonorous gullet of the triune boatswains, and "spring, you damn'd rascals!" squeaking from the faint lungs of the peurile midshipman, were all our sentiments and vocal music of the day. From the third until the eleventh of July, nothing but one incessant bustle and cry of "come here," and "go there," was to be heard. One officer orders a man to do one thing; a second immediately comes and orders him to do another thing: then he is flogged by the first for leaving his work, and ordered back to it: then served in the same manner by the second. A third comes—"what are you about, you d—'d puppy," and orders him to a new place:—"not a word!" if he attempts to parley—"a rope's-end!" if he refuses to obey his officers *tacitly*—"no jaw, you d—'d scoundrel!" if he essays to reason, or complain of exorbitant commands—"stubborn villain!" if he looks serious—"impertinent one," if he smiles. Thus he is alternately verberated and harrassed for not executing what, if he had the strength of Hercules, and as many hands as Briareus,[2] he could not possibly perform.

On the twelfth, we dropped down to Fort Penn, where we took in our guns, lay several days, and then fell down the river as far as Newcastle. Here we took in water, provisions, &c. and prepared for sea with all possible dispatch. We had now received hammocks, and the difficulty of getting clews, nettings, and lashings, and our ignorance and want of experience in the sublime art of slinging and lashing them up, was truly deplorable; for it was attended with serious and painful consequences. And surely no ignorance is more to be lamented, than that which subjects a man to corporeal punishment; and no inexperience more to be regretted, than that which exposes a man to censure, curses, scoffs and stripes. Our hammocks must be neatly fitted for critical inspection, at a short and stated time; and no provision made for rope-yarn or cordage; none allowed from the boatswain; no seaman permitted to take any, on pain of punishment, and yet every man that was found destitute was surely flogged. He *must not* leave his work to attend to his hammock; if he *did*, he was surely *flogged*. He *must* leave his work to attend to it; if he *did not*, he was surely flogged. In a word, a man must be omnicient, omnipotent, omnipresent, and be able to create things out of nothing, at a moment's notice, on board of a man of war, or he will surely be flogged: and yet, by nothing short of miracles, I always had the good fortune to escape.

As I lost the minutes of a journal which I had kept on board when we were taken in Tripoli, I will not pledge myself for correctness in naming the dates of events; but as to the veracity of them, no deviation shall be recorded. A mistake in the time of an action, does not prove that the action never took place; but can only prove, that it did not take place at that time.

The first person, if I mistake not, that was legally and publicly punished, was one Thomas Higgins, an able and skilful seaman, who had deserted from on board a British man of war, where he had been impressed and detained upwards of five years, and had now placed himself under the protecting wings of Columbia's genius. Fatigued with unremitting labours, in the dead of night, he sunk into a momentary repose, on the forecastle of the ship, the place where he was stationed, but not then on duty. A midshipman moping and blundering about in the dark, happened to detect him in the horrid act of *sleeping!* He went to the head, got a bucket of water, and dashed it into his face, and all over him. Starting from slumber, supposing it to be some one of his comrades, he began to "swear his prayers." But finding it to be a mighty midshipman that had performed the priestly act of baptizing him, he made an apology, by saying, "I did not think it was one of the *gentlemen*, (as sailors are taught to call these puny brats of despotism) or I should not have sworn as I did; for I did not think a gentleman would do such an action."

It is very surprising that the *gentleman* had sense enough to feel conviction; but it is not surprising at all, that he went to the officer of the deck, and entered a complaint that the "villain said he was *no gentleman*["]; which, if he had possessed common sense, he must have known was no more than the truth. The strutting potentate of the quarter-deck, ordered a boatswain's mate to call Higgins. He appeared—"What is this you have been saying to an officer, you damn'd rascal?"—said the dread umpire of the fate of tars. "I thought, Sir,"—"You thought, you damn'd rascal, who gave you liberty to think? Boatswain's mate! call the master at arm's—here master at arms, put that son of a bitch in irons." His orders were instantly obeyed, and the man was manacled, both hands and feet. The next night following, Peter Whelan, a marine, was found nodding in the cockpit, while on sentry, by a midshipman; reported to the officer of the deck, and put in irons. He was an aged veteran—had served in the army of the United States twenty-eight years—was covered with the scars of honour—had bled in the cause of freedom—was seven times wounded in the revolutionary war, and several times in St. Clair's defeat—had grown grey, and was nearly superanuated, in the defence of our rights; and this was the first time, he positively affirmed, that he was ever put in irons. He had excellent recommendations from General Wilkinson, and several other officers, under whom he had served, of his valour, good conduct, and patriotism; and the ingratitude of his country now, drew tears from the old man's eyes. After having been confined several days—"all hands to punishment!"—was bellowed from the boatswain, and his mimic mates. We assembled on the gun-deck, abreast of the main hatchway, to witness the exemplary operations of naval justice. The culprits were brought to the tragic stage, and ordered to strip. Whelan plead his scars—acknowledged, that worn down with toils, he had trespassed on the rigid rules of martial discipline, and implored mercy. Many could not refrain from tears—The scene was affecting—perhaps he had sons—how should I feel, if he were my father! He had contributed his blood to the purchase of our Independence—he was aged, poor, and friendless, and looked up to our government for succour and support. His fault, if a fault it could be called, was that of nature. How I then wished that I possessed, not only the power of pardoning, but the means of maintaining him for life. At length, the angel of Pity, descending from the highest seat save God's, in heaven, with a finger dipped in the fountain of mercy, touched the hard heart of war. The trembling, weeping, feeble, and grateful old man, was forgiven.

Higgins was then tied. He attempted to exculpate himself, by saying—"I thought, Sir, it was one of my companions"—for it was evident that what he first said was the cause of his being reported. "You thought! you have no right to think, damn your blood; you tell an officer he is no gentleman—I'll cut you in ounce pieces, you scoundrel—boatswain's mate! do your duty!" He was then flogged without feeling or mercy. That a man had no right to *think*, was a theorem I had never heard of before, not even under the most arbitrary governments, among the most flaming zealots in polemical theology. It was worse than the blue laws of my native state—worse than the inquisition of Spain—worse than the Bastile of France. Votaries of Justice! What do you think of a smockfaced, pickshank, fopdoodle of an officer, sporting with the feelings, the liberty, and the very life and health of one of our gallant tars, and for a trifling mistake, or a just retort, to have him chained, mutilated, and disgraced. Votaries of humanity! What do you think of an effeminate, pragmatical, sapling of an officer, who could have the turpitude, the effrontery, and the barbarity to report a worthy veteran, for shutting his eyes a few moments, when he had nothing to place them on deserving his vigilance? The midshipman who complained of Higgins, after having shamefully abused him, and trifled with his toils, was an imported British gasconade, who had learned his first lessons of nautical tyranny in the school of the English navy. And I could not but remark, that every cruel officer that we had on board was a warm partisan for British precedents, and of course a serious federalist.[3]

The next person that was put in irons, and punished at the gangway, was one Nugent, a marine. He was taken into the wardroom to wait on the lieutenant of marines, and had the charge of a sixteen gallon keg of brandy. He was found drunk, lying in the surgeon's birth, and, on examination, it was found that he had nearly emptied the brandy-keg, by giving bottles of brandy to a launch corporal, who had a doxy on board, and who was the first to bear witness against him, after having over persuaded him to do it. It cannot be said that he was unjustly or unlawfully punished. A few days after, as he was exercising or drilling on the quarter-deck, abaft the mizen, not knowing his musket was loaded, he snapped it, and a ball did but just escape the head of the officious corporal, and passing through the hammocks in the quarter nettings, communicated fire to the cloths. He was immediately reported by the corporal, and again put in irons; but having been so recently punished, and this being considered as accidental, rather than premeditated, in the plenitude of rich clemency there was found forgivness.

The next, making allowance for anachronisms, was John Tharpa, seaman, and cockswain of the barge. He had been master's mate, on board of the frigate United States, and entered on board the Philadelphia, with flattering promises of speedy preferment, and getting a little intoxicated on shore, was reported by a midshipman, put in irons, and a good round dozen was the first step towards his promotion.

About the same time, David Burling, a marine, was punished for sleeping on post. On being detected a second time, in the act of dozing, he was put in irons, confined to the coal hold, and there kept until we struck the shoals off Tripoli. But this last did not happen until we had been out a considerable time. He was to have been tried by a court-martial; for Capt. B. emphatically declared that it would give him "infinite pleasure to see him hanging at the yard-arm." It is known and acknowledged, that according to the articles of war, "any sentinel sleeping on his post, on being convicted, thereof shall suffer death or such other punishment as a courtmartial shall adjudge." But whether this is meant to apply, except in actual service, in times of imminent danger, is not for me to say. The marines had to take their tours of duty, keep themselves clean, and go to every call of all hands besides; and therefore, great allowance ought to have been made for their being constantly driven and harrassed night and day; and it is more than probable, that if they had been justly dealt by, and regularly relieved from sentry in due time, very few would have merited stripes or chains.

While we were lying here, Capt. Wharton came on board, and paid us some money. We put into a common stock a few dollars each, to send on shore and purchase some sea-stores. We gave the money to one Collins, a mizen-top boy, who belonged to the jolly-boat. He deserted, and I have never seen nor heard of him since. Perhaps some prophetic spirit whispered in his ear that we were bound to a Turkish prison. We had, as yet, no canns to draw our rum in, and tin pots and cups were very scarce amongst us. The serjeant of marines drew our rations from the purser's steward, and undertook to serve it out to us. We were classed in messes of eight men each. He would not give any part of the rum to any one of our mess except we found a vessel large enough to take the whole. We could not do it, and he kept the rum to himself. As the water was very bad, the men much fatigued, and the most of us not very averse, at any time, to the cheering beverage of spirits, this flagrant outrage committed on our rights—this glaring embezzlement of our rations, was spurned by all with indignation, and threatened revenge. But the officer of marines being on shore, before a complaint could be made to him, and the very night following, our serjeant, having so much more than his ordinary measure of rum, got intoxicated, and making considerable tumult in his birth, was ordered, by a midshipman in the steerage, who had heard him accused of purloining our rum, to "keep silence, and put out his light." Deeming himself an officer, co-ordinate with a midshipman, he refused to obey. The midshipman flew from the steerage, doused the gleam, and dragged the serjeant from his hammock, into which he had sprung, and gave him a hearty and severe basting. The general thirst of revenge was now allayed, although the person who executed justice had no more right to strike the serjeant than he had to drink our rum. The serjeant complained to the lieutenant of marines but could get no satisfaction, and he afterwards went and remained on shore. Lieutenant Jones arrived from New-York with between thirty and forty men, which he had shipped there. Being now fully prepared, and our pilot on board, we descended the river, and time will never efface the impressions I then felt. The tranquility, order, and harmony of the delightful shores, contrasted with the tumult, confusion and discord of the hateful ship, appeared now to have charms never before contemplated. *There*, liberty, equality, peace, plenty, and all the rural beauties of nature, held a halcyon reign. *Here*, oppression, arrogance, clamour, indigence, and all the hideous deformities of art, and implements of bloodshed, struck the mind with horror and dismay. It is a trite but true saying, that the blessings of life—the pleasures of sense, never appear so valuable, so lovely and so enchanting, as when they are about to depart from us; and a friend never appears so amiable, so engaging, and of such inestimable worth, as when we are bidding him a final adieu. Heaven-favoured farmers! how ineffably happy, how supremely blest would you be, did you but know how to appreciate the privileges you enjoy, and feel the same relish for the sweets of your fields, as one who is bound to meet the terrors of the god of war, and reap the horror of the midnight storm. On the twenty-seventh day of July, we dismissed the pilot, and in a short time lost sight of the happiest shores on earth.

CHAPTER VI

A Voyage

Invocation to Neptune

Neptune, attend, god of the vast profound!
Whose will controuls it; and whose pow'rs surround!
When lightnings flash, tremend'ous thunders roar,
And liquid mountains tumble to the shore,
Thy awful mandate, sounding from afar,
Can hush the dim of elemental war;
The restless billows lull to slumb'ring peace,
And bid the whirlwind and the tempest cease!
O make, in answer to our fervent pray'r,
The Philadelphia thy peculiar care.
To winds propitious all our sails unfurl'd,
Bearing the ensign of a glorious world;
Should in our cruise some hostile flag be seen,
The Moor, Tripolitan, or Algerine—
Should blood-stain'd Mars his hideous front display,
And menace carnage to obstruct our way—
As stern Ulysses, as Achilles bold,
Or warlike Hector, in the days of old,
The martial look of Bainbridge shall inspire
The dauntless ardour of heroic fire;
His sword shall triumph in the vengeful blow,
And deal destruction to the recreant foe.
So taught the muse prophetic—but the song
Prov'd in the sequel, the prediction wrong.

We were divided into two watches; but all hands being kept constantly on deck in the day time, we had not more than four hours, out of twenty-four, for relaxation and repose; and, consequently, at every muster of the watch, during the night, stupified with lassitude, more or less would be sound asleep below. Sometimes fifteen or twenty at a muster would be ranged along the gangways, to receive the reward of their atrocious actions—the punishment due to the incestuous crime of yielding to the embraces of mother nature, by resting their heads a few moments in her lap; not on a downy pillow of somniferous poppies, but more frequently on the soft side of a plank; and an almost unceasing cry of men excrutiating under the torturing operations of a rope's end, was to be heard through the dreary night. The ship was yet a chaos of disorder, and a frequent call to quarters in the dead of night, was attended with broken shins, bruised backs and battered noses. A midshipman had to muster the marines' hammocks, which were stowed in the quarter nettings. Mr. B. from Philadelphia, was commissioned, one morning, with this important charge. It must be previously understood, that when a marine officer musters his men, by calling them by name, they are not allowed to answer "here, sir," as the sailors are taught to reply to their officers, but "here," only. The most of us had the presence of mind, and fortunate precaution to consider, that, as Mr. B. was not a marine officer, perhaps we ought not to take hold of a name so brightly polished, without putting a handle to it; and we luckily added "sir" to the "here." But two of our marines, who very likely had been flogged by some marine officer for answering "here, sir"; O, fatal hallucination! O, impudent fellows! replied as they had been taught, with a bare "here." The little captious, amphibious animal flew into the most outrageous passion, and seizing an end of the mizen hallyards, gave each of those audacious wights twenty or thirty blows with all the strength of his little arms; while so remote were they from meaning any insult or disrespect, that when he had exhausted all his might and fury, they did not know what trespass they had committed—for what they had been beaten. Luckily for them, he was no Mendoza,[1] or he might have pounded them to jelly. They entered a complaint to the marine officers, but got no redress!!! They were marines, and that alone was enough to damn them. Lovers of equality! Cultivators of your independent soil! The only lords of America! what do you think of these things? Are such cruelties authorized by the constitution of our country? Or, is the constitution violated by those paltry imps of despotism? Are the officers of our navy legally invested with such absolute power? or, is such power as unlawfully assumed as it is arbitrarily exercised? Are we in want of seamen and soldiers, or are we not? Is it a crime so atrocious—a thing so degrading, to enter voluntarily into the service of the United States, that a man must be no longer considered as a citizen of America? And are citizens of this free country to be treated with as much contempt, as great barbarity, and as villainous injustice as the sable vassals of the West-Indies? Does it not reflect disgrace upon human nature, to suppose that mankind are incapable of being governed, even in a man of war, but by the iron rod of tyrannical power? Has a man, because he is no officer, no right to speak in his own justification? no right to complain? no right to seek redress if he is injured? Or is he so vile, so contemptible, so abandoned by God and man, that he cannot be injured? Has a sailor no emulation? no feeling? no resentment? And must a brat of an officer, a boy of twelve or fourteen years of age, be permitted to strike, to insult, to trample on, to swagger over men grown venerable by age, and honourable by wounds in the service of their country? And, above all, does a man's being a marine sink him to the very depths of debasement and infamy? Ye honest tillers of the ground! You, from whom all legitimate political power and authority originate; why do you suffer your hirelings to abuse the power you commit to them? Why do you not wrest the rod from their hands? How would you like to see a son of yours bleeding beneath the hands of your servant? You who were the purchasers of Independence, and next to God himself, the fathers of plenty, and of all the blessings and privileges we enjoy—you, who are the very life and soul of our liberty, why do you permit your servants to treat your sons like slaves? Or, are you ignorant of their perversion of your authority? Or, is a man, when he is once on board a man of war, dead to all justice, to all humanity, to all sense of feeling? and must he be treated like a slave—an out cast of society—a villain—a beast?

I cannot dismiss this subject without mentioning a circumstance which took place a few days after we were liberated from Tripoli; on board of the United States frigate Essex, while we were lying at Syracuse. Amongst a number of men that were sent in a boat to paint the ship's sides, was James Gallagher; who was one of the Philadelphia's crew, just emancipated from a Turkish prison—sickly, and emaciated. He had been destitute of shoes for a long time before he came on board, and there were none in the ship. In working amongst so much black paint, some of it unavoidably adhered to his feet. It was impossible to wash it off, with salt water. The men were called out of the boar, up the gangway; and such of them as had dirty shoes, left them in the boat, and came on deck with clean feet. Gallagher tried to wash his feet before he stepped on deck, but it only made them worse; and when he walked along the gangway, he left the vestiges of his feet. The officer of the deck called him and asked him where were his shoes? He answered that he had none, and could not possibly get any. He was snarled at, and asked, why he did not wash his feet then? He answered, that he had tried; but could not wash off the paint, unless he had soap and fresh water. He was then damned for a dirty rascal, ordered to take off his jacket, a boatswain's mate called, and told to give him about two dozen, with a large rope's end. He was a good seaman, had been several years in our service—a person of a peaceable and excellent disposition, and was beloved by all the prisoners in Tripoli. What bosom is there that would not burn with a sympathetic indignation and resentment at such a scene as this? That a man, but just escaped from the sanguinary clutches of Tripolitan barbarians, weak, palid, and broken with toils, chains, and hunger, should so soon be treated worse than by those savages—beaten, among his own countrymen, for not performing impossibilities, was enough to awaken the spirit of indignation in the bosom of a fainted anchorite.[2]

Shades of departed heroes! who fought, bled and died in the sacred cause of liberty, how are your blessed manes insulted; how is your blood contemned; how are your ashes profaned; how are your names reproached; how are those hallowed rights, transmitted to your sons, trampled upon, violated, and destroyed, if such things are winked at by our government. It will be answered that severe discipline is indispensably necessary on board a man of war. It is granted. But is there not some difference between disciplining men, and murdering them? How is it that men are made to perform duty on board of a merchantman without flogging? Perhaps it may be said that these statements are not true, or that they are exaggerated. So far from being falsehoods, that they are truths excused—truths that can be proved by every seaman that ever sailed in our service. So far from being exaggerated, that the worst I have yet said, is but a paliation of enormities.

Have you not heard of the man who was stabbed by an officer on board of the Constitution, while in action with a French frigate, merely for looking pale, and making a false step? Have you not heard of a man who was struck by an officer, on board the Essex, a few years since; and who, in consequence, died? Have you not heard of a man being kicked in the stomach or bowels, by an officer of the Constitution; and who, in consequence, died? Who has not heard of the man who was stabbed in his own house, in Baltimore, by Lieut. P.———,[3] and who, in consequence, died instantly? But, these are British precedents—imitations of British examples.

The British have the most powerful navy on the ocean, and the best seamen in the world; and if they treat their tars with cruelties, so must Americans. If they murder their sailors and soldiers, so must Americans. With shame to our navy be it said, that I have seen Americans who had been impressed, and had remained, for years, in the British navy, who have said, and will say, that they found better treatment in that execrable service—under that detestable government, which tears from the bosoms of their families and friends, their seamen, by infernal press-gangs, than in their own service, and under their own government. And it is a well known fact, that while part of our squadron was lying at Gibraltar, several of our seamen deserted to the British fleet. Amongst our crew, in the Philadelphia, I may safely say there were one hundred who had sailed in that navy, and not one of them all but would say, he fared better than in our own.

But, as I have before observed, we must not include the whole of our navy officers in this charge. The brave man is never a cruel one. The dauntless Preble[4] is said to be as humane as he is brave; as just as he is humane; and as merciful as he is just. The intriped Decatur[5] is as proverbial, among sailors, for the good treatment of his men, as he is for his valour. Not a tar, who ever sailed with Decatur, but would almost sacrifice his life for him. Capt. Bainbridge[6] was thought by many of our sailors, to be a good officer; but he trusted too implicitly to his subordinate myrmidons. His second lieutenant, Mr. Jones, was a calm, mild, and judicious officer, beloved by all the seamen. Mr. Hunt, his third lieutenant, treated me with distinguished kindness. Mr. Cutburt, a midshipman, was an amiable young gentleman. Midshipmen Gamble and Gibbons, were young gentlemen of merit. Mr. Osborn, lieut. of Marines, could not be called a tyrannical officer. But all this does not prove that the general complaint of ill usage in our service is unfounded. The commander of a ship may be a good man, and yet, confiding too much in his officers, or being absent, his men may be shamefully treated, without his knowledge; and custom, by imitating the British navy, having imposed such arbitrary rules, that a seaman dare not complain of an officer, they often suffer under a worthy commander. How is the captain of a ship to know that his men are mal-treated? He is not much on deck; the men do not complain to him; and for this reason he does not suppose they are wronged. If one of his officers punishes a man, he is made to believe by that officer, that the man deserved it. If a man is reported by an officer, it is the duty of the captain to punish him, at the officer's instance. The great fault; the chief cause of so much tyranny, of so many just complaints of cruel officers, is the practice of giving warrants to boys—to the upstarts, the fops, the base, unprincipled, inexperienced mammets of licentiousness; who are trained up to exercise undue authority over men, "the lachet of whose shoes they are not worthy to unloose." What necessity, what propriety, what justice is there in giving a boy of eleven or twelve years of age a warrant, with liberty to command, to insult; to strike in the face, men old enough to be their great grand-fathers? How can human nature brook such abuse? Does not the very establishment, then, give licence to the school of tyranny, and plant the nursery of despotism? Such things might plead excuse in any other country, under any other government but ours; but how does it comport with our boasted freedom? But the British do the like; and we, who pretend to discard British precedents, in almost every thing else, still retain them in this. This boy of an officer, draws nineteen dollars a month, when an able, and skilful seaman has but twelve. Is there any equity in this? It is true, we must have officers; but why are they not made officers by merit? Why are they not taken from among the seamen—men of experience? Or, is there no men of merit amongst them? Another thing to be noticed, is the provision made for the vultures of the navy, by sinecure offices. What is the advantage of a purser, on board of a man of war? Or, if there is a real necessity for one, where is the justice in his charging seamen fifty cents a pound for tobacco—fifty cents for a jack-knife, and more than one hundred per cent. on all his slops;—when, by law, he is allowed to charge no more than ten per cent? Where does the amount of this enormous profit go to? The purser has his wages besides the profits of his slops. How is this? Is he allowed to rifle from the sailors their hard earned wages to his own private benefit alone; or does he go snacks with other officers, who defend him in his peculations? Where is the justice in giving a chaplain forty dollars a month, and two rations, for doing nothing at all—not even so much as reading prayers? Or do they think the prayers of the wicked avail nothing? What justice is there in giving two idle surgeon's mates, each thirty dollars per month, for doing worse than nothing—for embezzling and devouring the rations allowed to the sick? for drinking their wine, and giving them cold water in the place of it?

Farmers! this is the way your money goes! to such purposes are your taxes appropriated! If a neighbour of yours, in the common transactions of business, defrauds you of a few pence, how ready are you to resent it; and will you suffer your servants, to whom you delegate your power, to pick your pockets before your face? The contributing of your taxes, to the support of such a naval establishment as may be deemed necessary, for the protection of our commerce, is no evil to you; because, commerce increases the demand for, and raises the price of your produce; so that, on the whole, it may probably put more money into your pockets than it takes out of them. But this is no reason that a man, whom you may hire to labour for you, because the profit of his labour is great, to seize on it as his own, or squander it away. Will any one pretend to say, that the foregoing predications, and remarks, are too circumscribed, too light, or unimportant, to be the subject of reasonable declamation, or serious reflection? That, for the general good, individual evils must be dispensed with—that, to secure liberty to all, a few must suffer slavery; and, that a handful of sailors and soldiers, being treated with every severity of injustice and oppression, ought not to be exposed to public investigation, as a matter of momentous concern? If our commerce cannot be protected—if our navy cannot be supported—if the ground of national honor and national defence cannot be maintained but by such flagrant violations of justice, of liberty, of humanity, and of the rights of man, freedom is a jest, and our constitution a mere burlesque on her name. And now, with all the logic of speculative politicians—all the criminations of public functionaries—all the noise of congressional debates—all the buzz and bustle of the alien and sedition laws—the stamp-act—the whisky insurrection—all the whoops of political office-hunters—all the warfare of editorial partisans—all the prating of federal-republican, quid, &c. Is it not of greater importance that one citizen of the United States should be chained, stripped, tied, and whipped like a dog, by an officer commissioned by our Executive, for not the least shadow of a crime? Yet this has been done, not to one man only, but to hundreds. Not only whipped like dogs, but immolated like bullocks. And who could witness such scenes with indifference? who could refrain from exclaiming with Cicero against Verres[7]——"O liberty! O sound, once delightful to every American ear! O sacred privilege of American citizenship! once sacred, but now trampled upon." That the preceding reflections may not be considered as the overflowing ebullitions of outrageous revenge for personal abuses, I would mention, as before observed, that I was never chastised while I was in the service; and as a proof that I was not considered as one of the most incorrigible men on board of the Philadelphia, I shall cite the following extract of a letter, written by one of our officers in Tripoli, to a gentleman in Philadelphia, which was published in the Port Folio, as an introduction to some pieces of poetry. He says—"I cannot omit mentioning a marine, whose extraordinary merit has attracted the attention and notice of all the officers; his name is Ray," &c. And Capt. Bainbridge, after he had returned to America, in a letter to a friend of mine, says—"Ray has conducted himself in such a manner, as not only to gain my good opinion, but also, the respect and good will of all the other officers." By which it will appear, that, as I had the good opinion of the officers, it is not probable I was much punished by them; and if I was not much punished by them, it is not very probable that in making these remarks I have been actuated by selfish revenge.

CHAPTER VII

Exercising Ship

Now for the rock our warlike frigate bore,
Nor storms were felt to beat, nor heard to roar—
"Clear ship for action!" sounds the boatswain's call—
"Clear ship for action!" his three mimicks bawl;
Swift round the decks, see war's dread weapons hurl'd,
And floating ruins strew the watry world!
"All hands to quarters!" for and aft resounds,
Thrills from the fife, and from the drum-head bounds;
From crouded hatchways scores on scores arise,
Spring up the shrouds and vault into the skies!
Firm at his quarters each bold gunner stands,
The death-fraught lightning flashing from his hands!
Touch'd at the word, tremendous cannons roar,
The waves rush, trembling, to the viewless shore!
From crackling muskets whizzing balls are sent,
And, darting, pierce the liquid element!
The fearful nations of the deep below,
Fly the dire signals of impending woe;
Air's wild inhabitants in clouds convene,
And wing impetuous from the frightful scene;
Men seek the spoils of the eventful fight,
Lo! not an enemy nor a sail in sight!
What then? must poets ne'er record a deed,
Nor sing of battles, but when thousands bleed?
Can naught but blood and carnage yield delight?
Or mangled carcases regale the sight?
Which shews more God-like, men to save—or kill?
Their *sweat*, by exercise, or *blood* to spill?

Which sounds more grateful to the man humane,
To hear of hundreds' health, or hundreds slain?
No blood here flows, no hero's dying groans,
No squadrons vanquish'd, and no broken bones;
But each more eager to the grog-tub ran,
Than when the foeless contest first began.

HAVING now been at sea for several days, it became expedient for us to practise in the art and discipline of war; and accordingly a time was appointed to exercise ship. The day was remarkably fine. We were prepared, by previous notice, and furnished with eight rounds of cartridges for small arms. The cannon were also made ready for the occasion. At ten o'clock in the morning, the boatswain piped, and the drum beat to quarters! We soon opened a tremendous fire upon our *imaginary* foes, and went through all the manoevres of a naval engagement. It was truly ludicrous to see three hundred men earnestly engaged in combatting the visions of fancy—running fore and aft the ship with naked, glittering cutlasses, and other weapons of bloodshed—flourishing their swords, hurling their battle-axes, and brandishing their pikes to prevent the enemy from boarding.

Perhaps if we had fought the Tripolitans with as much courage and pertinacity, as we did the fierce chimeras of our prolific brains, and opposed the great Bashaw with as much fortitude and as little trepidation as we did old Neptune, we might not have been captured without bloodshed; fortunately none were wounded—no lives were lost in either action; but the weather being very sultry, this might, with great propriety, be called a *warm* engagement. From the time we left the Capes, we were on an allowance of half a gallon of water, for each man, per day. The necessity of putting men on so short an allowance of water, while the weather was good and the wind fair, and while we had a plenty of it on board, could not have been very urgent; and certainly while we were lying in harbour, as afterwards, it was very arbitrary and unjust. This, notwithstanding, is practised by most of our ships of war.

On our passage, about this time, John House, a marine, died. When he first came on board he appeared to be very healthy, was florid and vivacious. I do not know what disease was the cause of his death; but I very well know that he was treated with less attention and more contemptuous neglect than if he had been an officer's dog. Our surgeon's mates could not possibly stoop to the low employment of attending a sick marine. He died insane, and in the greatest extremity of anguish, mental and corporeal.

Still on our course, the Western-Isles we past,
And fam'd Gibraltar heave in sight, at last;
Close in we stood at our commander's word,
The harbour enter'd and the frigate moor'd.
View'd, from the ship, what prospects here arise!
The rock's bold summit tow'ring to the skies,

Roll'd in eternal clouds, through time has stood,
Nods, threats and frowns terrific on the flood!
To guard the fortress and the port command,
Round its wall'd base repulsive batt'ries stand,
Rows above rows, huge cannon wide extend,
And groves of muskets glitt'ring terrors blend!
But flow'ry gardens soon relieve the sight,
And, side by side, lie horror and delight.

We had, for the most part of the way, a very fine breeze and pleasant weather. It was about the 26th of August, if I mistake not, when we arrived at Gibraltar. We lay here a few days when the frigate New-York, Commodore Morris,[1] the Constitution, Capt. Preble, and the John Adams, Capt. Campbell, arrived from the Mediterranean. The brig Vixen, Lieutenant Smith, also arrived from Baltimore. Information was received that a vessel, with Barbary colours, was cruising off the Rock, and we went in pursuit of her; she bore away, and we gave chase. Our ship was under English colours. We fired a number of guns before she would come to. About sun-set we came within hailing, and our captain ordered one of our seamen, who could speak Spanish and the Lingua-franca,[2] to speak her; which he accordingly did, and asked where she was from? They answered—"Morocco." Where are you bound?—"Morocco." What news?—"The Emperor of Morocco has given us orders to capture all American vessels." Have you taken any?—"Yes, we have captured a brig." Where is she?—"Ahead." Are any of her men on board?—"Yes, the captain and four men." You may judge something of their consternation and confusion when we let fall our English ensign, hoisted the American, and ordered them to strike. They instantly doused their colours and humbly deprecated our vengeance. Being ordered, they sent their boat on board of us, with their officers and captain of the American brig. Mr. Cox, our first lieutenant, with several midshipmen, about forty sailors, and a serjeant, corporal and eight marines, was sent on board to take command of the prize. The prisoners were disarmed and put under hatches, with sentinels over them. The ship carried twenty-two six pounders, and about one hundred men. Their guns were badly mounted, the ship filthy, and the men meagre, grisly and shabby. They had onions of the mildest flavour and largest size I ever beheld; I believe they were nearly six inches in diameter. Their sea-bread was from barley-meal, baked in large loaves, cut into slices and dried in an oven like what we call rusk. Their beef, or mutton, was boiled, cut into small pieces, mingled with flour, fat and oil, and packed into kegs. Rice, oil, olives, and dried fish composed the remainder of their esculent stores. Our frigate, now in company with the prize, steered for the brig, and came in sight of her the following day in the afternoon. She led us a chase, and was very unwilling to come to; but when we came within hail, the affrighted master of her cried out—"Morocco! Morocco!" and struck his colours. It was pleasing to witness the ecstacies of our countrymen on being thus unexpectedly and happily rescued from the power of their fierce predaceous captors. They had been stripped of their clothing, robbed of their chests and cash, plundered of every thing valuable in their cargo, and confined below in irons. We took the brig in tow, the prize in company, and sailed for the Rock. Knowing themselves to be pirates, and conscious of their crimes, the Moorish captives manifested great concern for their lives, by frequently putting their fingers across their throats, and asking us, by interpreters, if we did not think they would all lose their heads. At the Rock of Gibraltar the prisoners were all sent on board of the Philadelphia. Lieutenant Cox remained on board of the Moorish ship, as prize-master. The prisoners were kept on board of the frigate for a considerable time, and then sent to their own ship again. While they were with us, they were treated as prisoners of war—not insulted or abused—not put in irons, and had as much provisions allowed them as they could devour. Notwithstanding they were Mahometans, and, by their religion interdicted the drinking of spirituous liquors, and the eating of pork, many of the would indulge to excess in the former, and swallow, with voracity, the latter, in preference to any other meat. To supply the place of Mr. Cox, as first lieutenant of the Philadelphia, Mr. Porter came on board; and Mr. Renshaw, to fill the vacancy of Mr. M'Donough, who remained with Mr. Cox. James Ingerfon, Daniel Shays, Nathaniel Brooks, and Charles Rhilander, having been shipwrecked on the coast of Portugal, were sent by an American Consul, in a Portuguese ship, to the American Consul at Gibraltar. They were Americans, from Boston; had suffered much, and earnestly solicited him to provide them a passage to America, which he promised, and which was no more than his official duty to fulfil; but the perfidious misanthropes, instead of sending them on board of some of our shipping then lying in harbour and bound to America, sent them to our frigate, then bound up the Mediterranean, on a two years' cruise. The treacherous Consul told them that the ship to which he would send them was bound to America, and they were unsuspicious of any device, until they were safely on board of us, and informed to the contrary by our crew. Was this any better than impressing? The Consul's name is Gavino, and his conduct ought to be execrated by every American seaman. Him these four unfortunate Americans might thank for their chains in Tripoli. They applied to Captain Bainbridge, informed him of the Consul's finesse, and sued for permission to leave the ship and seek one bound to their native shores; but he told them, that as they had been sent by order of the American Consul, he could not possibly discharge them—encouraged them with the hope of our not being long out, and endeavored to persuade them to enter on the ship's books; but they were chagrined and contumacious, and positively refused, either to enter, or do duty. Some time in October we sailed for Malta, in company with the Vixen, and arrived there towards the latter part of the same month. Here we landed several boxes of dollars which we took in at Gibraltar. I need not inform the intelligent reader that this is the Island which in St. Paul's day was called Melita, the place where he was shipwrecked, when the viper fastened on his hand, and where "the barbarous people shewed him no little kindness." The town is large and populous. The harbour is spacious, safe and commodious, and nearly environed by the town. The houses are built of a cream-coloured stone easily hewn in any shape, though not too friable, and are handsome and durable. The numerous churches, priests and friars—the almost incessant ringing of bells, in every part of town, as signals for prayers, loudly proclaim the reign of superstition and fanaticism over genuine morality and rational devotion. While we lay here, two of our men, Walker and Kelly, deserted from a boat that was sent ashore for water. Walker had been cruelly flogged a few days before, for no crime or fault at all, by order of Lt. P. and he was heard to swear that if he found no opportunity to desert, he would jump overboard and drown himself sooner than stay in the ship during the cruise. There was a general murmuring among the men of insufferably bad usage, and it is my real opinion, that had we not been stranded, a mutiny would have ensued. Lt. P. when he first came on board, and before they knew his voice, ordered some men who were in a boat to come on deck, in order to do something to the rigging. It was very dark, and they, not judging it to have been the first lieutenant of the ship, made a reply, neither indecorous nor insolent, but not quite so obsequious and parasitical as to please the ear of consummate arrogance. He, therefore, called them up, and ordered a boatswain's mate to give them a severe flogging, before they knew, or he told them what it was for. And because they did not pull their hats off, while under the operation, in token of begging his mercy, he ordered a second flogging. Suppose an officer had coolly and deliberately stabbed a man in Baltimore, and had to fly from the pursuit of justice, and dare not return to America for fear of the halter, could any thing better be expected from such an officer, than that he would treat his men with the cup of torture? We now sailed for Tripoli, and, for what reason I know not, parted with the brig.

On the 31st day of October, early on Monday morning, a sail was discovered on our larboard bow, and orders were immediately issued to give her chase. She made towards the shores of Tripoli, and we soon distinguished that she carried Barbary colours. The white walls of our destined residence in captivity, soon hove in sight. Every sail was set, and every exertion made to overhaul the ship, and cut her off from the town. The wind was not very favourable to our purpose, and we had frequently to wear ship. A constant fire was kept up from our ship, but to no effect. We were now within about three miles of the town, and Captain Bainbridge not being acquainted with the harbour, having no pilot, nor any correct chart, trusted implicitly to the directions of Lieutenant Porter, who had been here several times, and who professed himself well acquainted with the situation of the harbour. We, however, went so close in that the captain began to be fearful of venturing any farther, and was heard, by a number of men, to express to Lt. P. the danger he apprehended in pursuing any farther in that direction, and advising him to put about ship. Lieut. P. answered that there was no danger yet, and that we would give them a few shots more. A moment of two afterwards, and just as we were preparing to come about, she struck upon the shoals and remained fast! The impudent pirate now, for the first time, hove to, and returned fire. Lt. P. looked much like the paper on which I am now blackening his name. Dismay was conspicuous in ever countenance. The sails were put aback, anchors cast ahead, and other means exerted to throw her off, but without effect. Three gun-boats were immediately under weigh from the wharves, and one of them, coming within reach, began to spit her fiery vengeance. I could not but notice the striking alteration in the tone of our officers. Burling was taken from our bastile, the coal-hold. It was no time now to act the haughty tyrant—no time to punish men for snoring—no time to tell men they had "*no right to think*," but every man could not snoaze and cogitate as much as he pleased. It was not "go you damn'd rascal"—but "come, my good fellow, my brave lads." The forecastle guns were run abaft on the quarter deck—the guns on the main deck hauled aft, but to no effect. The gun-boats kept throwing their balls; but they all went too high, none of them touched our hull, and but very few went through the rigging. It was thought if our guns were thrown overboard, it might cause her to swing clear; it was accordingly done, excepting those on the quarter-deck, and in the cabin; but no hopes were visible. Her foremast was cut away—all would not do—she seemed immoveable. Her stern was partly demolished, to make way for our guns to bear upon the enemy the better, but our shot had little or no effect. Mr. Hodge, the boatswain, suggested the experiment of casting a stern anchor, but this attempt was rejected by the officers, and he afterwards persisted in his opinion, that if this method had been adopted, she might have been thrown off with facility. Now was the juncture, at which we required the aid of the brig we had left.

It was a little past twelve oclock when we struck the shoals, and we continued firing at the boats, and using every means in our power, to get the ship afloat, and annoy the enemy; when, about four o'clock, the Eagle of America, fell a prey to the vultures of Barbary—the flag was struck!!

Many of our seamen were much surprised at seeing the colours down, before we had received any injury from the fire of our enemy, and begged of the captain and officers to raise it again, preferring even death to slavery. The man who was at the ensign halyards, positively refused to obey the captain's orders, when he was ordered to lower the flag. He was threatened to be run through, and a midshipman seized the halyards, and executed the command, amidst the general murmuring of the crew.

There was only one gun-boat that could bear upon us, although there were two more lying to leeward, between us and the shore, afraid to come nigher. It is true there were two or three more making ready and getting under way, but it was afterwards thought they would not have attempted to board us for that night; and by the next morning she was afloat!!

In fact, the Turks were so pusillanimous, that after our colours were struck, they dare not, for they did not attempt to come any nearer, until we sent a boat, and persuaded them that it was no farce, no illusion, assuring them that our frigate had in reality struck to one gun-boat, and entreated them to come and take possession of their lawful booty!!

While the boat was gone, the clothes, chests, and provision barrels were brought on the gun-deck, and every man was allowed free access. The ship was scuttled, and water let into the magazine—the cabin furniture destroyed—battle-axes, pikes, cutlasses, pistols, muskets, and all implements of war, thrown over-board. All hands were then called, to muster on the quarter-deck. Captain Bainbridge read a clause in the articles of war, stating, that our wages would continue, while we were prisoners of war; encouraged us to hope for ransom, by our country, and advised us to behave with circumspection and propriety, among our barbarous captors.

To witness the odd appearance of our provident tars, at this solemn hour, would have excited risibility in the muscles of an expiring saint. Some of them with three or four pair of trowsers, and as many shirts on, with handkerchiefs stuffed with handkerchiefs round their necks, and their bosoms crammed with clothes and provisions, bore the resemblance of Blunt, in puppet-show, or Falstaff, in comedy.

CHAPTER VIII

Remarks on Dr. Cowdery's Journal

I SHALL now take some notice of extracts from Doctor Cowdery's journal, as published in the Balance, of Hudson, and republished in the Albany Register. As far as he adheres to strict veracity, I shall coincide with his observations; but when he deviates from correctness, or exaggerates on facts, take the liberty of differing with the learned Doctor's diary. He says—"After the signal of the Philadelphia was struck, and the officers and crew waiting the pleasure of their new masters, the Tripolitan chiefs collected their favourites, and, with drawn sabres, fell to cutting and slashing their own men who were stripping the Americans and plundering the ship. They cut off the hands of some, and it is believed, several were killed." It is true there was a sort of mutiny and clashing of arms amongst them; but for my part I never saw any hands amputated, nor do I believe there were any lives lost; for myself and a hundred others were in the ship much longer than the Doctor, and none of us ever saw or heard of this carnage amongst themselves. After they had borrowed about ten dollars of the Doctor, and wrested his surtout from under his arm, he says—"Whilst they were picking its pockets, and quarrelling with each other for the booty, I sprung for the next boat which was waiting for me. In my way I met a little fellow who seized me and attempted to get off my coat, but I hurled him to the bottom of the boat," &c. This was certainly the most heroic action that has ever been read of any of the Philadelphia's officers. Surrounded by those horrific brigands, with "drawn sabres" and "cocked pistols," for a man, at such a critical and fearful crisis, to have the courage to collar an enemy, on his own ground, must be considered as a specimen of heroism not very common to be found among empirics of our navy. And when the Doctor mentions "hurling the *little fellow*," the reader, not acquainted with the person of the said Doctor, would really suppose him to be a mammoth of a man—quite the reverse. He further says—"they then began upon Mr. Knight, sailing-master, Mr. Osborn, lieut. of marines, and all the officers in the boat, and plundered their pockets; and took their handkerchiefs from their necks. They then landed us at the foot of the Bashaw's palace, where we were received by a guard, who conducted us into the palace, before the Bashaw. He viewed us with the utmost satisfactions, and had us conducted into an apartment where we found the captain and several officers, who arrived in another boat just before us. Here was a table set in the European style. The servants appeared to be Maltese and Neapolitan slaves. Here we stripped; after which it was announced that another boat had arrived with our officers and men, who were before the Bashaw. Captain Bainbridge requested me to go and look for Doctor Harwood, whom it was feared was killed. I found him with the carpenter, before the Bashaw, stripped of every thing but their shirts and trowsers. They afterwards informed me that they were stripped in the boat when I lost my surtout, and when they got within a few rods of the shore, they were thrown into the sea, and left either to drown or swim ashore. The Bashaw gave them dry clothes, and we were all conducted before the Bashaw and formed into a half circle. He was seated on his little throne, which was decorated in the Turkish order, and made a handsome appearance. He is a good looking man, aged about thirty-five. He counted us, viewed us with a smile and seemed highly pleased with us. We were then conducted, by the minister of axterior relations and a guard, to the house formerly occupied by the American Consul, a very good house, with a large court, and room enough for our convenience. We were seated here about 9 o'clock in the evening. Captain Bainbridge got permission from the Bashaw to send for the Danish Consul, who paid us a visit, and offered every assistance in his power. We slept upon mats and blankets spread upon the floor, which was composed of tiles." Although the Doctor here makes no discrimination between men and officers, it must not be understood that he includes the former when he says *we*, excepting servants—no, no, it was only the officers who were treated to a supper, and lodged in this comfortable mansion, and had mats to sleep on. You will, therefore, please to remember, that when the Doctor says *we*, it is the very same as if he had said *we officers only*; for he does not think proper to descend to the task of relating how the crew were provided for, or whether they were but half alive or all dead. I must, therefore, inform the interested and humane reader, that as soon as we were huddled in to the boats, all, or the most of us, were stripped of all our clothing excepting a shirt, trowsers and hat; some, however, who were in the first boat, under the eye of our officers, fared a little better, and kept the most of their clothes. When we came near the shore, we were all precipitated into the foaming waves; for the wind blew very fresh, and left to the free exercise of our talents at swimming or wading ashore. At the beach stood a row of armed men on each side of us, who passed us along to the castle gate. It opened, and we ascended a winding, narrow, dismal passage, which led into a paved avenue, lined with terrific janizaries, armed with glittering sabres, muskets, pistols and tommahawks. Several of them spit on us as we passed. We were hurried forward through various turnings and flights of stairs, until we found ourselves in the dreadful presence of his exalted majesty, the puissant Bashaw of Tripoli. His throne, on which he was seated, was raised about four feet from the surface, inlaid with mosaic, covered with a cushion of the richest velvet, fringed with cloth of gold, bespangled with brilliants. The floor of the hall was of variegated marble, spread with carpets of the most beautiful kind. The walls were of porcelain, fantastically enamelled, but too finical to be called elegant. The Bashaw made a very splendid and tawdry appearance. His vesture was a long robe of cerulean silk, embroidered with gold and glittering with tinsel. His broad belt was ornamented with diamonds, and held two gold-mounted pistols, and a sabre with a golden hilt, chain and scabbard. On his head he wore a large white turban, decorated with ribbons. His dark beard swept his breast. He is about five feet ten inches in height, rather corpulent, and of a manly, majestic deportment. When he had satiated his pride and curiosity by gazing on us with complacent triumph, we were ordered to follow a guard. They conducted us into a dreary, filthy apartment of the castle, where there was scarcely room for us to turn round. Here we remained an hour or two dripping and shivering with the chills of the damp cells, and the vapors of the night. The Neapolitan slaves were busily employed in bringing us dry clothing to exchange for our wet. We rejoiced to see men who wore the habiliments of Christians, and sincerely thanked them for their apparent kindness. We thought them disinterested, generous and hospitable; for we expected to receive our clothes again when dry; but the insidious scoundrels never afterwards would make us any restoration. The clothes which we gave them were new, and those which they brought us in exchange were old and ragged. We were then taken to a piazza, nearly in front of the Bashaw's audience hall, where we lodged for the night. It was floored with tiles and arched above, but open, on one side, to the chilling blasts of intemperate night, and as many of us had wet clothes on, and nothing to cover us with; add to this the gloomy prospects before us, and the painful apprehensions of chains, stripes and dungeons, and you may well suppose we had not a very refreshing night's repose. In the morning, about eight o'clock, an old sorceress came to see us. She had the complexion of a squaw, bent with age, ugly by nature, and rendered frightful by art. She looked round upon us, and raised a shrill cry of *bu-bu-bu-bu*, struck her staff three times upon the pavement, and then went through and examined us. There was a black man amongst us, and him she selected and placed aside from the rest. We supposed she had chosen him for herself, but he remained in the castle, as one of the cooks for the Mamelukes. This frightful hag is held, by the Bashaw and all the Tripolitans, in the highest veneration, not only as an enchantress, but as a prophetess also. It is said by them that she predicted the capture of the Philadelphia, and believed by them that the ship struck the shoals in consequence of her incantations.

The potent Bashaw presently made his appearance, and we were ordered to rise and pull off our hats. He walked past us, into his balcony, and we were permitted to ramble for a while, through the various divisions of this chaotic pile. Some of our men had saved a little cash from the ruffian hands of our hostile pillagers; but there was nothing eatable to be purchased in the castle. We had eaten nothing for twenty-six hours, and began to feel our appetite. The Neapolitans, by paying a certain share of the profits, were permitted to retail *aqua-deut*, a spiritous liquor distilled from the fruit of the date-tree, and similar to our whisky. This they kept to sell in their cells, in the castle, around the doors of which, our shivering men thronged, and such as had money shared it with such as had not. But these villainous, mercenary knaves, taking advantage of our ignorance in the price of the liquor, and of the money which they gave us in change, allowed no more than about one fourth of the real value of a dollar.

We were now collected together again, in front of a large window, which looked into a back yard. The Bashaw, his son, the renegade Scotchman, commodore Lysh,[1] and several of the Bashaw's officers, appeared at the window, and the Commodore began to interrogate us respecting our Captain, &c. He asked us whether we thought our captain a coward, or a traitor? We answered, neither. He replied, "who with a frigate of forty-four guns, and three hundred men, would strike his colours to one solitary gun-boat, must surely be one or the other." We told him that our ship being fast on the shoals, we had no chance to defend ourselves, having thrown our guns overboard, and that although we were in no immediate danger, except from one gun-boat, we judged, and feared, that as soon as night favoured their designs, they would surround and cut us to pieces, giving no quarters. He said there was no necessity for throwing our guns overboard; that we might have known she would be got off, as soon as the wind shifted, and assured us she was already afloat—that if we had not struck our flag, they would not have ventured to board us, and highly ridiculed our captain's cowardice, if, in fact, it was owning to want of courage; he persisted in the idea that the ship was given up by design; for he said, the captain not bringing a pilot with him, and leaving the brig, when he acknowledged himself unacquainted with the harbour, and then running so nigh in so precipitately, were circumstances weighty enough to overbalance all doubts of his treachery, or, at least, indubitable evidences of his want of judgment, and proofs of his pusillanimity. The Bashaw was very inquisitive to know the number of shipping and strength of America. We gave him surprising accounts of both. The commodore asked us, if there were any mechanicks amongst us, and said, that such as were willing to work at their trades, should be paid for their labour; if not, they would be compelled to do other work. He was informed there were ship carpenters and blacksmiths amongst us. They were selected from the rest, counted, and then mingled with us again. We were then collected in a body, and marched through dark and winding alleys, to the principal gate of the castle, and different from the one at which we entered. Passing out of this, we were conducted to an old magazine, as they called it, filled with sacks of grain, meal, lumber, and useless combustibles, which we were ordered to remove to another old building, not far distant. This was the first of our labour. Our drivers began to display their ferocity, by beating several of our men, who were rather dilatory in obeying their new boatswains. When we had finished removing the rubbish, we were given to understand, that this was to be the place of our confinement. It had once been occupied as a prison, by the Swedish captains, who had shared a fate similar to ours. The prison was about fifty feet in length, twenty in breadth, and twenty-five in height, with a sky-light, and two front, grated windows. It had a most dreary appearance, was dark and fuliginous. Not a morsel of food had we yet tasted, and hunger, like the vulture of Prometheus, began to corode our vitals.

Towards evening, some coarse, white bread, was brought, and we were all ordered out of the prison, and as we were counted in again, each one received a small white loaf, of about twelve ounces. This was all we had for the day. About sun set, our keepers came, and ordered us all out, to be counted in. We were under the disagreeable apprehensions of being separated, and sold into distant parts of the country, and at every call of all hands, painful sensations would disturb our breasts. We were counted in, one by one, and as we passed the grim jailor, were under the humiliating injunction of pulling off our hats. Those who refused this devoir were sure of a severe bastinading.[2] We had nothing to keep us from the cold, damp earth, but a thin, tattered sail-cloth; the floor of the prison was very uneven, planted with hard pebbles, and as we had nothing but a shirt to soften our beds, and nothing but the ground for a pillow, and very much crouded in the bargain, the clouds of night shed no salutary repose. Let us now return to our officers.

Doctor C. says—"This morning, Nov. 1st. the Danish Consul, Mr. Nissen, paid us another visit. Captain Bainbridge engaged him to furnish us with provisions, and such other necessaries as we might want. Our dwelling was furnished in a plain style, and we were supplied with fresh provisions that were tolerably good. We were allowed to go to the front door, and walk on the terrace, or top of the house, which commanded a handsome prospect of the sea, the harbour, the palace, and the adjoining country. Here we could see our ship on the rocks, full of Turks, and surrounded by their boats; and a constant stream of boats going to, and bringing off the plunder of the ship. We could see those robbers running about town with our uniform coats and clothing on. The minister of exterior relations promised to be friendly, and collect as much of our clothing and effects as he could, and return them to us."

The Doctor does not think it worth mentioning, that almost the whole crew were suffering intolerably, by hunger and nakedness; and it is very evident, that he thought more of uniform coats, than of his naked countrymen, who had no coats to put on. He says, also, that the ship was lying on the rocks, which was positive mendacity, for she floated clear, early that very morning! And I have observed, in all the public letters, that this circumstance has been carefully concealed.

"This day, Captain Bainbridge wrote a letter to the Secretary of the Navy, with the lamentable tale of our misfortunes, containing a brief statement of the circumstances of our capture; requesting, that arrangements might be made to meet the exigencies of himself, the other officers and officers' servants, and adding, that the remainder of the crew would be provided for by the Regency."

How did he know this? What assurance had he from the Bashaw, that he would provide for us, any more than for himself and his favourites? It is true, he might suppose that the Bashaw would put us to labour, if we were not provided for by our government, and that, for his own benefit, he would allow us sufficient food to sustain existence; but, was this any reason, that no farther notice should be taken of us? That government should make no appropriations for the mitigation of our sufferings? How did he know, but that benevolent characters in America, might initiate charitable contributions for the palliation of our miseries? How did he ever know, but that Congress might interpose for our relief? Or, how did he know but that the department of the navy might see fit to allow us some part of our rations or wages? But his declaration, that we would be provided for by the Regency, precluded, at once, the necessity of any executive, legislative, public, or private aid whatsoever. No doubt, had Captain Bainbridge made a just statement of our situation to the department of the navy, representing, that we were wholly dependent on the clemency of a faithless fratricide[3] for the support of life, and soliciting, in our behalf as well as for his train of servants, that some provision might be made for us, a liberal and patriotic spirit would have granted us laudable and adequate alleviation, until a ransom, or enfranchisement could be effected. For certainly those who were compelled to labour, were under greater necessity for temporary aid, and governmental munificence, than those who were cloistered in idleness. At numerous times, when we were on the very brink of starvation, and petitioned Captain Bainbridge for some part of our pay or rations, he invariably gave us to understand, that it was entirely out of his power to do any thing for us. No wonder, when he had impressed, not only the government, but all the people of the United States, with the belief that we stood in no need of assistance. The fact is an obvious one—He had committed a most flagrant blunder, and to parry off the shafts of obloquy, would hold up the idea of moderation in his demands, and frugality in his expenditures of the public money. Or, if not, his conduct evinces a total disregard and dereliction of his crew. How could an officer feast and fatten on the public benefaction, and, at the same time, be unmindful of his men, who had an equal claim on the government for similar favours? How could he be the means of debarring that claim, by asserting, that we would be provided for without it? Had not the Captain as much reason to expect that the Bashaw would make provision for him and his officers, and his officers' servants, as for us? Or, were the men whom he had brought into this distress by his blunders, totally unworthy of his regard? We were completely ignorant of this duplicity, until we returned to America, and verily thought, that Captain Bainbridge had done every thing in his power to meliorate our condition. What must we, then, think of a commander, who would give up his men to the enemy, contrary to their wishes, and then abandon them to starve, or rely on the mercy of sanguinary barbarians?

Nov. 2.—Before sunrise, the horrid clanking of huge bolts, announced the early vigilance of our keepers, who ordered us all out. They told the carpenters to stand by themselves—the blacksmiths by themselves, also—the coopers the same, and each company were appointed to their several employments, under the direction and command of Turkish masters; but they did not effect much, for a considerable time. The remainder of the men were distributed into different gangs, as we called them; some to the castle, to carry stone, dirt, lime, and mortar, where they were making repairs. Some were sent as cooks in the castle, and ten men were taken from among us, to be denominated cooks. Their employment was to bring water from a well, about a quarter of a mile distant, for the whole of us to drink—to bring, and serve out, the bread and oil to us, and sometimes, to boil what the Turks call *coos-coos*, which is barley ground very coarse, and neither sifted nor bolted; with which they occasionally fed us. Some were sent on board the frigate, and remained all night. About twelve or one o'clock the cooks were called, to go for bread, and presently returned with a quantity of black barley loaves, coarse, and full of straws and chaff, weighing about twelve ounces each. Of these they gave us two apiece, and, bad as they were, our men seized them with avidity. This was our allowance for twenty-four hours.

Nov. 3.—"The Bashaw sent for the carpenter to go on board the ship; he went, and found six feet water in the hold. The carpenter's crew and fifty men, were ordered, and carried on board, to work. At night, a gale of wind, and a heavy sea, hove the ship off the rocks, and the carpenter returned."

No doubt, as the Doctor says, there was six feet water in the hold; but he ought to have mentioned, that the ship was scuttled by us; otherwise, it conveys the idea, that the ship filled in consequence of the shock at first, or injury on the shoals.

If our men, and all the Turks, have not uttered wilful falsehoods, or been very egregiously mistaken, the ship was hove off the rocks, the very next morning after she was captured. This morning, after a large company was sent to the ship, and the most of our crew disposed of in different avocations, and at various employments, a considerable number of us were told, after having been counted, to return into the prison, and be ready, at a moment's warning, for any emergency. Some of them, however, strayed away, went into the town, and returned intoxicated. Our keepers perceived it, and proceeded to exhibit exemplary punishment, and sate, at once, their thirst of revenge. The instrument with which they prepare a man for torture, is called a bastone; It is generally about four or five feet long, and as thick in the middle as a man's leg, tapering to the ends. At equal distances from the centre, it is perforated in two places, and a rope incurvated, the ends passed through the holes, and knotted. This forms a loop. The person is then thrown on his back, his feet put through the loop, and a man at each end of the stick, both at once, twist it round, screw his feet and ancles tight together, and raise the soles of his feet nearly horizontal. A Turk sits on his back, and two men, with each a bambo, or branch of the date tree, as large as a walking-staff, and about three feet in length, hard, and very heavy, strip or roll up their sleeves, and, with all their strength and fury, apply the bruising cudgel to the bottoms of the feet. In this manner they punished several of our men, writhing with extreme anguish, and cursing their tormentors. They were then hampered with a heavy chain at each foot, but the next day they were taken off.

Our men began to complain much of hunger, having for this day but the two loaves of filthy, black, and sour bread. Some of them, however, who had the good fortune to save a little money, were permitted to go to the market, to purchase vegetables. Their market makes a wretched appearance. On each side of the main street in the town, commencing at the principal gate, a long string of low mud-wall huts, on each side the way, is all the market they have; at the doors of which, seated cross-legged on the ground, and a blanket wrapped round them, the Turks retail pumpkins, carrots, turnips, scallions, oranges, lemons, limes, figs, &c. &c. with a thousand trinkets, and haberdashers' wares.

At night most of our men returned from the frigate, and brought with them beef, pork, and bread, which was generously shared with those who had none, and though raw, devoured with voracity. The floor of our prison was not large enough to contain, or admit us all, stretched at full length, and many of us were obliged to sit, or stand, all night. This occasioned a strife, or crowding, at the prison door, to be the first, or, at least, not the last counted in, for the first were considered as being lawfully entitled to the spot of the ground for the night, and no one attempted to eject or oust them. It was surprising to witness the invincible spirit of our tars, and a person would be at a loss, whether to ascribe it to a philosophic fortitude, or natural apathy. In the most desponding aspect of times, they would caper, sing, jest, and look as cheerful, many of them, as if they had been at a feast or wedding.

Nov. 4.—A large number of our men were again sent, and employed in bringing ashore the product of the frigate. The officers were prohibited walking on the terrace of their prison. Some of us were every day referred for sudden avocations; to go and carry burthens, in different parts of the town, and for any other enterprize. At every emergency, or call for men, a wardman, or keeper, would enter the prison, take such as fancy, or accident pointed out, and if there was the least hesitation in obeying his commands, a severe beating was the result of such contumacy. Four of us were chosen to be the pack-horses of some unknown expedition. We were led by a grisly emissary of the Bashaw, through many crooked and dirty alleys, until we came to a house, at which he ordered us to halt. He went in, but soon returned, and gave us signals to follow him. He led us through a gloomy passage to a large court-yard. Our breasts palpitated on the way, but our fears were dissipated when we found ourselves surrounded by a dozen beautiful females, who came from the piazzas above. As the women in the streets are constantly wrapped and muffled up in blankets, which conceal their shapes and faces, except one eye, this, to us, was a novel sight; for the ladies were exposed to view, as much as the half-naked belles of our own towns. They were fantastically wrapped in loose robes of striped silk; their arms, necks, and bosoms bare. Their eye-lids stained round the edges with black. Their hair braided, turned up, and fastened with a broad tinsel fillet. They had three or four rings in each ear as large in circumference as a dollar. Several of them were very delicate and handsome. They brought us dates, olives, oranges and milk. They expressed or manifested great surprize at our appearance, and, like other ladies, were full of giggling and loquacity. Our driver then bade us follow him again into another yard, where he shewed us a large copper kettle, and ordered us to take it up and follow his footsteps. We carried it about half a mile to another house, where there was a number of women, one of which would have killed us if she had not been prevented by our master. He made us understand that her malignity arose from her husband having been killed by the Americans, in the boat at which we fired when we were on the shoals. Here we left the kettle and returned to the prison. The streets are not paved, never swept, and are full of sharp pebbles, and having no shoes, I suffered intolerably both by the cold and in carrying burthens, until they became indurated by use.

November 5.—"Our new masters came and closed up the passage which led to the top of the house, and a guard was set at the front door to prevent our going into the street. The minister sent his chief secretary with a parole of honour, written in French, which we all signed." The Turks informed us that the reason of their closing up the passage was a suspicion that we men were concerting with the officers some plan of escape, and that the suspicion was raised from a report of this kind fabricated by the infamous Wilson,[4] in hopes to ingratiate himself with the Bashaw. Our prison door was more effectually secured at the same time. This day several of our seamen, who were born under British colours, flattered themselves with the fallacious hope of obtaining emancipation by throwing themselves under the protection of the British government, and claiming from the English Consul the privileges or exemptions of British subjects. For this purpose they went to him and he registered a number of their names, promised to write to his government, and, if possible, effectuate their release. They returned highly elated with the prospect of freedom. But a large majority of our patriotic tars, who had adopted America as their country, laughed at their credulity and hissed at their project, positively declaring that they would not be released by a government which they detested, on account of its tolerating the impressment of seamen, and swearing that they would sooner remain under the Bashaw than George the third.

November 6.—Our treatment and provisions much the farce. "The English Consul, Mr. M'Donough, paid our officers a visit, and offered them every assistance in his power." As I was walking the streets, on a return from carrying a bundle of faggots into the town, I met with a Mahometan who spoke English tolerably fluent. He informed that he had been in America, in the time of our revolution, a servant to General Fayette; and when his master returned to France, he continued in America for two years, then went to his native country, and was a soldier in the French revolution, went with Bonaparte's army to Egypt, and when the French evacuated that country, his life was despaired of, and he was left in a wretched hospital, and would have perished had it not been for the fraternal kindness of a benevolent Mussulman, who took him to his house and treated him with the affectionate attention of the nearest consanguinity, and who was the means of saving his life. While in a debilitated state both of body and mind, he was pursuaded by his benefactor, whose importunities it seemed ungrateful to resist, to embrace the religion of Mahomet. He was now on his way to Tunis with a travelling company, appeared to be well respected by his comrades, was decently dressed, and seemed to have plenty of money; but he asked me a thousand questions concerning America, and seriously regretted his ever having left it, and of his transmutation of religion; but he still had hopes of making his escape. He gave me a Spanish dollar which he insisted on my accepting, shook hands and bade me adieu.

November 7.—Several of our men were much indisposed from sleeping on the damp ground, and being almost destitute of clothes. A small apartment or cell adjoining our prison was appropriated for the use and retirement of the sick, and Dorman, who was loblolly-boy[5] on board of the frigate, was appointed to attend them. Another room, contiguous to that was the receptacle of our provisions, and the men who were called cooks were permitted to sleep in it by themselves. Another cell, at a different part of the prison-yard, was set apart for the carpenters, coopers, and blacksmiths to sleep in; so that our prison was not quite so much crouded as at first.

November 8.—"The Bashaw sent for Capt. Bainbridge and told him that John Wilson had informed him, that Captain Bainbridge, before hauling down the colours, threw overboard nineteen boxes of dollars, and a large bag of gold. Captain Bainbridge assured him it was false, and gave him his word and honour that no money was thrown over to his knowledge, but that the money in question was left at Malta. In the evening the Bashaw, not being satisfied, sent for the captain's servant, and ordered him flogged if he did not tell the truth concerning the money. The boy denied having any knowledge of it. After repeating that several times, and the boy insisting on his not knowing any thing about the money, he was acquitted. Wilson had turned traitor, and given the enemy all the assistance in his power. He now acts as overseer of our men." This perfidious wretch was a quarter-master on board the frigate. He was born in Germany, and spoke the lingua-franca very fluently. He as yet mingled amongst us, and acted as a spy, carrying to the Bashaw every frivolous and a thousand false tales. He had not as yet assumed the habiliments of the Turks, so that he was the more dangerous. The Basahw rode out this day, and as he returned, was to pass, with his retinue, through our prison-yard, which is approximate to the castle. Wilson came and told us that it was the Bashaw's orders that we should parade, in single file, in front of our prison, with our hats off, and when he should make his appearance we must give him three cheers. He presently made his entrance into the yard, and being marshalled according to orders, some of our silly asses swung their hats and brayed like the animal they personated; but the most of us refused, with a laudable spirit of indignation, this mean and sycophantic testimonial of a tyrant's applause. His return from his cavalcade was announced by the firing of cannon from the castle, and crackling of muskets on the beach. He was preceded by a foot-guard at some distance. Next to the foot-guard was the high constable of the town police, mounted on an elegant Arabian grey, in his hand he held perpendicularly before him a three-pronged sceptre, richly ornamented. His majesty was mounted on a milk-white mare, sumptuously caparisoned and glittering with golden trappings. He was dressed much the same as when we first saw him, excepting a white robe, which had a head like a hood, and on the top a large tassel. At his right hand rode a huge negro, who was made one of the Bashaw's principal officers, and admitted to this distinguished honour for having assassinated the Bashaw's brother, who was a powerful and dangerous rival. Three or four of his younger children went before him, seated on mules, with Neapolitan slaves running by their sides, holding with one hand the bridle of the mule, and with the other an umbrella over the head of the child. At his left hand rode his vizier, or prime minister, his chief officers of state, and was followed and attended by his Mamelukes, or life-guards, without order or arrangement, courting his approbation by numerous feats of equestrian agility. Two large boxes flung across a mule, led by a trusty Neapolitan slave, contained his principal treasures.

November 9.—"Our captain established a credit with the Danish Consul, who supplied us with necessary provisions, and with cloth for matrasses. A guard was placed at our door to prevent our going into the street, or purchasing any books or clothing."

November 10.—The Turks appeared very savage and spit at us, and on us, as we passed the streets. The keepers or drivers beat us without any pretext, and acted more like infernal than human beings. We did not then know the cause of this alteration for the worse, but perhaps the following will account for it. "Several Turks came in and informed Capt. Bainbridge that the Bashaw had been told that Capt. Rodgers, who commanded the United States frigate John Adams, treated the Tripolitan prisoners very bad, and that they feared we should suffer for it." Several of our men were sent for and interrogated very closely concerning the money Wilson had reported was thrown into the sea; but they all unanimously corroborated the assertions of Capt. Bainbridge, that there was no money sunk.

November 11.—As I was coming in at the principal gate of the town, having been out on the sands for water, I saw a hand and foot hanging at the outside of the gate fresh bleeding, and observing a cluster of people not far distant, I stepped to see the cause of their being collected. The object of their curiosity was a wretch with his left hand and right foot recently amputated, faint and almost expiring. The stumps had been dipped in boiling pitch. This is their mode of punishment for capital offences, and the miserable object is dragged out of town and left to breathe his last in the most exquisite agonies, and then he some times recovers; for you will see a great number of men in Tripoli hobbling about the streets thus mutilated.

November 13.—"The minister of exterior relations sent his droggerman[6] to Capt. Bainbridge, and informed him, that if he would send an immediate order to Commodore Preble to deliver up the Tripolitan prisoners, captured by Captain Rodgers, last summer, amounting to eighty in number, we might remain where we were, but if he did not comply we should fare worse. Captain Bainbridge replied that he could not command Commodore Preble, and therefore could not comply with his request. At nine in the evening a Tripolitan officer came armed with two pistols and a sabre, and said—"to-night, nothing; to-morrow, the castle." We accordingly prepared for the castle. This day we were employed in bringing pig-iron and shot from the boats at the wharf to the magazine in the navy-yard. I was very sick, and complained to the principal keeper that I was unable to work; but the only consolation I received was that of being called a *kelp* (dog), and told to do as I was ordered. At night our men returned from the frigate with some more beef and pork, which, eaten raw, hunger gave a delicious flavour.

November 14.—"Breakfasted early to be ready for our new habitation. At 9, A.M. a guard came and ordered us to the castle. We formed agreeable to rank, and marched to the castle. We were huddled into a gloomy cell amongst our men, where there was hardly room for us to stand. Here we spent the day without food, and were scoffed at by our foes until night, when, to our happy surprize, we were conducted back to our old place of abode." Poor Doctor! in this whining take there are several misrepresentations. That the officers were in the prison amongst us, contaminating fellows, is true; but the Doctor and his fellow-officers, though nobody doubts their feeling very big, must be gigantic monsters indeed, if they had hardly room enough to stand in a cell at least twenty-five feet high, and which contained every night nearly three hundred men, who were chiefly absent the whole day. Neither was our prison in the castle, as he intimates; and if he remained all day without food, after having eaten a hearty breakfast, it was owing to his own fastidiousness, for our men boiled some meat which was brought from the frigate, and invited all the officers to partake of it, and several of them made a hearty repast. If this famous son of Esculapius had been three days at a time without food, as we often were, perhaps he might have had an appetite for black bread and salt beef.

While Captain Bainbridge was amongst us, Wilson came with orders to get men for some kind of drudgery, when the captain accused him of informing the Bashaw of our sinking the box of money; he prevaricated, and attempted to extenuate, though he could not pointedly deny the crime. The captain told him that he would have him hanged for a traitor if he ever returned to America, and in a violent passion threw his chain at him. A few days afterwards, Wilson, probably fearing the reality of his threats, put on the turban, and confirmed his apostacy.

November 17.—The Danish Consul sent some fresh provisions for our sick, by the request of Captain Bainbridge. Our bread was very coarse and musty. This day I saw one of the Mahometan saints or Anchorites, who are held in the highest veneration by the Tripolitans. He was seated on a tomb within a small smoky cell, where he kept a lamp incessantly burning, which he said was the spirit of the dead. He offered me a piece of bread in the name of the prophet, pitied my situation, and really appeared to possess philanthropy.

November 18.—A number of us was sent to carry powder from the quay to the castle, which is about three quarters of a mile. The powder was taken from the frigate and was still wet. I was compelled to carry a cask of it, which was very heavy; and my feet being tender, gave me insufferable pain. What would the querimoneous Doctor think, if he had been doomed to such hardships?

November 20.—Thomas Prince was metamorphosed from a Christian to a Turk. He was a lad of about seventeen years of age, and had a mother, as he informed us, living in some part of Rhode-Island. Our men now began to construct what they termed cots. They were formed by fastening four pieces of timber at the corners, in the shape of a bedstead, and then weaving a net of ropes like a bed-cord. These were suspended from spikes driven in the wall, and composed a lodging much more comfortable and healthful than the moist earth; but materials for these cots being very scarce, but few of us could be provided with a luxury so rare and inestimable.

November 21.—Doctor Cowdery informs us that a man, one hundred and sixteen years of age, came to him to be cured of deafness. We do not know which to doubt most—the Doctor's veracity or the Turk's credulity.

November 22.—We wrote a petition to the Bashaw in behalf of the sick, praying for some kind of blankets or clothing to keep them from the earth, appealing both to his humanity and his interest. "The Bashaw refused to furnish necessary clothing for the sick; or any thing for them to eat but sour, filthy bread. Captain Bainbridge contracted with the Danish Consul to supply the sick with beef and vegetables for soup every day."

November 25.—Sixteen of us were put to boring cannon; the labour was intense, and having neither bread nor any thing else to eat, until four o'clock in the afternoon, hunger and weariness were almost insupportable. Some of our men, by some clandestine means, were found intoxicated; for which they were inhumanly beaten, and confined in shackels. Whenever instances of this kind occurred, *all* were sure to suffer for the misconduct of a *few*.

November 26.—To the disgrace of human nature be it said, that although we had an equal share of bread allowed us, some had the meanness, the selfishness, the brutality to steal from their companions in misery the only ligament of soul and body. We frequently divided our pittance, and kept one loaf over night to eat in the morning, and often when morning came we found ourselves pillaged of our stores, and nothing to silence the importunate calls of hunger. About twelve o'clock I received a small white loaf from the allowance of our officers, and never in my life did I taste a more luscious dainty. It came from Mr. Morris, who was or had been by a trade a baker, and the next day I sent him the following stanzas; friendship the strain, and gratitude the muse.

The Loaf

The best of all friends is the friend in distress,
  And more the rich morsel I prize,
Imparted when hunger and poverty press,
  Than thousands, did fortune suffice.

With gratitude, friend, to the parent above,
  And thanks to yourself not a few;
I took the sweet loaf as a token of love,
  And ate in remembrance of you.

To life-wasting hunger, to heart-piercing cold,
  To scourges of tyrants a prey;
Midst demons of slavery too fierce to be told,
  And comrades more brutish than they.

The least of my wants not a soul has reliev'd,
  Nor friendship invited a beam;
From you the first crust of regard I receiv'd—
  From you the first crumb of esteem.

Then take the fond lay as the yeast of return,
  For, while I thus indigent live,
Though my breast, like an oven, with gratitude burn,
  'Tis all I am able to give.

CHAPTER IX

A Petition

When in the pow'r of foes, we must be civil,
And sometimes supplicate a king, or devil.

ON the 27th of November, we presented a petition to the Bashaw in the following language.—

TO HIS EXCELLENCY THE GRAND BASHAW OF TRIPOLI.

The petition of the American prisoners most humbly sheweth—That when your petitioners were captured, in the United States frigate Philadelphia, they were plundered of all their clothing, and are daily sickening and suffering most intolerably by the inclemency of the season, and by not having any thing to sleep on to keep them from the cold, damp ground, but a thin and tattered sail-cloth: and also, that your petitioners, not receiving sufficient food and nourishment to enable them to endure the hardships and perform the hard tasks assigned them, are frequently most inhumanly bastinadoed for the lack of that strength which adequate nutriment would restore and supply. Your petitioners, therefore, pray that his Excellency, consulting his interest as well as his honour, by contributing to our relief, would graciously be pleased to grant us more comfortable clothing, and more nutricious food; and your petitioners, while they continue your prisoners, will remain your most faithful, industrious, obedient and humble servants.

November 28.—In consequence of the foregoing petition, the Bashaw ordered us two barrels of pork from the frigate. It was really laughable to see with what ridiculous pride and pomposity our chief keeper performed the functions of a purser's steward; but it was not laughable to see with what greediness our half-starved crew seized and consumed their crude dividend of the meat.

November 29.—I was sent to work in the castle carrying dirt, stones, mortar, lime and sand, for repairing the walls. A little past 12 o'clock our overseer beckoned to me to follow him. I obeyed, and he took me to the cook-house and ordered me to take a dish of *coos-coos*, and follow him again. He led me through several gloomy, subterraneous cells, dimly lighted, smoked black by torches, where were large iron staples and chains, once the lot of some ill-fated object of a tyrant's wrath, until we came to a dungeon strongly bolted. My grim conductor loosened the door, and a wretch appeared, ghastly and loaded with chains. The dish was handed in without saying a word, and we returned to our labour. I durst not express the curiosity I felt to know what was his accusation. His head was afterwards struck off, and carried on a pole through the streets of the city.

November 30.—"One of our men attempted to kill himself, but was prevented, by the Turks, when in the act of cutting his throat; the wound did not prove mortal." This was C.R. one of the four persons previously mentioned, who was taken in at Gibraltar, and were so unlawfully detained. The wound, however, was a mere scratch, and the lycanthropy, which was the cause of it, was occasioned by taking a little to much aqua vitæ. Nothing of very great importance for a considerable term of time. West, one of our carpenter's crew, had turned Turk, and had a number of men employed in building gun-boats, repairing gun-carriages, and works of circumvallation. Some of our men were assisting to repair fortifications in mason work—some sent into the country every day to cut timber for ship and boat building—some boring guns—some coining buckamseens in the mint in the Bashaw's castle, twenty-five of which are equal to a Spanish dollar—some carrying mortar from cisterns in different parts of the town. Our rations continued the same, two black barley loaves and about three-fourths of a gill of oil per day—more or less bastinading continually, and once a fortnight we received a little beef and pork. A number of Spanish carpenters were employed in building boats and other vessels for the Regency; and on the 15th of December they had a schooner ready for launching. In the afternoon the consuls all hoisted their colours, three guns were fired from the battery, and the schooner was precipitated into the waves, amidst the acclamations of a shabby multitude of idle spectators. "At sunset, a firing from the batteries announced the commencement of the Mahometan Ramadam, continuing a lunar month, in which they neither eat, drink nor smoke, while the sun is above the horizon, but feast at night. In walking through the town to visit my patients, I found the mosques and principal houses illuminated, and the people rejoicing."

On the 17th, as I was returning with a crock of water from the sands, not far from the large eastern gate, I saw a man walking towards me leading a child by the hand. Another Turk was just before me leading a large fiery courser, wild, and prancing by his side, and as they met the harmless child passing very near to the horse's heels, struck him with a switch. The haughty, majestic animal, as if conscious of the indignity, let fly his hoofs and dashed him into eternity in the twinkling of an eye. The father of the child, as I supposed it to be, looked at him for a moment—raised him up, and perceiving he was past all remedy, laid his right hand on his breast, lifted his left, raised his eyes to heaven, made a short ejaculation, seeming to say—"It is done—and I acquiesce in thy righteous dispensations,

O omnipotent God!" He seemed perfectly composed, took the corpse in his arms, and walked pensively towards the country. The surrounding spectators beheld this pathetic scene of paternal affliction—this sudden stroke of death, with brutal indifference.

December 20.—"The market was so poor that we could get nothing for dinner but the shoulder of a poor dromedary." What the Doctor here complains of in such dolorous language, would have been a feast and produced strains of joy with us. Had he been compelled to labour as many of us, quite as good by nature, as himself, and been stinted to two small loaves of coarse, musty bread, the shoulder of a dromedary would have been a most delicious repast to the querulous gentleman and his dainty companions.

December 22.—One hundred and fifty of us were sent to raise an old wreck deeply buried in the sand, near the beach, eastward from the town. It was now the coldest season of the year; we were almost naked, and were driven into the water up to our arm-pits. We had to shovel the sand from the bottom of the water, and carry it in baskets to the banks. The chilling waves almost congealed our blood, to flow no more. The Turks seemed more than ordinarily cruel, exulting in our sufferings. We were kept in the water from sunrise until about two o'clock, before we had a mouthful to eat, or were permitted to sun ourselves. Then brought us some bread and a jug of acqua-deut. When we had snatched a short repast, we were driven again into the water, and kept there until sunset. Having no clothes to change, we were obliged to sleep on the ground in our wet ones; which gave many of us severe colds, and caused one man to lose the use of his limbs upwards of a year afterwards. With such usage life became insupportable, and every night when I laid my head on the earth to sleep, I most sincerely prayed that I might never experience the horrors of another morning.

December 25.—The different consul's colours were all hoisted, and the Neapolitan slaves permitted to attend mass; for there are no less than three Roman Catholic priests in this place. No relaxation was allowed us.

December 26.—Mr. Godby, late carpenter of the Philadelphia, had been taken out from among the officers, to work in the Bashaw's navy-yard. He returned every night to his usual lodgings with the officers. His being employed in giving strengths and furtherance to our enemy, raised suspicious umbrage in the breasts of many of our officers, because they said he was not constrained to do it. Some of his messmates were Mr. Erving, serjeant of marines—Mr. Morris, purser's steward—and Mr. Leith, ship's cook. Mr. Godby returning home at night a little fuddled, began to vaunt his liberty, and the privileges he enjoyed superiour to his messmates. They also had been kissing black betty,[1] and no doubt gave him some pungent retort. Blows ensued, and the carpenter found his timbers too weak, and something shattered by the attack. The next morning, Godby went to the Bashaw, and entered a complaint against the three persons above mentioned. Wilson, the renegade, was now highly in favour with the Bashaw, and the serjeant, while they were on board the ship, had given Wilson a severe drubbing, for interfering with the duty of a sentinel, and this was a fine opportunity to feed revenge. Wilson acted as interpreter for Godby, and no doubt exaggerated all he said. About 10 o'clock, the three men were brought to the castle, before the Bashaw. Judgement was already passed against them, and the Bashaw ordered them bastinadoed. Wilson stood by, and dictated the punishment, telling them, when they came to Erving, not to spare his flesh. They were all most unmercifully beaten, on the soles of their feet, and on their posteriors; then hampered, with a huge chain at each leg, and sent to the prison with us, where they remained for one night, and the next day were sent to their wonted residence. Godby was as cruel to our men who were under his command as any of their other drivers, and we all supposed he would now turn Turk. Doctor Cowdery does not mention this in his journal, or, at least, it has not been published. What is the reason? Why, the reason is as plain and prominent, as the action was dastardly and flagitious. Godby was a warranted officer, and officers must not expose each other's secret villainies. What was the reason he was not reported to the commodore, after his liberation, and dealt with according to his demerit? Why, for the very reason above mentioned. Would you believe, that instead of a haltar, he received his full pay and rations, for volunteering his services in the Bashaw's employ—building gun-boats, and instructing the enemy in the arts of defence, and means of repelling our friends, and their foes? Yes, I have never heard that he was ever even reprimanded for his conduct. The case with us was quite different. We were compelled to work, or perish in tortures. He was under no compulsion, but solicited the undertaking, and executed his business so effectually, that he received from the Bashaw, one hundred dollars at a time, for his services.

January 2.—"As I passed out of the gate of the city, I saw a man's head sticking on a pole. On enquiry, I found that it was the head of one of the Bedouins, who, about a year before, had killed the Bashaw's son-in-law, who commanded the army in collecting the taxes, in the back part of his dominions. About a quarter of a mile from the gate, the road passed through a burying ground, full of graves. After this I came into a well cultivated country, which was laid out in squares of from one to six acres of ground, each, surrounded with date trees, interspersed with orange, fig, olive, lemon, and other trees."

The head, which the Doctor here speaks of, belonged to the person whom I saw confined in the castle. That the Doctor should have seen a "burying ground, full of graves," is very astonishing, indeed! It is as wonderful as if he had seen a town full of houses.

January 8.—"Went to the Bashaw's garden, where I met the minister and the prince, the Bashaw's eldest son. They politely conducted me through the garden, which was ornamented with a great variety of fruit trees, loaded with fruit, particularly with oranges, lemons, and limes. John Hilliard died in the evening."

The Doctor is as laconic in mentioning the death of our seamen, as he was remiss in attending to them. The company of a "prince," in a flower-garden, was much more pleasing to the Doctor, than the company of a languishing sailor, in a dreary cell. The gratification of his vanity was obviously anterior to the offices of humanity. He frequently informs us of his prescriptions for the Bashaw and his family, but seldom mentions the sickness or sufferings of his own countrymen. Hilliard died of a flux, which might have been greatly mitigated, if not cured, had he received proper medical attention.

Elegy

On the death of JOHN HILLIARD, *who died Jan. 3d,* 1804, *in the prison of Tripoli.*
[Published in the Port Folio.]

HILLIARD, of painful life bereft,
Is now a slave no more;
But here no relative has left,
His exit to deplore!

No parent, no fond brother, stands
Around his clay-cold bed;
No wife, with tender, trembling hands,
Supports his dying head.

No sister follows or attends
His melancholy bier;
Nor from a lover's eye descends
The soft distilling tear;—

But foes and of a barb'rous kind,
Surround him as he dies;
A horror to his fainting mind,
And to his closing eyes.

What though no monumental stone
Bespeaks a guilty name,
By splendid trophies basely won,
Damn'd to eternal fame;

If but an honest heart he wore,
If virtue's paths he trod,
He was, so poets sung of yore,
The noblest work of God.

His fellow-pris'ners strove to cheer
His sad departing soul,
And bade the sympathetic tear
In free profusion roll.

Mourn not—'twas Heav'n's allwise behest,
And merciful decree,

That gave his wearying sorrows rest,
And set the captive free.

January 4.—William Anderson died. He had been sick ever since we fell into the hands of the Turks. Both him and Hilliard were placed on cots, carried by four of our men, and interred, with as much decency as possible, on the beach, at the western part of the town, without the gates, and near the wall.

January 12.—"The Bashaw's eldest daughter was married to Selim, the Bashaw's chief casileda or treasurer. Wilson received 500 bastinadoes, for quarrelling with the noted Lysle." The new moon appeared, and the Ramadam ended. The Turks were all looking at the moon, and muttering some kind of prayer or thanks. Several of the castle guns, and a salute from the frigate, which now lay moored in the harbour, was fired at sun set. Joy seemed to brighten the gloomy visages of all the Tripolitans.

January 15.—The feast, called Byram, commenced. Every gun in Tripoli proclaimed the day. The Turks all appeared arrayed in new suits of their best attire. The markets teemed with the richest productions I had ever seen them; but this, to us, was only a tantalizing prospect. Their bakers were too much engrossed with the pleasures of the feast, to attend to their business, and we had nothing but the camelion's rations for this day.

January 16.—When hope is nearly expiring under the torturing hand of despair, what a small anodyne will revive her. Captain Bainbridge, in company with all the consuls, visited the Bashaw, and this we considered as a presage of pacification.

January 17.—The feast ended this evening. The consuls' flags, which had been flying for three days, were struck, and the people resumed their usual vocations. We were now supplied, every Sunday, with fresh provisions and vegetables, for soups.

January 20.—Happening in at a Greek's shop, he showed me a sacred relict of the holy Cross, which he had purchased at, and brought from Jerusalem. It was about four inches long, of no intrinsic value, and yet this superstitious fanatic said he would not give it for all the wealth of the Bashaw. I reached my hand to take it, but he said I must not touch it, unless I had recently partaken of the eucharist. I told him I would not give him a buckamseen for it. He said I was a great infidel then, and asked me if all the Americans were so impious, kissed the toy, with holy rapture, and put it in his bosom.

January 25.—I saw a man, at the castle gate, undergo the shocking operation of having his left hand and right foot amputated. It was performed with an axe, in the shape of a half moon, and the executioner was one of our keepers. The wretched victim never uttered a word, nor even a groan. The stumps were dipped in boiling pitch, and he was dragged to the gate, and thrown on the mercy of mankind.

February 3.—"Was conducted to the castle, to visit the Bashaw, whom I found, after passing several sentinels, and fifty fierce, yelping dogs, and three heavy doors, loaded with irons and bolts; which were opened for us by armed Mamelukes." Our men were frequently called before the Bashaw, both by night and by day, and it is very strange that none of them ever saw any thing of these yelping dogs. We must therefore suppose, that the Doctor, in this particular, is very much mistaken.

February 16.—Towards evening two vessels were seen standing in for the harbour. Our men were much rejoiced at the sight, for they were confident they were Americans, and as the season of the year was not favourable for an attack, they flattered themselves that very probably they had come with proposals of amicable accommodation. The Bashaw had ordered us a barrel of pork, and another of beef, and all our men appeared more than ordinary cheerful. About 11 o'clock at night, we were alarmed by the screeches of women, the clattering of footsteps through the prison yard, the harsh, loud voices of men, mingled with a thundering of cannon from the castle, which made our prison tremble to its base. Tumult, consternation, confusion, and dismay reigned in every section of the town and castle, and it was verily believed, that if we had been at liberty, and armed, we might with ease have taken the castle, and every fort in the town; for the most of the people in the town supposed we had already risen and taken the castle, and were afraid to come nigh it. In the confusion of voices we could often hear the word American, and therefore hoped that some of our countrymen were landing, to liberate us; but the true cause of so much clamour, we did not learn until morning.

February 17.—Early in the morning, and much earlier than usual, our prison doors were unbolted, and the keepers, like so many fiends from the infernal regions, rushed in amongst us and began to beat every one they could see, spitting in our faces, and hissing like the serpents of hell. Word was soon brought, that the wreck of the frigate Philadelphia lay on the rocks, near the round fort, almost consumed by fire. We could not suppress our emotions, nor disguise our joy at the intelligence, which exasperate them more and more, so that every boy we met in the streets, would spit on us and pelt us with stones; our tasks doubled, our bread withheld, and every driver exercised cruelties tenfold more rigid and intolerable than before.

Eight Turks had charge of the ship; two of them escaped, and made the report, that an American schooner and three boats set fire to the ship, and carried the other six Turks away. By what we could learn, Captain Decatur, who was commander in this heroic action, had taken some Maltese with him in the boat, and when they were hailed, as they approached the frigate, they answered, that they were Maltese, had been in a gale, and were in want of water. They were permitted to enter the ship, when they instantly secured the hands, all but two, and set fire to her.

February 18.—All hands were sent to get the remains of the frigate from the rocks, under the controul of Mr. Godby, who, to court favour from the Turks, struck several of our men, and behaved more like one of the Bashaw's myrmidons, than like an American fellow-prisoner. They did not succeed in clearing the wreck, but brought off copper, bolts, spikes, &c.

February 19.—A tent was pitched in front of our prison, and a strong guard kept over us at night, and we received no more beef or pork from the Bashaw's stores. The militia began to collect from the country; they were repairing their ramparts, and making every preparation to repel the expected invasion.

March 1.—Our officers, with a strong guard, passed through our prison yard, for the castle. We were not permitted to exchange words; Captain Bainbridge, however, bid us be of good heart, although he looked very much dejected himself. They were confined in a prison very dreary, with a grated sky-light.

March 4.—"Captain Bainbridge received a letter from the ministers, repremanding him on account of three men who floated ashore, a few days after burning the frigate. The Turks pretended that they were murthered after they were made prisoners, by the Americans." That mean, detestable spirit of revenge, which seeks retaliation on the innocent connexions, or affinity of those who have injured us, blackens and disfigures one of the most conspicuous features in the portrait of a Tripolitan. Every time there was any attack upon the place, or even an American vessel in sight, we were sure to suffer for it.

March 7.—The Turks got the guns from the wreck of the frigate. They mounted them on their batteries, and in proving them several burst—killed one Turk, and wounded four.

March 26.—Early in the morning, some of our men returned from the beach, and with joy sparkling in their countenances, informed us, that a frigate with American colours was standing in for the harbour. About 8 o'clock our joy was increased by observing the flag which she carried to be a white one. The Bashaw soon responded to the signal, by hoisting a white ensign on the castle. What a contemptible opinion of the Tripolitans' character must we form—Yesterday they would stone us and spit in our faces, for the burning of the frigate, which we had no hand in destroying—and to-day they would flatter and caress us, because there appeared a pacific signal, which we had no more agency in raising, than in burning the ship. As we walked the streets, the Turks would pat us on the shoulder, and say, American *bono* (good). About 9 o'clock, Consul O'Brian landed on the beach, and went up into the castle. In about half an hour he returned, and went on board the frigate. We could not learn the business or result of this short interview. Various were the reports, and our conjectures. Some said, that peace was concluded on, and that the Commodore had gone to Malta, for the money to ransom us; but when the white flag dropped, with the most of us, our spirits flagged; and the frigate departing, bore away the anchor of hope which she had brought us.

Our allowance continued the same—our men, many of them, began to be as naked as the natives of Pellew. A few shirts and trowsers had been alternately issued amongst us, but not sufficient for all. We made a most pitiable appearance. Many of the men had to drag a heavy waggon five or six miles, over the sand, into the country, and back again, every day, before they had any thing to eat, except sometimes a few raw carrots, which they plundered on the way. We were turned out every morning regularly, before sunrise, and locked in at sunset. We were much afflicted with vermin, and not having any clothes to change, the only way we had to keep ourselves from becoming insufferably filthy, was to go on the beach and strip off our shirts, going naked until we washed and dried them, and then our trowsers, in the like manner.

April 15.—We felt the Syroc winds; they are very sultry and suffocating. The Turks do not walk the streets during the prevalence of these morbid gales. We now began to grow economical. We found that we could sell our bread in market, for four paras a loaf. Three hundred of these paras make a dollar; and with the avails of one loaf, we could purchase as many vegetables as three men would eat at a meal, made into a soup, with bread and oil. We put ourselves into messes, as we chose, some of three or four men each, and thus, by sparing two loaves out of our day's rations, we could purchase carrots and scallions enough to make a handsome little pot of soup, for these vegetables were very cheap. We also contributed our mites, and purchased an earthen vessel, large enough to cook for four men, for about two buckamseens, 25 paras. We then boiled the vegetables, threw in some bread to thicken the soup, and added oil and salt. We were allowed to get some chips from the navy-yard, to cook it with, and when prepared, we eat it sitting on the ground, with wooded spoons. By this management we began to live rather more comfortable. There are also little shops in the market, in which they keep *tirsha* for sale; which is made of either carrots or turnips, cut into small pieces, and boiled; then mashed with a ladle, and beat with salt and water until it becomes pulpous; to which are added red pepper, pulverized and mixed with water, and a measure of oil—a lemon is squeezed into it, and over the top are strewed fennel seed. It is of the consistence of apple-sauce, and so strong of pepper, that it is quite disagreeable at first, but by frequent use it soon becomes palateable. This is a cheap and salubrious dish; of which the poorer sort of people eat much, and you will see those little hovels of shops almost constantly crouded with Turks, sitting on a ground-floor, and with their fingers load their greedy mouths. The Bashaw, to excite them to industry, occasionally called the carpenters, the masons, the coopers, and the blacksmiths into the castle, and distributed amongst them a few buckamseens. Those who dragged at the cart were sometimes encouraged with the like gratuity.

April 24.—Departed this life, John Morrison, in the 27th year of his age. He was an able and skilful mariner, captain of the fore-top, on board the frigate, and supported the character of a true and brave American tar. His death was occasioned by a hurt which he received, in assisting to load a large piece of timber on the waggon, about two miles from the town. He was brought in on a litter, by four men, and lay three days in the most excruciating pain. The night previous to his death, Doctor Ridgby was permitted to visit him, in company with Lewis Hexiner, who was one of our crew, transformed into a Turk, and now acted as interpreter to our officers. An old Algerine, who was one of our drivers, came in to see him, while he was dying, and insisted that nothing ailed him; but that he was shamming sickness, to avoid labour. He went to the dying man, told him to rise, called him an infidel and a dog, and struck him several times with his cane. How our men burned to immolate the ferocious villain. He was interred the following day, by the side of his late shipmates. Part of the American fleet was now in sight, and as has been observed, the unreasonable Turks always made this a pretext for doubling their severity. Our spirits, however, were cheered at the sight, and hope again returned, to cheer our desponding bosoms, till, on the 26th, the squadron disappeared. We now began to abandon all hopes of release by negociations of peace, and only expected, from the force of arms, carnage and emancipation.

May 11.—The squadron again appeared. The Turks were in great trepidation, and expected an attack. They sent us to carry powder and balls, from the castle to their forts, and beat us without mercy. I was now taken sick, with a bilous complaint.

May 16.—Ten of our officers were permitted to walk into the country. They passed several of our men, at a cart, and scattered them some buckamseens.

May 20.—"A party of us, under escort of four Turks, walked to the desert, about four miles from our prison. We ascended a large bank of sand, where we had an extensive view of the country. The deserts have a singular and grand appearance. They extend to mount Atlas, which we could see at a distance of two days' journey. The sand is in heaps, like snow-drifts in our country. There was not a house nor any other object to be seen to intercept the sight, but it appeared like an ocean of sand." The sap of the date-tree, which they call lagby, now began to be plenty in the market and elsewhere. It is of a whitish colour, like whey, and as it comes from the tree has the spirit of wine. It tastes something like mead, and can be bought for about three cents a quart.

May 27.—Doctor Ridgby paid a visit to our sick, and informed me that Captain Bainbridge had exerted his influence with the prime minister, and had procured me an exemption from labour. He called the keepers and told them that it was the Bashaw's orders not to send me to work any more while I was a prisoner.[2] As I never had been much accustomed to, nor was I remarkably fond of labour, especially among the Turks, these were glad tidings of great joy.

May 28.—A number of our men were employed in cleaning and fitting up a prison for us in a different part of the town.

May 29.—"A party of us, under escort as before, took a walk into the desert. On our return, we dined in the Bashaw's garden, under the shade of orange trees. The dinner was prepared in the Turkish style, and we ate with wooden spoons—it was simple and good." Two of our brigs were lying off the harbour, and in consequence, as usual, we had severe treatment.

June 10.—We were ordered to remove to our newly prepared prison, which was adjoining the wall at the eastern part of the town. We found it much more strong, spacious and cleanly than the other, but the yard was much smaller. About one hundred of the Neapolitan slaves were confined with us, making upwards of three hundred and fifty of us in one apartment. Our sick were kept in a separate cell, at one end of the yard, the wall of which was very high, and at the entrance was a gate of enormous weight and strength. Within the gate was a guard-house, where a dozen armed Turks kept sentry every night, and the keepers, or drivers, in the day time. There was a guard also on the top of the prison. This day our weekly rations, from the captain, was discontinued.

June 18.—"The Bashaw's eldest wife, called the queen, was delivered of her ninth child. She was twenty-three years of age. It was said to be common to marry at ten." This may be true, but it looks a little like mendacity.

June 27.—Mr. Hodge, our boatswain, Mr. Fenton, our first master's mate, and Mr. Douglas, sail-maker, were taken from their prison, in the castle, to oversee our men in their several departments. An upper story of a building, occupied by our sick in the prison-yard, was fitted for and received them and Mr. Godby.

July 4.—A few of us got permission to go out on the sands to purchase and drink lagby. The benevolent Danish Consul had made me a small present to enable me to celebrate the day. We retired to a stone platform, the ruins of an ancient reservoir, under the cooling shade of a luxurient orange-tree, open to the refreshing breezes of the sea. Here we sat and regaled ourselves with this delicious beverage until we almost forgot that we, who were offering a libation to the birth day of liberty, were ourselves but wretched slaves. Towards sunset, three or four of our squadron appeared in sight, and we returned to our gloomy prison with several jugs of this wholesome and cheering liquor.

July 15.—The most of our men were employed in carrying furniture and baggage from the castle to the Bashaw's seat in the country, about two miles distant. At night the Bashaw and his family left the castle and went thither.

July 25.—The Constitution, Commodore Preble, appeared again off the harbour. Every preparation of defence was now making by the Turks with the utmost dispatch. The American squadron now consisted of the frigate Constitution, brigs Syren, Argus and Vixen; schooners Nautilus, Enterprize and Scourge, two bombs and six gun-boats. The whole number of men 1060. The bomb vessels were about thirty tons, and carried thirteen inch brass sea mortar and fifty men. The gun-boats twenty-five tons, carried a large iron twenty-four pounder in the bow, with a complement of twenty-five men. They were officered and manned from the squadron, excepting twelve Neapolitan bombardiers, gunners and sailors attached to each boat; who were shipped by permission of their government. The bomb-vessels and gun-boats were loaned us by his Sicilian majesty, nearly one hundred and fifty of whose men were slaves in Tripoli. The commodore now proceeded to make the necessary arrangements for an attack on Tripoli as soon as the weather would permit. Tripoli was impregnably walled, protected by batteries judiciously constructed, mounting one hundred and fifteen pieces of heavy cannon, and defended by more than twenty-five thousand Arabs and Turks. The harbour was protected by nineteen gun-boats, two gallies, two schooners of eight guns each, and a brig mounting ten guns, all ranged in order of battle, forming a strong line of defence, at secured moorings, inside a long range of rocks and shoals, extending more than two miles to the eastward of the town, which forms the harbour, protects them from the northern gales, and renders it impossible for a vessel, of the

Constitution's draft, to approach near enough to destroy them, as they are sheltered by the rocks, and can retire under that shelter to the shore, unless they choose to expose themselves in the different channels and openings of the reefs, for the purpose of annoying their enemies. Each of these gunboats mounts a heavy eighteen or twenty-six pounder in the bow, and two brass howitzers on her quarters, and carries from thirty-six to fifty men. The gallies have each one hundred men; schooners and brigs about the same number. For several days the weather was very boisterous, and the gunboats were in great danger of being lost.

August 1.—The gale subsided, and the squadron stood towards the coast; every preparation was made for an attack on the town and forts.

CHAPTER X

Commodore Preble's Engagement with the Tripolitans

No more of TRUXTON:[1] PREBLE all outbraves—
A greater hero never rode the waves:
'Round the drear coast his squadron's wings are spread,
And hungry billows crave the future dead.

AUGUST 3.—The wind east, pleasant weather, and the squadron stood in towards Tripoli. About 12 o'clock, the squadron was within two or three miles of the batteries. Some of our men, who had been at work on the fortifications, came running in, and informed us that the whole coast was lined with our shipping. The whole town was in an uproar, every Turk had his musket and other weapons, and wild disorder rang through every arch. We were all locked into the prison, and a formidable guard set over us. Their batteries were all manned, and several of their gun-boats and gallies had advanced in two divisions without the rocks. The commodore, observing this, was resolved to take advantage of their temerity. At half past 12 o'clock the commodore bore off, and made a signal to come within hail, when he communicated to each of the commanders his intention of attacking the enemy's shipping and batteries. The gun and mortar boats were immediately manned and prepared to cast off. The gun-boats in two divisions of three each. The first division commanded by Captain Somers, in No. 1; Lieutenant Decatur, in No. 2; and Lieutenant Blake, in No. 3. The second division by Captain Decatur, in No. 4; Lieutenant Bainbridge, in No. 5; and Lieutenant Tripp, in No. 6. The two bombards were commanded by Lieutenant-commandant Dent, and Mr. Robinson, first lieutenant of the Constitution. At half past one o'clock, having made the necessary arrangements for the attack, the commodore wore ship, and stood towards the batteries. At two, signals were made to cast off the boats; at a quarter past two signal for the bombs and gun-boats to advance and attack the enemy; at half past two general signal for battle; at three quarters past two the boats commenced the action by throwing shells into the town. In an instant the enemy's shipping and batteries opened a tremendous fire, which was promptly returned by the whole squadron within grape shot distance; at the same time the second division of gun-boats, led by the gallant Captain Decatur, was advancing with sails and oars to board the eastern division of the enemy, consisting of nine boats. Our boats gave the enemy showers of grape and musket balls as they advanced; they, however, soon closed, when the pistol, sabre, pike and tommahawk were made good use of by our brave tars. Captain Somers being in a dull sailer made the best use of his sweeps, but was not able to fetch far enough to the windward to engage the same division of the enemy's boats which Captain Decatur fell in with; he, however, gallantly bore down with his single boat on five of the enemy's western division, and engaged within pistol shot, defeated and drove them within the rocks in a shattered condition, and with the loss of a great number of men. Lieutenant Decatur, in No. 2, was closely engaged with one of the enemy's largest boats, which struck to him, having lost a large proportion of men, and at the instant that brave officer was boarding her to take possession, he was treacherously shot through the head by the captain of the boat that had surrendered, which base conduct enabled the paltroon to escape.

Captain Decatur, after having, with distinguished bravery, boarded and carried one of the enemy of superiour force, took his prize in tow, and gallantly bore down to engage a second, which, after a severe and bloody conflict, he also took possession of. These two prizes had thirty-three officers and men killed, and twenty-seven made prisoners, nineteen of whom were badly wounded. Lieutenant Trippe, of the Vixen, in No. 6, run along side one of the enemy's large boats, which he boarded with only midshipman John Hinly, and nine men, his boat falling off before any more could get on board; thus was he left to conquer or perish with the odds of thirty-six to eleven. The Turks could not withstand the ardour of this brave officer and his assistants; in a few moments the decks were cleared and her colours hauled down. On board of this boat, fourteen of the enemy were killed, and twenty-two made prisoners, several of whom were badly wounded; the rest of their boats retreated within the rocks. Lieut. Trippe received eleven sabre wounds, several of which were very severe.

During the action, our men were taken out of the prison several times to carry powder and shot from the magazine in the castle to the forts, and were almost beaten to death—stoned and cudgeled by every Turk in the streets.

At half past four, the wind inclining to the northward, the commodore made a signal for the bombs and gun-boats to retire from action, and immediately after to tow off the gun-boats and prizes; which was handsomely executed by a heavy fire from the Constitution, which was two hours under the fire of the enemy's batteries, and the only damage which she received was a twenty-four pound shot nearly through the centre of her mainmast, thirty feet from the deck; main-royal-yard and sail shot away; one of her quarter deck guns damaged by a thirty-two pound shot, which, at the same time, shattered a marine's arm; sails and rigging considerably cut. The commodore imputed his getting off thus well to his keeping so near that the batteries overshot him, and to the annoyance our grape-shot gave the enemy. They are, however, wretched gunners. Lieutenant Decatur was the only officer killed; but in him the service has lost a brave and valuable officer. He was a young man who gave strong promises of being an ornament to his profession. His conduct in the action was highly honourable—and he died in a noble cause. The enemy suffered very much in killed and wounded among their shipping, but as few of the shells burst on shore, not so great execution was done as might be expected, or as has been reported. This was, undoubtedly, owing to unskilful bombardiers. The officers, seamen and marines of the squadron behaved in the most gallant manner. The Neapolitans, in emulating the conduct of our seamen, answered the commodore's highest expectations. All the officers and ship's company of the Constitution gave full satisfaction. The commodore was much gratified by the conduct of Captain Hall, and Lieutenant Greenleaf, and of the marines belonging to his company, in the management of six long twenty-six pounders on the spare deck, Captain Decatur spoke in the highest terms of the conduct of Lieutenant Thorn. The boat which was first boarded by Captain Decatur was obstinately defended, and was not surrendered until seven-eighths of her crew were killed or wounded. Having manned his prize, and being left with only nine Americans besides himself, he determined to board another boat. Being only ten Americans to twenty-four Turks, a scene of combat ensued of the most daring effort on the one part, and determined resistance on the other. The Turks made a powerful defence, and were not subdued until twenty-one of them had fallen. Captain Decatur was, at different times, most critically circumstanced. At one time, while engaged with the Tripolitan captain in front, a Turk, in his rear, aimed a blow with a sabre, which one of the seamen most nobly interposed to defend, and which split his skull. In a subsequent encounter he was engaged by a Turk with a pike, which he endeavoured to cut off with his sword when the blade broke and left the hilt in his hand, and he then received a thrust in his arm. Not having time to draw a pistol until the thrust would be repeated, he closed with his antagonist, who, being the strongest man, threw him, but his activity placed him above his adversary, who drew his dagger, as Captain Decatur did his pistol which prevailed. The list of killed and wounded is as follows.

Killed—Gun-boat No. 2, Lieut. James Decatur.
Wounded—Constitution, one marine.

Do. Gun-boat No. 4, Captain Decatur, slightly—one serjeant of marines, and two seamen.

Do. Gun-boat No. 6, Lieutenant Trippe, severely—one boatswain's mate, and two marines.

Do. Gun-boat No. 1, two seamen.

Do. Gun-boat No. 2, two seamen.

Total—one killed and thirteen wounded.

The number of killed and wounded among the Turks cannot be ascertained; it is thought, however, to be very considerable. Three of their gun-boats were sunk in the harbour and three captured. Two Turks swam ashore and came to the Bashaw, who gave them a few dollars and a suit of clothes.

August 4.—All our men were employed in repairing damages done to the forts, and in carrying powder and shot to replenish them. The infuriate Turks, wherever we met them, would strike, spit upon and stone us. From the circumstance of our giving up the Philadelphia to one gun-boat, without bloodshed, they had, until now, entertained an opinion that the Americans were all cowards, but they now were impressed with a full conviction of the skill and bravery of our tars. The Turks told us that the Americans were all drunk, or they would not have ventured as they did, and fought so furiously.

August 5.—The squadron was at anchor about two leagues north from the town. A French privateer of four guns, which put into Tripoli a few days since for water, left it this morning, and was chased by the Argus, which soon came up with her. The commodore prevailed on the captain of her, for a consideration, to return to Tripoli for the purpose of leaving fourteen very badly wounded Tripolitans, who were put on board his vessel with a letter to the prime minister, leaving it to the option of the Bashaw to reciprocate this generous mode of carrying on the war. This act of humanity had but little effect on the minds of these barbarians, for they did not abate their cruelties to us in consequence of it.

August 7.—The French privateer went out and carried a letter from the French Consul to the Commodore, stating that his attack, of the 3d instant, had disposed the Bashaw to accept of reasonable terms, and advising him to send a boat to the rocks with a flag of truce, which was declined, as the flag was not hoisted on the Bashaw's castle. At nine o'clock, the light vessels, the gun and bomb-boats were ordered by signal to cast off, and stand in towards the western batteries, and the whole advanced with sails and oars. A light breeze from the eastward, and a strong current, obliged the Constitution to remain at anchor. The orders were for the bombs to take a position in a small bay, to the westward of the city, where but a few of the enemy's guns could be brought to bear upon them; but from whence they could annoy the town with shells. At half past two, P.M. the bomb and gun-boats having reached their station, the signal was made for them to attack the town and batteries. After the alarm gun of Tripoli was fired, the Turks all took their stations and performed Mahometan ceremony of prayer, by kneeling and putting their foreheads to the ground, with their faces towards the east, with as much regularity as a well disciplined military company grounding their arms. The moment the signal was made by the commodore, the bombs commenced throwing shells into the town, and the gun-boats opened a sharp and well-directed fire on the town and batteries within point blank shot, which was warmly returned by the enemy. The seven gun battery, in less than two hours, was silenced, except one gun. The walls of the other forts were considerably injured. At a quarter past three, P.M. a ship hove in sight to the northward standing towards the town. The commodore made the Argus a signal to chase her. She proved to be the United States frigate John Adams, Captain Chauncey. At half past three, one of our gun-boats was blown up by a hot shot from the enemy, which passed through her magazine. She had on board twenty-eight officers, seamen and marines, ten of whom were killed and six wounded. Among the killed was John S. Dorsey, midshipman, and James R. Caldwell, first lieut. of the Syren; both excellent officers. Midshipman Spence, and eleven men were taken up unhurt. Capt. Decatur, whose division this boat belonged to, and who was near her at the time she blew up, informed the Commodore, that Mr. Spence was superintending the loading of the gun at that moment, and, notwithstanding the boat was sinking, he and the brave men surviving finished charging, gave three cheers as the boat went from under them, and swam to the nearest boats, where they assisted during the remainder of the action.

The father of Mr. Spence was purser of the Philadelphia, and one of the American prisoners in Tripoli. All the officers and men behaved with the utmost intrepidity. Forty-eight shells, and above 500 twenty-four pound shot were thrown into the town and batteries.

"The Bashaw has a bomb-proof room in the castle, where he staid during the action. On hearing the explosion of our gun-boat, he ventured to take a peep, with the precaution of having a Marabewt or priest seal a small piece of paper on the top of his head, with a Turkish or Mahometan scrawl, with assurances that it would entirely secure him from all danger; but he soon returned to his cell. The Turks all wear a paper of this kind, sewed up in a little velvet bag, with assurances from the Marabewt, that it will protect them in the greatest danger. The Marabewt gets a sum of money for these blessings. If a Turk gets wounded, or killed, it is supposed the blessed paper is too old, or not placed in a proper manner. In the time of action, these Marabewts get upon some secure place, and cry to Mahomet, in the most dismal yells, to let them conquer their enemies, or beckon to the vessels to run ashore or be destroyed." In this action twelve men were killed and six wounded, two of whom mortally.

August 9.—The commodore went on board the Argus in order to reconnoitre the harbour of Tripoli; he stood in towards the town, and was very near being sunk by the enemy's fire. One of their heaviest shot, which struck about three feet short of her water line, raked the copper off her bottom under water, and cut the plank half through. This day a number of our men fainted and dropped beneath the weight they were compelled to sustain, and they were brought half dead to the prison. In the evening we petitioned the Bashaw in the following words.

TO HIS EXCELLENCY THE GRAND BASHAW OF TRIPOLI.

The petition of the American prisoners humbly sheweth:

That your humble petitioners, when doing, with all their power, as they are commanded, are most cruelly beaten by our wardens, stoned, insulted and spit upon by the soldiers and others; required to carry burthens impossible for them to sustain; and chafed and beaten until we are or soon shall be unable to labour at all. From the many acts of justice, kindness and generosity we have experienced from your Excellency, we cannot suppose that such conduct is authorised by your command; or that we should be punished for what is out of our power to perform, or for the actions of others which we have no agency in, and which we cannot prevent. Returning your Excellency our sincere and humble thanks for your bounty and privileges heretofore shewn, and relying on your goodness for protection; we therefore most humbly pray, that your Excellency would interpose your royal authority, and grant us speedy relief. And your petitioners, as in duty bound, will remain your Excellency's most humble, faithful and obedient servants.

On the petition being explained to the Bashaw, by Hexime, or Hamet American, his new name, the Bashaw forbid the Turks striking us; but his orders were insincere and illusive, for the very next day he stood by and saw several of us severely beaten innocently, without the least apparent dissatisfaction.

August 10.—At ten o'clock in the forenoon, the French Consul hoisted a white flag, at his flag-staff, under the national colours, which was a signal that the Bashaw was ready to treat. The commodore sent a boat into the harbour, and took this opportunity to forward to Captain Bainbridge letters from three friends. The boat was not allowed to land, but returned in the afternoon, and brought the commodore a letter from the French consul, advising that the Bashaw was ready to receive five hundred dollars for the ransom of each of the prisoners, and terminate the war without any consideration for peace or tribute. This was 350 thousand dollars less than was demanded previous to the action of the 3d inst. These terms the commodore did not hesitate to reject, as he was informed by Captain Chauncy, that it was the expectation of our government, on the arrival of four frigates, to obtain the release of the officers and crew of the Philadelphia without ransom, and dictate the terms of peace. This is the commodore's statement respecting the truce which, no doubt, is a correct one; and if it is, what a monstrous blunder has the Doctor again committed. He says at this same time, "Our squadron hoisted a flag of truce, sent in a brig and schooner, and fired a gun. The Bashaw did not, and swore he would not answer it; and said he would not treat with Commodore Preble. A truce, however, was afterwards held. Consul O'Brian wished to come on shore, but was refused." And again he says,

August 13.—"Another truce was held, when the Bashaw demanded one million of dollars for our ransom. One hundred and twenty thousand dollars were offered and refused." Here is a wide difference between the Com.'s and the Doctor's statement. The Doctor has only given his patient, the public, too large a dose of exaggeration; which has proved the fatal bane of unbelief.

August 17.—Fifteen dead Americans were found drifted ashore on the beach, westward of the town. By an epaulette on his shoulder, one of them was known to be a lieutenant. Doctor Cowdery asked permission of the Bashaw to go with some of our men and bury them. He promised they should be buried the next day. The inhabitants had chiefly moved out of the town for fear of another bombardment; and the Bashaw ate, drank and slept in his bomb proof room. The beach was covered with a despicable multitude of horse and foot soldiers, with rusty muskets without locks, and fired with a match. They were half naked, meagre and totally undisciplined.

August 18.—We were not permitted to bury our dead, according to the Bashaw's promise. At night our squadron stood to sea.

Aug. 19.—Mr. Church, whom we called the English merchant, was shot through the head, in the streets, as he was returning, at night, to his lodgings.

August 20.—The ketch Intrepid arrived from Syracuse, with fresh provisions and vegetables for our squadron. Capt. Chauncy had brought word to the commodore that Commodore Barron[2] was to sail for the Mediterranean four days after his departure; and, in consequence of this information, Commodore Preble expected him every moment, and was waiting for his arrival to make another attack, which he believed would be final and effectual. He had dispatched the Enterprize to Malta with orders, to our agent there, to hire transport to bring our squadron fresh provisions, water and other stores. On the 22d she returned, but brought no intelligence of the long expected frigates. A ship arrived from Malta, the same day, with live stock and water for the squadron.

August 24.—"In the morning, about two o'clock, and at day light, two of our small vessels hove about thirty shells, as was supposed, for the round fort, but they fell short of the mark. Such attempts serve rather to encourage than intimidate the Tripolitans, and the Bashaw was in high spirits on the occasion."

August 26.—The fellow who murthered Mr. Church was executed in the afternoon, on the ground where the act was perpetrated. It had hitherto been the custom, in this country, when a person had committed murder, to fly to the tomb of a Marabewt, where they were protected from justice, and fee to the Marabewt would procure them absolution. This fellow fled to a place of this kind immediately after killing Mr. Church. The English Consul, Mr. Langford, on being informed of the murder, addressed the Bashaw and demanded justice. The Bashaw then found out by a boy, who accompanied the murderer when he committed the crime, the particulars of the affair, and immediately sent a file of men and ordered them to prevent any one from carrying food or drink to the murderer. They watched him until night, when the Bashaw sent his Marabewt, who coaxed him away and brought him to the castle and confined him in irons. The next day the Bashaw called his Divan, when it was decided the person was guilty of wilful murther, and should suffer death. It appeared by the evidence and confession of the prisoner, that Mr. Church had lent a sum of money to the Spanish master-carpenter in this place; that Church had pressed him for payment, and that the carpenter's wife had hired the Turk to kill him, for forty dollars. The boy who accompanied him was bastinadoed with five hundred blows.——The carpenter's wife was ordered to leave Tripoli. At three, P.M. the commodore weighed anchor and stood in for Tripoli. He was employed, until eight, P.M. in making arrangements for attacking the town—all the boats in the squadron were officered and manned and attached to the gun-boats. The two bomb vessels could not be brought into action, as one was leaky and the mortar-bed of the other had given way. The John Adams, Scourge, transports and bombs were anchored seven miles to the northward of the town. Captain Chauncy, with several of his officers and about seventy seamen and marines, had volunteered their services on board the Constitution. At one, A.M. the gun-boats, in two divisions, led by Captains Decatur and Somers, were ordered to advance and take their stations close to the rocks, at the entrance of the harbour, within grape-shot distance of the Bashaw's castle. The Syren, Argus, Vixen, Nautilus, Enterprize and boats of the squadron, accompanied them. At three, A.M. the boats anchored with springs on, within pistol shot of the rocks, and commenced a brisk firing on the shipping, town, batteries, and Bashaw's castle, which was warmly returned, but not as well directed. At day-light, perceiving that the gun-boats had nearly expended their ammunition, the commodore weighed with the Constitution and stood in for the harbour; Fort English, the Bashaw's castle, crown and mole batteries, kept up a constant fire as he advanced. At half past five, the commodore made a signal for the gun-boats to retire from action, and for the brigs and schooners to take them in tow. The Constitution was then within two cables length of the rocks, and commenced a heavy fire of round and grape on thirteen of the enemy's gun-boats and gallies which were in pretty close action with our boats. They sunk one of the enemy's boats, and at the same time two more, disabled, run in on shore to avoid sinking. The remainder immediately retreated. The commodore continued running in until he was within musket shot of the crown and mole batteries, when he brought to, and fired upwards of 300 round shot, beside grape and cannister, into the town, Bashaw's castle and batteries. He silenced the castle, and two of the batteries, for some time. At a quarter past six, the gun-boats being all out of shot and in tow, the commodore hauled off, after having been three quarters of an hour in close action. The gun-boats fired upwards of four hundred round shot, beside grape and cannister. A large Tunisian galliot was sunk in the mole; a Spanish ship had entered with an ambassador from the Grand Seignior, and received considerable damage. The Tripolitan gallies and gun-boats lost many men and were much cut. Captains Decatur and Somers conducted their divisions with their usual firmness and address, and were well supported by the officers and men attached to them. The brigs and schooners suffered considerably in their sails and rigging. The damage which the Constitution received was principally above the hull; three lower shrouds, two spring stays, two top-mast back-stays, trusses, chains and lifts of the main yard shot away. Her sails had several cannon shot through them, and besides were considerably cut by grape; much of her running rigging cut to pieces; one of her anchor stocks and larboard cable shot away, and a number of grape shots were sticking in different parts of her hull, but not a man hurt!

> The hero's life a miracle shall save,
> For partial fortune will protect the brave
> Through many dangers; but, when e'er they fall,
> 'Tis heaven in mercy that directs the ball.

A boat belonging to the John Adams, with a master's mate (Mr. Creighton) and eight seamen, was sunk by a double-headed shot from the batteries, while in tow of the Nautilus, which killed three men, and badly wounded one, who, with Mr. C. and the other four, was picked up by one of our boats. The only damage our gun-boats sustained was in their rigging and sails, which were considerably cut by the enemy's round and grape shot.

August 30.—Doctor Cowdery "took a ride upon a mule, about 8 miles to the westward of the town, in company with Hamet, a Turkish officer, and several footmen." Here they saw a boat which had drifted on shore, with a dead man, and several muskets and swords in it. The man appeared to have been shot through the body with a cannon ball, which had also pierced the bottom of the boat. The Turkish officer collected about twenty Arabs, who hauled the boat up the beach, dragging the dead man out of it, stripped him entirely naked, and left him on the beach. They were scattered on the shore for miles, and were torn to pieces by dogs.

August 31.—A vessel arrived from Malta, with provisions and stores for our squadron, but brought no news of Commodore Barron or his frigates.

September 2.—The bomb vessels having been repaired, and ready for service, Lieutenants Dent and Robinson returned the command of them. Lieut. Morris, of the Argus, took command of No. 3, and Lieut. Trippe having nearly recovered of his wounds, resumed the command of No. 6, which he so gallantly conducted on the 3d. ult. Capt. Chauncy, with several young gentlemen, and sixty men, from the John Adams, volunteered on board the Constitution. At 4, P.M. the Commodore made signal to weigh—kept under sail all night. At 11, P.M. general signal to prepare for battle. A Spanish Polacre, in ballast, went out of the harbour to the Commodore, with an Ambassador from the Grand Seignior on board; who had been sent from Constantinople to Tripoli, to confirm the Bashaw in his title. This ceremony takes place in the Barbary regencies every five years. The Captain of the vessel informed the Commodore, that the shot and shells made great havoc and destruction in the city, and that a vast number of the people had been killed; but his accounts were much exaggerated, for very few of the shells burst, and consequently did no great injury.

The weekly allowance of meat and vegetables, which we received from the Danish Consul, by order of Captain Bainbridge, had been discontinued ever since the 10th of June, as has been noticed, and in consequence of several petitions made to Capt. Bainbridge, stating, that it was almost impossible for the men to exist, under the severity of treatment, and increased labour to which we were doomed, since the invasions of Commodore Preble, we received from the Danish Consul, by order of Capt. Bainbridge, one pound of beef per man, with vegetables for soups, and one loaf of wheat bread, in addition to the Bashaw's allowance. The meat and vegetables we were to receive only twice a week, the bread every day. As I was exempt from labour, the task of superintending the drawing and dividing of the provisions was enjoined on me. There had been much dissatisfaction and murmuring among the men, respecting the division of their late rations, and as every ounce of meat, to men half starving, was considered of the greatest value and importance, to prevent any just complaints, by giving every one his exact dividend, I classed the men into messes of eight, and made them choose their messmates; then numbered the messes, as on board the ship. The meat was then cut up by two of the petty officers, and divided into as many heaps as there were messes, and particular care was taken that each heap should be alike in quality. Each lot was then exactly weighed, and made equivalent. Our vegetables were pumpkins, turnips, and scallions, which were as exactly divided as the meat, and in the same manner. As many numbers as there were messes, were then made of paper, and stuck on the meat, and in like manner to the vegetables. Another set of numbers was made, put into a hat, and shook together. The number of the messes being called, one by one, whatever ticket each one drew, entitled him to a corresponding number of meat and vegetables. This was a lottery without any blanks, and a method that prevented any more complaints. The bread was easily divided. This was a great alleviation to our hunger-pained breasts. But to return to our squadron.

September 3.—At half past two, P.M. the signals were made for the gun-boats to cast off, advance, and attack the enemy's gun-boats and gallies, which were all under weigh in the eastern part of the harbour, whither they had been, for some time, working up against the wind. This was certainly a judicious movement of theirs, as it precluded the possibility of our boats going down to attack the town, without having the enemy's flotilla in the rear, and directly to windward. The Commodore accordingly ordered the bomb vessels to run down within proper distance of the town, and bombard it, while our gun-boats were to engage the enemy's gallies and boats to windward. At half past 3, P.M. our boats having gained their stations, to which they were directed, commenced throwing shells into the city. At the same time, our gun-boats opened a brisk fire on the gallies, and within point-blank shot, which was warmly returned by them and fort English, and by a new battery, a little westward; but as soon as our boats arrived within good musket shot of their gallies and boats, they gave way, and retired to the shore, within the rocks, and under cover of musketry from fort English. They were followed by our boats, and by the Syren, Argus, Vixen, Nautilus, and Enterprize, as far as the reef would permit them to go with prudence. The action was then divided; one division of our boats, with the brigs and schooners, attacked fort English, whilst the other was engaged with the enemy's gallies and boats. The Bashaw's castle, the Mole, Crown, and several other batteries, kept up a constant fire on our bomb vessels, which were well conducted, and threw shells briskly into the town; but, from their situation, they were very much exposed, and in great danger of being sunk. To prevent which, the Commodore ran within them with the Constitution, to draw off the enemy's attention, and amuse them while the bombardment was kept up. The Commodore brought to, within reach of grape, and fired eleven broadsides into the Bashaw's castle, town, and batteries, in a situation where more than seventy guns could bear upon him. One of the batteries were silenced. The town, castle, and other batteries considerably damaged. By this time it was half past four o'clock. The wind was increasing, and inclining rapidly to the north-ward; the Commodore made a signal for the boats to retire from action, and for the brigs and schooners to take them in tow, and soon after hauled off, with the Constitution, to repair damages. Our gun-boats were an hour and fifteen minutes in action. They disabled several of the enemies gallies and boats, and considerably damaged Fort-English. Most of our boats received damage in their rigging and sails. About 50 shells were thrown into the town, and our boats fired about 400 round shot, besides grape and canister. They were led into action by Captains Decatur and Somers, with their usual gallantry.

It is very unaccountable, that among so many shells as were thrown into the town, so few of them burst. It must have been owing to want of skill, and not treachery in the bombadiers. The Bashaw gave a bounty for every shell that his people brought to him, and they were found in plenty. A large number went directly over our prison, and fell innoxious in the sand. Three or four shot struck our prison, but did no damage of consequence.

It must be remembered, that most of the foregoing account of Commodore Preble's operations, is taken from his letter to the Secretary of the Navy, and nearly in his own words. The Commodore further says—"Desirous of annoying the enemy, by all means in my power, I directed to be put in execution a long-contemplated plan of sending a fire-ship, or infernal, into the harbour of Tripoli, in the night, for the purpose of endeavoring to destroy the enemy's shipping, and shatter the Bashaw's castle and town. Captain Somers, of the Nautilus, having volunteered his service, had, for several days before this period, been directing the preparation of the ketch Intrepid, assisted by lieutenants Wadsworth and Israel. About 100 barrels of powder, and 150 fixed shells, were, apparently, judiciously disposed of, on board her. The fuses, leading to the magazine, were calculated to burn a quarter of an hour.

"September 4.—The Intrepid being prepared for the intended service, Captain Somers and Lieutenant Wadsworth made choice of two of the fastest rowing boats in the squadron, for bringing them out after reaching their destination, and firing the combustible materials which were to communicate with the fuzes. Captain Somers' boat was manned with four seamen from the Nautilus, and Lieutenant Wadsworth's with six from the Constitution. Lieut. Israel accompanied them. At eight in the evening the Intrepid was under sail, and standing for the port, with a leading breeze from the eastward. The Argus, Vixen, and Nautilus, convoyed her as far as the rocks. On entering the harbour, several shot were fired at her from the batteries. In a few minutes after, when she had apparently, nearly gained her intended place of destination, she suddenly exploded, without their having previously fired a room, filled with splinters and other combustibles, which were intended to create a blaze, in order to deter the enemy from boarding whilst the fire was communicating to the fuzes, which led to the magazine. The effect of the explosion awed the batteries into profound silence, with astonishment. Not a gun was afterwards fired for the night. The shrieks of the inhabitants informed us, that the town was thrown into the greatest terror and consternation, by the explosion of the magazine, and the bursting and falling of shells in all directions. The whole squadron waited with the utmost anxiety, to learn the fate of the adventurers, from a signal previously agreed upon, in case of success, but waited in vain; no signs of their safety were to be observed. The Argus, Vixen, and Nautilus hovered round the port till sunrise, when they had a fair view of the harbour. Not a vestige of the ketch or the boats were to be seen. One of the enemy's largest boats was missing, and three others were seen, very much shattered and damaged, which the enemy were hauling on shore. From these circumstances I am led to believe, that those boats were detached from the enemy's flotilla, to intercept the ketch, and without supposing her to be a fire-ship, the missing boat had suddenly boarded her, when the gallant Somers, and heroes of his party, observing the other three boats surrounding them, and no prospect of escape, determined, at once, to prefer death and destruction of the enemy, to captivity and torturing slavery, put a match to the train leading directly to the magazine, which, at once, blew the whole into the air, and terminated their existence. My conjectures respecting this affair are founded on a resolution which Captain Somers, Lieutenants Wadsworth and Israel had formed, neither to be taken by the enemy, nor suffer him to get possession of the powder on board the Intrepid. They expected to enter the harbour without discovery, but had declared, if they should be disappointed, and the enemy should board them before they reached the point of destination, in such force as to leave no hopes of a safe retreat, they would put a match to the magazine, and blow themselves and their enemies up together; determined, as there was no exchange of prisoners, that their country should never pay ransom for them, nor the enemy receive a supply of powder through their means. The disappearance of one of the enemy's boats, and the shattered condition of three others, confirm me in my opinion, that they were an advanced guard, detached from the main body of the enemy's flotilla, on discovering the approach of the Intrepid, and that they attempted to board her before she had reached her point of destination, otherwise the whole of the shipping must have suffered, and perhaps would have been totally destroyed. That she was blown up before she had reached her station, is certain; by which the service has lost three very gallant officers. Captain Somers, and Lieutenants Wadsworth and Israel, were officers of conspicuous bravery, talents, and merit. They had uniformly distinguished themselves in the several actions—were beloved and lamented by the whole squadron."

Far from wishing or endeavoring to detract from the merits of those immortal heroes, who lost their lives in attempting to effectuate our emancipation, a strict regard to correct information, as far as it can be traced, induces me to make the following enquiries and remarks:—

I would ask any reasonable person, is it probable, that Captain Somers, Lieutenants Wadsworth and Israel would have voluntarily sacrificed their lives by a premature act? Or, in other words, would they have fired the train had they not been boarded by the enemy, or surrounded in such a manner as to banish all hopes of escape? And if the enemy had boarded them, would they not have shared promiscuous destruction, as has been reported from conjecture? And if the enemy did suffer, or were thus destroyed, should not we have been informed of it through some of the means following?—

The Neapolitans, who were servants to most of the chief men in Tripoli, who were slaves, and anticipated freedom from our squadron's success, who brought us with avidity, every intelligence of our enemy's loss or defeat; who perfectly understood the language of the Tripolitans; never gave us any information; and, of course, never heard that any of the Turks were destroyed by the explosion of the infernal. There were many Jews and disaffected Turks, Greeks, and Maltese, who were ready to communicate to us every unfavourable circumstance of the enemy, and we never heard from them, that any of the Turks perished in the explosion. The Christian Consuls, and especially the Danish one, who was our particular friend, never informed us that any of the Turks were killed by the explosion of the fire-ship. Lewis Hexiner, who had turned Turk, but seriously repented it, and who was promised, and expected to be given up to us on our liberation, by covertly befriending us, while in full confidence of the Bashaw and all the Turks, never gave us information of the kind, and of course never heard such a report amongst the Turks. Doctor Cowdery, who lodged in the same room with Hexiner, does not mention it in his journal. Is it not, therefore, more than probable, that through all these channels of communication, if a circumstance so extraordinary as the destruction of one or two hundred Turks, some information of the event would have reached us? It is therefore very evident, that no Turks were destroyed; and if none were destroyed, is it not full as evident, that the train communicated to the magazine sooner than was expected, and that the explosion happened before our men could possibly avoid a catastrophe so much to be lamented? Doctor Cowdery says, that "The fire-ship sent in by Commodore Preble, did but little damage, and that the Bashaw and his people held a thanksgiving to Mahomet on the occasion," which would not have been, had he lost a boat and two hundred men by it. But from whatever circumstance or accident they lost their lives, it is certain that they died meritoriously, and while valour, patriotism, and heroic actions, meet with admiration, gratitude and applause the names of Somers, Wadsworth, Israel, and their brave companions in death, will live and shine on the annals of fame, and be registered in the catalogue of American martyrs in the cause of liberty.

The weather continuing to wear a threatening aspect until the 7th of September, and the ammunition being reduced to a quantity not more than sufficient for three vessels to keep up the blockade, no intelligence of the expected reinforcement, and the season so far advanced as to render it imprudent to hazard the gunboats any longer on the station, the Commodore gave orders for the John Adams, Syren, Nautilus, Enterprize, and Scourge, to take the bombs and gun-boats in tow, and proceed to Syracuse with them; the Argus and Vixen to remain with the Constitution, to keep up the blockade.

This day 14 bodies of Americans, supposed to be destroyed by the explosion of the fire-ship, were interred by permission of the Bashaw. John M'Donald, who had long been in a decline, departed this, he hoped, for a better life. But turning from such gloomy subjects as death and the grave, let us attend Doctor Cowdery in another of his excursions.

September 9.—"The Bashaw took us with him and his suit to his country seat, where we spent most of the day. We went to see the great Marabewt, in whom the Bashaw had great faith, and thought he could foretell events. It was thought, by the Turks, that he foretold the stranding and capture of the Philadelphia, and that he got offended with the Bashaw, and caused and foretold her being burnt. He now said, the Commodore's ship would never return to America; that she would either be blown up, or run on shore, and that the Bashaw would have success in his warfare with America. It appeared, that this great prophet was a sojourner, and that he only came to Tripoli when the Bashaw was in want of a prophet. He was encamped on the sandy desert, at a tomb of an ancient Marabewt. When we came near him, we all dismounted. The Bashaw went to him, kneeled before him, and kissed his hand. The Mamelukes followed the example. The Marabewt then sat down, and was followed by the Bashaw and suite, forming a circle on a mat. During this time I stood by my mule, with my hat in my hand, about five rods from the scene. I was soon called, and ordered, by the Bashaw, to take off my shoes and feel the Marabewt's pulse. I left my shoes at the edge of the mat, or holy ground, and stepped on. I laid my hat on the edge of the mat, in preference to laying it on the sand, but it was immediately taken off. I was then ordered to approach his holiness and kiss his hand. I felt his pulse, but before I had time to prescribe for him, he put his hand against me, and gave me to understand, that I must go off the holy ground. I immediately stepped off, put on my shoes, took my hat, and went to my mule. The Bashaw called me back, and asked me what I would do for the Marabewt. I recommended bleeding, but the Marabewt shook his head, and gave me to understand, that he wanted nothing of the kelp (dog.) I was then told to withdraw, which I did, and took a walk around the tomb, which I found to be very ancient. The Bashaw spent about half an hour with the Marabewt, when he kissed his hand, and we all returned to the country palace. The Bashaw apologized for the impoliteness of the Marabewt, and said, that they had a foolish antipathy to all but Mahometans."

September 10.—The United States ship President, Commodore Barron, and Constellation, Captain Campbell, hove in sight, and soon joined company, when the command of the squadron was surrendered to Commodore Barron, with the usual ceremony. Commodore Preble continued in company with the squadron until the 12th, when three strange ships hove in sight, standing directly for Tripoli. Chase was given, and two of them boarded and taken possession of by the Constitution; the President in company, about four leagues from Tripoli, but not more than four miles from land, while the Constellation and Argus were in chase of the third. The two boarded by the Constitution were loaded with about sixteen thousand bushels of wheat. Tripoli was in a state of starvation, and there can be no doubt but those cargoes were meant as a supply and relief to our enemies. No farther operations were carried on against Tripoli for the season.

Commodore Preble left the station and returned to America by the first convenient opportunity, where he met with that warm, generous and honourable reception, which our countrymen are ever ready to evince towards those who have distinguished themselves by valour, patriotism and magnanimity. He left a lasting impression on the mind of the Bashaw, and all the barbarians of Tripoli, of American bravery. Such unparalleled heroism appalled their savage bosoms, and struck them with the profoundest astonishment. That a single frigate should dare venture under the batteries, in the manner that Preble did, they imputed to madness, and that she ever lived to return was ascribed, by them, to some superiour agency's invisible protection. He was considered as a prodigy of valour and dread as the minister of destruction. He was not an idle, *barron* Commodore. His labours produced effect—it won laurels and bore them.

Respecting the damage done to the town of Tripoli, various reports have made erroneous statements. There was but little damage done to the town, for it is wholly built of incombustible materials, and they who have reported that the town was set on fire by the shells, might as well have informed us that a conflagration of the Mediterranean was effected with a taper. In every attack upon the place we were taken out, at intervals, to carry powder to the different forts, and treated worse than can be represented by words. They would place a barrel of powder on a man's back, and make him run every step, without resting, from the castle to the batteries, three quarters of a mile, with a driver behind him dealing blows at every breath, amidst the pelting of stones from the soldiery, and every insult and indignity that could be offered or endured. A great number of shells and balls went over and fell near our prison, but none of them did any material damage. One ball went through our cook-house, adjoining one end of our prison—one struck the front, obliquely, and spent its fury without harm, and several more glanced over the corners and terrace of it. A ball went through the Danish consul's observatory, the moment he had left it, in the exact direction where he stood. It is great pity the commodore had not found more skilful bombardiers, for though they could not fire the houses, had they all burnt, great damage, as well as great consternation, must have been the result. Two of the guns burst, in the last action, and killed two Turks in the castle.

Before our squadron had left the coast, and previous to the last engagement, I received a line from one of our officers, mentioning that Lieutenant James Decatur[3] was killed, on the 3d of August, and requesting me to write an elegy on his death; which was attempted in the following strain.

CHAPTER XI

Elegy

On the death of Lieutenant JAMES DECATUR, *who fell August 3d*, 1804,
in an action with the Tripolitan gun-boats.

Through these drear walls, where fiends horrific reign,
Chill the faint heart and rend the frantic brain!
Where, void of friends, of pleasure, food or rest,
Tormenting slavery preys upon our breast;
From yon thick squadron, whence we hope to hear
The voice of freedom charm the captive's ear,
Sounds the sad tale, DECATUR's name deplore,
For that young hopeful hero breathes no more!
He left, to free us from barbarian chains,
Columbia's blooming groves and peaceful plains;
Forever sacred be those arms he wore,
The cause that mov'd him, and the barque that bore,
'Twas heav'ns own cause—'twas freedom's injur'd name,
The love of country, and the voice of fame
Call'd forth his active marshal skill to go
Scour the wide deep and scourge the tyrant foe:
Dauntless he fights, where dying groans resound,
And thund'ring carnage roars tremendous round—
'Till heav'n beheld him with propitious eyes,
And snatch'd his kindred spirit to the skies.
When from the Turks his mangled form they bore
With glory cover'd, bath'd in streaming gore,
Bewailing his friends his ghastly wounds survey'd,
Which bid defiance to all human aid,
When life stood trembling, ling'ring in its flight,

And heav'n's blest visions dawn'd upon his sight;
The radient shades of heroes hov'ring round,
Midst harps of angels, with reviving sound,
Sooth'd the last pangs of his undaunted breast,
And wing'd him, convoy'd, to eternal rest.
Could worth have rescue'd, or could virtue save
Her heav'n-born vot'ries from the destin'd grave;
Could sacred friendship's hallow'd pray'rs bestow
The gift of immortality below;
Could thousand's sighs and tears, that ceaseless roll,
Call from the shores of bliss th' angelic soul:
(Though the bold wish be impious deem'd, and vain.)
Death ne'er had reach'd him, or he'd live again.
But fate's decrees, irrevocably just,
Doom'd his frail body to the mingling dust;
In yon cold deep it finds unwak'd repose,
Far from th' embrace of friends or reach of foes;
Till the last trumpet's loud eternal roar
Call forth its millions from the sea and shore,
Nor till the final blast, and awful day,
Shall that brave soul reanimate its clay.

Our men were employed in repairing the damages done in the several attacks upon the forts and batteries—laying new platforms, building new gun-carriages, hauling timber and stone to build boats and erect fortifications, and nothing, worthy of remark, transhaped our fortune for a considerable time.

October 21—was the last day we saw any of our shipping. The Tripolitans took their arms and ammunition from their gun-boats, and extracted the charges from the cannon on the forts and batteries. It seems the Bashaw, as yet, had but very inadequate conceptions of the force of his foe; for he this day told Doctor Cowdery (so he informs us) that if he had three frigates he would blockade America. He fancied he could do it as easily as one frigate and a schooner could blockade Tripoli.

October 23.—No bread to be had. The Turks told us, that in consequence of the blockade which our shipping had maintained, we now had to suffer, and advised us to petition to our Commodore in Syracuse, to make peace and take us away. The Bashaw issued an edict, prohibiting the inhabitants from purchasing, and the venders of grain from selling to any but the castellany. Money would not command bread, and starvation was whetting her teeth to devour us. Commodore Lysle, disregarding the Bashaw's proclamation, purchased some barley. An altercation ensued between them. Lysle insisted on his right to purchase grain in the public marts. The Bashaw was outrageous, flew at him, struck him, and commanded his guard to disarm and confine him, which was done, for a few hours, when the Bashaw ordered him released, and gave the person, who had fomented the fracas, 500 bastinadoes. For three days we never tasted bread, and for eleven days more we had but a very little, subsisting on dates pressed into a cake, and vegetables, with oil.

November 9.—The meat and vegetables, which we had drawn by order of Capt. Bainbridge, were discontinued. Philosophers may prate what they will, of the feasibility of our enjoying happiness under all circumstances, and in all conditions. Let one of those sticklers for contentment be placed in our situation, with an empty stomach, a heavy burthen on his back, and a fell fiend at his heels, dealing flagellation at every step, and I am pretty well convinced, that he would feel disposed to relinquish his tenets.

The Bashaw had a fit of the epilepsy. His people imagined him possessed of the devil; a Marabewt performed many exorcisms, which at length dispelled him.

November 20.—A great scarcity of bread still prevailed, and our men were obliged to sell the clothes which they had lately drawn, and for which they were suffering, to procure something to sustain life. The cravings of hunger predominated over the calls of external wants, and our clothes were sacrificed for a mere trifle; but trifles are of magnitude when they preserve life. During the extremity of famine, one of our men, impelled by imperious hunger, taking advantage of the Jews' Sabbath, who had the charge of the distillery, clambered over a wall twenty feet high, broke or unlocked three doors, and got into the still-house, where a little shop was kept for retailing aqua-deut, and brought off a pitcher full of Buckamseens, which he distributed amongst his companions so profusely, that he was suspected, and subsequently convicted of the robbery; but he greased the fists of his keepers, who, for a share, put him in irons, and gave him a slight punishment. Some of our tars had the ingenuity to counterfeit the Bashaw's coin. When a specimen of the fraud was shewn to the Bashaw, he laughed heartily, and said that the Americans were all wizards and devils, and protested, that if the person was detected, he could not punish, but reward his invention.

December 7.—It was said, that the Bashaw, impatient for the money which he forestalled as the price of our ransom, gave orders to our wardens, to treat us with the utmost severity, in order to extort from us supplications to our country for a speedy peace. For several days we had been without bread or money, for the Bashaw sometimes ordered us cash, when bread was not plenty, and the men were unanimously determined not to labour any more unless one or the other was allowed us.

December 10.—Our keepers or drivers, as usual, unlocked the prison doors early in the morning, and ordered us *tota fora* (all out.) Not one of us moved. The most of us had now provided ourselves with cots, as before described, which were ranged one above another, to the top of the prison, making it difficult for the drivers to come at us. A few, however, slept on the ground, and to those the furious elves had free access, and began to beat them. We then all spoke, and told them, that we were resolved, if death should be the consequence, not to turn out another day without food. They threatened to call the soldiers, and fire in upon us, and when they found they could not move us by the threats nor blows, they left us, and informed the Bashaw of our refractory conduct. They soon returned, and assured us, that if we would peaceably and tacitly obey their orders, we should have bread at twelve o'clock—this was agreed to, and the stipulation was fulfilled.

December 21.—At night the Bashaw's eldest son, the Bey of Tripoli, was married to his cousin, eldest daughter of the Ex-Bashaw. The bride was very beautiful, and said to be but twelve years old. Our boatswain, carpenter, sail-maker, and first masters-mate, who had been at liberty, on parole, since the 27th of June, were put in close confinement with our other officers, on a suspicion of conspiring with the crew, to rise and take the castle. It is true, such a plot was in cogitation, but it was a very preposterous one. It was meditated for us to rush into the castle, when the gates were first opened in the morning—to seize on the armoury and magazine—liberate our officers—secure the guard and the Mamelukes, and make a prisoner of the Bashaw and his family. At the same time, to plant a 26 pounder, loaded with grape, at each gate, and point the guns of the castle into the town. This, doubtless, might have been effected with but little loss; but the question is, how long could we have maintained our ground. The Turks might have brought their cannon, from the different forts, to bear upon, and battered the castle to prostrate ruins. Could such a plot have been carried into operation, when our squadron was cruising off the harbour, it might have been terminated with success; but under the then existing circumstances, before relief could have reached us, destruction must have swallowed us up.

December 25.—In compliance with a petition which we preferred to Captain Bainbridge, he sent orders to the Danish Consul, to have us supplied with a collation of fresh beef and vegetables, with an additional allowance of one loaf of bread per man; the whole to be washed down with a cask of wine, yielding a dividend of one quart to each individual. We also petitioned the Bashaw, for a respite from labour, for the day, and he was graciously pleased to vouchsafe our request. In the morning, at the usual time of unlocking our prison, the wardens came, and informed us, that some cordage and other articles were missing out of the Bashaw's naval magazine, (as they called it) and that some of the Americans were suspected of the robbery, and, unless we would give information of the perpetrator, no holiday should be allowed us; but, that we should spend the day in close confinement, and without food. They kept us in until about ten o'clock, when it being discovered, that Selim, the Bashaw's son-in-law, who carried the keys of the stores, had committed the crime, by selling the cordage, clandestinely, to a Tunisian merchant, we were allowed to come out, and bring our provisions and wine to the prison. The Bashaw ordered his son-in-law 500 bastinadoes; but he fled to a Marabewt, and escaped punition. The remainder of the day was spent, if not with the greatest festivity, with a decent propriety, and was ended in perfect unanimity. Among a number of songs, in the evening, the following, though not composed on the occasion, and, perhaps, not applicable to the particular genius of the day, was, nevertheless, sung by unanimous request.

Song

Tune—"*Madam you know my trade is war.*"[1]

1. Columbia! while the sons of fame
Thy freedom through the world proclaim,
And hell-born tyrants dread the name
  That wills all nations free;
Remote, on Barb'ry's pirate coast,
By foes enslav'd, a miscreant host,
No more the rights of man we boast;
  Adieu, blest Liberty!

2. How fearful lour'd the gloomy day,
When, stranded on the shoals, we lay
Expos'd, our foremast cut away,
  To the rough-dashing sea;
When hostile gun-boats thunder'd round,
And no relief, nor hopes were found,
The mournful words swell'd ev'ry sound,
  Adieu, blest Liberty!

3. In helpless servitude, forlorn,
From country, friends, and freedom torn,
Alike we dread each night and morn,
  For nought but grief we see;
When burthen press—the lash we bear,
And all around is black despair,
We breathe the silent, fervent pray'r,
  O come, blest Liberty!

4. Mem'ry, to mis'ry e'er unkind,
Brings present, to the painful mind,
The woes oblivion, else, would find,
  And evils cease to be;
And fancy, when we're wrapp'd in sleep,
Conveys us o'er the boundless deep;
But, wak'd to sigh, we live to weep,
  Adieu, blest Liberty!

5. And when invading cannons roar,
And life, and blood, from hundreds pour,
And mangled bodies float ashore,
  And ruins strew the sea;
The thoughts of death, or freedom, near,
Create alternate hope and fear;

Oh! when will that blest day appear,
That brings sweet Liberty!

6. When rear'd on yonder castle's height,
The naked flagstaff's drest in white,
We gaze, enraptur'd at the sight;
How happy shall we be!
When thund'ring guns proclaim a peace,
Our toils all o'er, our woes shall cease;
We'll bless the pow'r that brings release,
And hail sweet Liberty!

We sent our thanks to Captain Bainbridge, for his compliance with our request, and, on the first of January, he ordered us the same quantity of provisions and wine as before. I was told to take eight men, go to the Danish Consul's, and get the wine. Our men were the tapsters, and the Consul requested me to keep an account of the measure. The good-natured, benevolent man, told us all to drink as much as we wanted, while it was drawing, and came, several times, urging us to drink. The tapsters accepted of his liberal invitation with such unreserved cordiality, that, by the time they had finished drawing, they were not able to carry the cask to the prison. Another set of bearers was collected, and the Consul made them drink, until they were nearly as much intoxicated as the first; and when we were departing, he distributed a handful of money amongst the whole. Our tars pronounced him the best fellow they had ever met with, and swore he must have been a sailor, or he would not be so generous with his cash and his grog.

January 28.—A strong guard was placed in our prison-yard, and we were forbid to go out. The infamous Wilson had informed the Bashaw, that we were all armed, and prepared to rise and take the town. They searched our prison, and found the report false.

February 1.—George Griffeth, gunner's-mate of the late Philadelphia, having inveigled the Bashaw with the project, that he could construct an air-furnace, to cast guns, shot, and shells in, was provided with masons, and nine of our crew, and set to the work. He received a doubloon, on commencing, and was promised one hundred dollars for the first specimen of his skill. After lavishing more than five hundred dollars, in making the experiment, it this day proved abortive, by premeditated design.

February 13.—

Another tar has weather'd storms and strife,
And burst the bonds of slav'ry and of life.

As a number of our men were at work, under a corner of the castle wall, a part of it fell, and crushed out the entrails of Jacob Dowerdishu, who died instantly.

February 20.—Our bread, which we drew from, or by order of the Captain, growing light, we petitioned him to let us receive a buckamseen a piece, each day, in the place of it, to which he complied, and which we received, daily, until the termination of our captivity. The sum amounted to ten dollars and three quarters, which I received, every morning, from the Danish Consul, and divided amongst the men. Such as laboured at the cart, and a large number who were employed in building up a corner of the castle, received a buckamseen a day from the Bashaw, and my task was to muster them, at evening, and mark the number of days each one had laboured, and receive and pay them the money. The men were often defrauded, by the embezzling of the keepers.

March 1.—An American frigate appeared off the harbour. The Turks repaired to their quarters, and manned their gun-boats. They began to resume their wonted cruelties on such occasions.

March 4.—Hassan Bey, the Bashaw's Aga,[2] was appointed to the command of an expedition to Derne. A great number of our men were employed in packing up ammunition and provisions for the expedition. Two frigates and a brig, supposed to be American, appeared off the harbour. The inhabitants, expecting a siege, began to move their families and effects into the country.

March 16.—The mansion lately occupied by our officers appeared to be full of people, and a guard on the terrace, and at the door. They were the nearest relatives of those officers who had gone on the expedition, and held as pledges of their loyalty, fearing they might attach themselves to his brother, the Ex-Bashaw.

March 18.—The Bashaw sent Selim, his son-in-law, into the country, to raise troops for the defence of Tripoli.

March 21.—A frigate in sight. "Several of the sons, and most esteemed friends of the Bashaw's chiefs in the country were brought into the castle, as hostages for their fidelity to the present Bashaw."

March 29.—Two large, stout negroes, were hanged at the city gate, for murder and robbery. They were executed in a most barbarous manner. A thick clumsy straw rope was fastened round each of their necks; they were placed at the foot of the wall, the ropes passed through the embrasures of the wall, and then five or six Turks seizing hold of it, ran away with the bight, and dragged them to the top, where they were made fast, and in which situation they lived three or four hours. They had no caps over their faces, and nothing on but shirts. They were not taken down until night, hanging from about 9 o'clock in the morning.

March 30.—Selim, who had been sent into the country to collect or enlist troops, returned with but a handful of men. The people had been oppressed by his exorbitant demands for money, and their women had been stripped of their rings, bracelets and jewels, and they refused to fight for the Bashaw.

April 12.—The Regency received information from his agent in Malta, of the formidable armament of the Americans in preparation. The Spanish Consul presented the Bashaw three hundred stands of arms, and a number of pistols; and, it is said, advised him to keep up the war, and force the Americans to pay his demands.

April 13.—"The Bashaw declared that if the Americans drove him to extremities, or attacked his town, he would put every American prisoner to death."

April 27.—A very oppressive Syroc wind, and two of our men, who were sent into the country with a cart, dragging it, loaded, over the burning sands, fainted and were brought in almost lifeless. The remainder were nearly exhausted by heat and fatigue. Several companies of Arabs passed through the town, and paraded under the Bashaw's balcony, in the navy-yard. There were about three hundred horse and seven hundred foot, and both made but a despicable appearance.

May 3.—The great Marabewt, who has been mentioned, assured the Bashaw that two American frigates more would be destroyed; and that the powder of the whole American squadron would be so damaged that they would not be able to fire a gun. He agreed to attend the Bashaw, to keep the balls and shells from hurting him.

May 14.—Doctor Cowdery received a letter from Captain Bainbridge, stating the inconveniences which the officers suffered by being in close confinement, and breathing unwholesome air. The Doctor spoke to the Bashaw on the subject, and humbly solicited that our officers might be removed to the American house. The Bashaw replied, that the war between him and our country was at first about money; but now it was whether he or his brother should be the Bashaw; and that the Americans had bound themselves to his brother in such a manner that it was not in their power to make peace with him; and that his brother and the Americans were determined to take Tripoli, and put him to death. He swore by the prophet of Mecca, that if the Americans brought his brother against him he would burn to death every American prisoner except the Doctor; that he should be spared because he had saved the life of his child when very sick.

May 19.—Antonio, a Neapolitan slave, who had recently paid his own ransom, returned from Malta and Syracuse, whither he had been sent by the Bashaw as a spy. He bro't news that the American squadron sailed for Alexandria, Egypt, about twenty days before; that they were to take on board the former Bashaw, and proceed along the coast of Tripoli, and take the principal towns, and then to attack and take the town of Tripoli, and put in possession the Ex-Bashaw. The Bashaw and his people were much alarmed at this news. As the residue of Doctor Cowdery's journal approaches very near the truth, we must do him the honour to copy it nearly verbatim.

May 22.—"I was informed that, in a letter which the Bashaw received the evening before, it was stated that Hassan Bey and his army were taken in Derne, by the Americans and Sidi Hamet, the Ex-Bashaw. I was desired not to mention it, because it was a great secret, and the Bashaw called a council of his chiefs, and proposed to put all the American prisoners to death, but it was agreed to postpone this measure for that time."

May 23.—"Twenty-four of our men were sent with a cart, for timber, into the country. The wind from the desert was very heavy and hot. The men almost perished in the sand, which flew and drifted like snow-storm in our country. They stopped through fatigue, and asked their driver, who was a Turk, for liberty to drink at a well which was near there. The Turk replied that they were Rama kelps

(Christian dogs), and said they should have no water. He gave them all a severe beating with a club, which he always carried with him to beat them with, and made them go on with the cart, which the poor fellows had to drag, loaded with timber, thro' the burning sand. They returned towards night, almost perished." This is true, but no more than what occurred almost every day.

May 24.—"At night the Bashaw dispatched a boat, loaded with powder, musket-balls and money, for his troops who were collecting to oppose the approach of his brother Hamet, the Ex-Bashaw. The eldest son of Hamet was confined in the castle, by order of his uncle. The Bashaw was so much agitated at the news of the approach of his brother, that he this day declared that if it were in his power to make peace and give up the American prisoners, he would gladly do it without the consideration of money." If this be true, what must we think of Col. Lear's[3] treaty? What must we think of sixty thousand lavished to no purpose? "His funds were so low that his steward run in debt for the supply of the kitchen. He gave his Mamelukes, domestics and myself but one meal per day. The rich Turks in town took turns in supplying his troops. He heartily repented for not accepting the terms of peace last offered by our country."

May 26.—"Three frigates in sight. About eleven, A.M. the smallest came near in and hoisted the banners of peace. The Bashaw asked his head men of the town, who were with him in the gallery, whether it was best to hoist his white flag. All, except one (the charge de affairs for Algiers) declared in favour of it, and of making peace, if possible. They expressed great contempt towards the Algerine Consul for his advice, and said that whoever would advise the Bashaw not to hoist the white flag at such a critical moment, must be his foe, and not his friend. The Algerine soon disappeared and left the castle. The Spanish Consul soon after came to the castle, and the Bashaw sent him in one of his handsomest boats with Shaws Hammad, to the frigate. They returned in the evening with the joyful news of a prospect of peace. There was a visible change from gloominess to joy in the countenances of all the Turks." And if it had this effect on the Turks, what must it have produced in the feelings of Americans in slavery? Our men were in paroxisms of joy, notwithstanding the issue was yet precarious.

May 27.—"Both Turks and Christians were all anxiously looking out for the frigates. It was said that Col. Lear promised to come on shore this morning, and that the Spanish Consul was preparing a dinner for the gentlemen who were expected to come with him. We were all agitated alternately by hope and despair. The terraces, and every eminence in town, were covered with people of all classes and ages, who were looking for the wished-for peace-maker; but not a frigate nor sail hove in sight during the day."

May 28.—"All looking out again for our squadron. A brig hove in sight in the morning, which we all at first thought was the flag ship. On discovering it was a brig, a gloominess again appeared on every countenance. The Turks began to think the frigate had gone to fetch the whole fleet, which they had heard consisted of sixty sail of different sizes. They thought that the flag of truce was only a plea of the Americans to find out the force of Tripoli, &c. But, at sun-set, three frigates and a brig appeared, which revived our hopes. The Bashaw shewed great anxiety for peace. He was sensible of the danger he was in from the lowness of his funds, and the disaffection of his people."

May 29.—"Three frigates and a brig bore down upon the town, and displayed the ensigns and signals of peace, which were immediately answered from the castle. The Spanish Consul, Fasah the Jew, and several Turks, went on board and did not return till late at night, when it was reported that negociations for peace were going on rapidly."

May 31.—"The Spanish Consul and Shaws Hammad went on board with the commodore, and returned at night. The Bashaw sent me to inform Captain Bainbridge that peace was agreed on, which I did to the great joy of our officers."

June 1.—"The truce continued. Captain Bainbridge went on board the commodore, and returned at night. Our mess were still drove to hard labour, and our officers confined."

June 2.—"I received a letter from Captain Bainbridge, stating that the terms of peace were agreed on, and that we should go on board the squadron. I immediately read this letter to our crew, who were so overjoyed that many of them shed tears. They were still drove to hard work, and many of them flogged."

Captain Bainbridge came himself to our prison, called us together and communicated the intelligence of a treaty being agreed on, but not yet signed; and cautioned us not to let the prospect of liberty transport us beyond the bounds of discretion, lest the preliminaries might yet be annulled. He delivered me a letter from a friend of mine in the United States, the only one I received while in Tripoli.

June 3.—"The articles of peace were signed, and about four o'clock in the afternoon the salute was fired from the frigates and batteries."

I shall not pretend to describe in adequate terms our various emotions for a number of days previous to this confirmation of our hopes. Sometimes our spirits were soaring buoyant on the wings of sanguine expectation; at other times, diving into the very gulph of despair.

But O! what joy when the saluting sound
Was heard to thunder through the arches round!
Enraptur'd lays the choral hundreds sung,
And that drear mansion once with gladness rung.

The Bashaw this morning called the American renegades Wilson, West, Smith, who had a wife and four children in Boston, Hexiner and Prince, and told them that peace was now concluded, the Americans were about to leave Tripoli, and if they, or either of them chose to go, it was left at their option. Unaware of the artifice, all, except Wilson, expressed their wish and anxiety to relinquish the turban and accompany us to America. Wilson, jealous of the Bashaw's sincerity, and perhaps afraid of the threatened halter, thanked his majesty for this generous offer, but told him that he preferred Tripoli to America, and Mahometanism to Christianity, and that he chose to remain, and would ever continue firmly attached to his service. Wilson was honoured and caressed by the Bashaw and his Divan for his singular fidelity—while the other four were sent into the country with a formidable guard. We had a glance at them as they passed our prison, and could see horror and despair depicted in their countenances. A number of our men went to the American house and remained all night with our officers, but the greater part were locked in the prison as usual. Our drivers were missing and a new guard over us.

June 4.—Lest our men might wreak vengeance on some of the Turks, and especially the keepers, for past cruelties, which would have inevitably involved us in difficulties and dangers, our men were kept locked in the prison until the arrangements were made to receive them all at the rendezvous, which was not until about ten o'clock, A.M. Here we all received new clothes, and were sent on board of different vessels in the afternoon; where some met with the warm reception of a good flogging before the next morning.

The fall of preceding we had drawn a subscription for the purpose of purchasing the ransom of a friendly Neapolitan. We obtained considerable encouragement at that time; but our own emancipation appearing so dubious, this humane project for that time was procrastinated. As soon, therefore, as our liberty was ascertained, we resumed the subject, and obtained upwards of three hundred dollars, wrote to Captain Bainbridge and had the money advanced and deducted out of our wages, and enjoyed the supreme satisfaction of giving liberty to one of our fellow-creatures. He was a servant to our chief wardeen, and not a task-master nor a driver over us as has been reported, in which capacity he had frequent opportunities of befriending us, and had rendered several of us very essential services. I have been informed, however, that when he found what severity was practiced in our service, he seriously repented of his leaving Tripoli!

We were upwards of nineteen months in imprisonment, and only six died out of more than three hundred men; and considering the hardships we endured, we had but little sickness—a sufficient proof that the climate is remarkably healthy. It was thought that the oil we mixed with all our food contributed greatly to the preservation of our healths. Abdallah, whom we called Captain Blackbeard, was our chief wardeen. He was a Moor, possessed great subtlety, insufferable pride, and was a "calm, thinking villain."[4] Soliman, whom we nick-named Scamping-Jack, was a Tunisian. He was sagacious, irrascible, fierce and cruel when provoked, and seemed to delight in mischief, strife and tumult. He was more serious and less vindictive than Blackbeard. Tousef, or Joseph, who was formerly the Ex-Bashaw's chief steward, was our third in authority. He was born of French parents, and came from Egypt to Tripoli when quite young. Like men disappointed and deprived of office, he was captious, querulous and malevolent. In a word, he was a quid.[5] The fourth was of Greek parentage, whom we called Bandy, from his having crooked legs. He had been a Mameluke of the Ex-Bashaw, and sincerely prayed for his restoration. He never struck any of us, seemed to symphathise in our sufferings, and was friendly and humane. Every one of our men would strive to be in his gang, and the old fellow, grateful for their preference, or proud of their partiality, would show them all the kindness and lenity which he dare. The fifth was an old Algerine, whom we named Blinkard. He was a sort of a doctor—cruel, passionate and ferocious. The last and most barbarous villain of the whole was a Tripolitan. Him we called Red-jacket. Whenever any of our shipping were firing on the town, he would take the opportunity to vent his infernal malice by beating and bruising our men with accumulated barbarity. The boatswain of the navy-yard was a Russian Mahometan, and was very inhuman to our men when they fell under his clutches. These wretches were the ready instruments of the Bashaw's will, wholly dependent on his smiles, and constant competitors for his favour. Mean, fawning, mercenary and cruel, they were held in as much contempt as slave-drivers in our own country, as jail-keepers in all countries, and as boatswains' mates of a man of war. I have often seen the citizens of Tripoli hiss them as they walked the streets. The prison which we last occupied was about one hundred and fifty feet in length, thirty in breadth, and twenty-five in height. It was built of stone, and its huge arches were supported by square columns, about ten feet distant from each other, extending from the inside of the wall nine or ten feet. Between these columns our cots were fastened or suspended, one above another, to the vertex of the arch. Out of our allowance of oil we saved enough to light our gloomy prison at night. There were three hundred and fifty persons, including Neapolitans, nocturnal inhabitants of this prison, and more than two hundred lamps burning every night. When every lamp was lighted, every arch, and every cot in each arch illuminated, the whole made a romantic, multiform and grand display of pompous misery.

CHAPTER XII

Description of the Place

Ye lurid domes! whose tott'ring columns stand,
Marks of the despot's desolating hand:
Whose weed-grown roofs and mould'ring arches show
The curse of tyranny, a nation's woe;
In ev'ry ruin—ev'ry pile I find
A warning lesson to a thoughtful mind.
Your gloomy cells expressive silence break,
Echo to groans and eloquently speak:—
"The Christian's blood cements the stones he rears;
"This clay was moistened with a Christian's tears;
"Pale as these walls a pris'ner oft has lain,
"Felt the keen scourge and worn the ruthless chain;
"While scoffing foes increasing tortures pour,
"Till the poor victim feels, alas! no more!"
Here thy brave tars, America, are found
Lock'd in foul prisons and in fetters bound.
Heav'ns! what sad times! must free Columbians bow
Before yon tinsel'd tyrant's murky brow?
Cringe to a pow'r which death and rapine crown?
Smile at a smile, and tremble at a frown?
Kneel at a throne, its clemency implore,
Enrich'd by spoils and stain'd with human gore?
Bear the sharp lash, the pond'rous load sustain,
Suppress their anger, and revenge restrain?
Leave a free clime, explore the treach'rous waves,
The sport of miscreants and the slave of slaves?
Heav'ns! at the sight each patriot bosom glows
With virtuous hatred on its country's foes;

At ev'ry blow indignant passions rise,
And vengeance flashes from resentful eyes.
But heav'n is just, though man's bewilder'd mind
To mystic ways of Providence is blind;
Else why are some ordain'd above the rest,
Or villains treated better than the best?
Why, martyr'd virtue, hang thy injur'd head?
Why liv'd an Arnold,[1] while a Warren[2] bled?
Earth's murd'rers triumph, proud oppressors reign,
While patriots bleed and captives sigh in vain.
Yet slumb'ring justice soon shall wake and show
Her sword, unsheath'd, and vengeance wing the blow:
Columbia's genius, glorious as the sun,
With thy blest shade, immortal Washington!
Unite to guard us from nefarious foes,
And heav'n defend, and angels interpose,
Devoted tyrants cause due wrath to feel,
Make Beys[3] and Bashaws in submission kneel;
Man's equal right, sweet liberty, restore,
And despotism fall, to rise no more.

TRIPOLI, including Barca, one of the piratical states of Barbary, on the continent of Africa, is situated between 10 and 30 degrees east longitude—30 and 34 degrees of north latitude; bounded on the north by the Mediterranean sea; east by Egypt; south by the country of the Beriberies, and west by Tunis and Biledulgerid; being about eleven hundred miles in length, and two hundred and forty in breadth. The city of Tripoli, the capital and largest town of the dominion, lies on the southern shore of the Mediterranean, in east longitude 14 degrees and 30 minutes, and in north latitude 38 degrees and 30 minutes. It is built on low sandy ground; the adjacent country is level, and as you approach the harbour, from the sea, being bordered on the east and southwest, beginning from about a mile distant, by tall, graceful and ever verdant date-trees, contrasted with the pale sands of the barren deserts on the west and southwest, the white walls, the horizontal terraces, the enamelous domes, the scattered ruins on the beach, whose wild and stubborn breasts repel, as they confront the furious foaming waves, maintaining an eternal warfare, exhibit to the wandering eye the picturesque scenes of nature and of art, and convey, to the fertile imagination, impressive lessons of the superstition, the folly, the duplicity and the turpitude of mankind. For here bribery, treachery, rapine, murder, and all the hedious offspring of accursed tyranny, have often drenched the streets in blood, and dealt, to the enslaved inhabitants, famine, dungeons, ruin and destruction. On yonder nodding tower, once waved the banners of the all-conquering Rome, when these fruitful regions were styled the Eden of that empire, now Gothic ruins, and barbarous inhabitants curse the half-tilled soil. The harbour is difficult and dangerous to enter, teeming with rocks and shoals.

The town is surrounded by intrenchments, and inclosed by a wall between twenty and thirty feet in height, thick, firm, and impregnable; flanked by forts, planted with heavy artillery, and formidable hosts of savage barbarians. There are three gates, two of which open to the east, into the country, and the other to the northwest, leading to a wharf, where cargoes from their shipping are landed, and freights received on board. These gates are opened precisely at the rising, and closed exactly with the closing day; but when the Bashaw takes his cavalcade excursion, they are not allowed to let the people pass through them, until his return.

At the northeast corner of the town, stands the Bashaw's castle, washed, on one side, by the waves. Like the government, it is built on ruins, without either taste, elegance, or grandeur; and exhibits an apposite specimen of barbarian folly. The foundation of it is said to have been laid more than twelve hundred years ago, and covers about an acre of ground. Its form is of an irregular square, and its altitude may be one hundred feet. Its principal gate looks towards the south, in front of which, a large portico contains a constant guard; the captain of which appears to be both a civil and a military officer, for both citizens and soldiers are daily brought before him, where, sitting cross-legged, on a carpet, or reclined on a sofa, he calmly listens to their clamourous accusations and defence, and if the culprit is found guilty of a petty crime, he receives instant punishment, on the spot, by bastinading; if of a capital crime, he is either committed to prison, and reported to the Bashaw, or carried immediately into his presence, where he is reheard, and meets from the Bashaw either a full and quick discharge, or a sure and accelerated death. There is a small gate at the east, and another at the west side of the castle, through which people on emergencies pass, when the grand part is closed. Towards the west, from the attic story, projects a gallery, rebuilt by our carpenters, and gaily painted by Smith, the renegade Yankee. Here the Bashaw may be seen from the navy-yard, several times a day, surrounded by his fawning parasites, taking a vista of the country, the sea, and great part of the town, the harbour, and fortifications. From this lofty eminence, the tumid potentate looks down on the groveling multitude, like fictitious Jove, from the summit of Olympus, and dispenses blessings, or curses, to the humble supplicants beneath his feet. After entering the front gate, a narrow, dark, and sinuous passage, leads into a handsome square, or court-yard, with a piazza on each side, sustained by colonades of marble. Within this court, stands the Bashaw's family mosque, to enter which, resorters must ascend a gradatory of white stone. Over the door, is an inscription, in Arabic characters—Sacred to God, and the Mahomet, the great prophet. The floor is of tessellated marble, and partly covered with rich carpeting. The walls are lined with porcelain, full of painted hieroglyphicks, and the Sanctum Sanctorum of the Mufti is very superb—hung with embroidered velvet tapestry. Christians are never admitted into their mosques in time of devotion; but a few of our men being sent to wash out the place, we had an opportunity to see the inside. Every afternoon, at about four o'clock, a band of music collect at this place, consisting of a kettle-drum, a French-horn, a clarinet, a hautboy, a timbrel, a bassoon, and several other tinkling toys. The chief officer of police, the same person who has been mentioned as always preceding the Bashaw on horseback, and who is his harbinger at all times, standing on the steps of the mosque until the band have finished their concert, which lasts about twenty minutes, delivers a brief harangue, extending his pronged sceptre three times towards Mecca, when the croud disperse, the gates are opened, and the people pass at pleasure.

There are in this castle, several arsenals, magazines for powder, repositories for provisions, a mint, a seraglio, and a bomb-proof room, where the dastardly Bashaw skulks from danger. Besides the apartments occupied by himself and about one hundred Mamelukes, there are a great number of rooms, once elegant, for that country, falling into ruins.

A large number of camels, horses, mules and asses are kept in the castle, and about five hundred persons attached to it, including servants and soldiers, and yet it is not half occupied. This huge pile overlooks the whole town, and is strongly fortified by heavy pieces of artillery, pointing in all directions. There are in the town three large mosques, a Roman chapel, and a Jewish synagogue. The inside of their mosques are spread with carpets, they are but dimly lighted, supported by collossian pillars of polished marble, and display a gloomy grandeur. Their outward appearance is uncouth, and their form of the Gothic order, their cornices adorned with antique engravings. The houses occupied by the different Christian consuls are large and commodious, built in the oriental style, with a square court two stories high, with handsome piazzas standing on lapideous columns, facing the court, and a cistern in the middle. That of the Swedish consul is decorated with elegant paintings, in imitation of porphyry. That of the American consul is contiguous to the Danish consul's, and is spacious and convenient. Its portico rests on eight pillars of Egyptian marble.

At the time of our manumission and departure from Tripoli, there were seven Christian consuls, residentiaries in the place, viz. American, Danish, French, Spanish, Swedish, English and Dutch.

The American consul, Doctor Ridgely, who was surgeon of the Philadelphia, possesses all the pathos of sensibility, and the suavity of the real gentleman, without the blandishments of the fop. The Danish consul, Mr. Nissen, is in every respect a most worthy character, and for the benevolent services which he rendered us in captivity, at the risque of his own safety, deserves the gratitude, not of us only, but of every American, and merits the applause of every votary of humanity and hospitality throughout the globe.

The English consul, Mr. Landford, like the most of his countrymen, is possessed of more national pride than individual merit; and is a vain and insolent bragadocia. Some of our tars, once British subjects, dragging at the groaning cart, one may as they were passing by him, attracted by a sympathy natural to compatriots, faintly ejaculated some appeal to his philanthropy; when the orgillous representative of Satan had the savage brutality to tell them that it was good enough for them having deserted his majesty's service. Some of them had the spirit to damn both him and his majesty, for which he threatened to cane them, but wisely restrained his hand. It is a singular but irrefragable fact, that let an Englishman meet an American where he will, especially on the ocean, he never fails to insult him; if not by a violation of all law and justice, by making a collateral desparity between the two countries, exalting the English and debasing the Americans; and yet the most of our navy-officers will cringe and act the spaniel to an English one. Some of our sailors made a handsome ship, neatly rigged, painted, &c. which they presented to their countrymen, in hopes of a generous remuneration. And what do you suppose his majesty's vicegerent gave them? one paltry dollar! which was not half so much as the canvas for the sails cost. They presented one to the Bashaw, of similar ingenuity, and he gave them a doubloon.

The houses of Tripoli are built of a free, whitish stone, brought from quarries at a considerable distance, and conglutinated by the Egyptian cement. In their ground stories, they have no windows towards the streets. Their roofs are nearly flat, and convey the rain-water into pipes, which spout it into large subterranean cisterns, whence it is drawn, as from wells, and is much superior to any other water, in or about the town. The floors of the common houses, like the roofs, are composed of mortar, which, when dry, forms a testaceous cement, firm and durable.

The streets of Tripoli are not paved, and are crooked, narrow and dirty. The houses, occupied by the shop-keepers, are one story high, small, and make but a wretched appearance. In the front of our prison, last occupied, is an exchange partitioned into numerous shops, where merchandize is cried by auctioneers running to and fro with rivalling agility, and harsh, vociferous voices. The building is about three hundred feet square, one story high, and its ponderous dome is supported by twenty enormous pillars. It has three large gates, which are shut every night, and the shops are all secure. Slaves are often exposed to sale in this noisy mart.

The whole number of artillery, which defend this place, is not less than 150, exclusive of those belonging to the flotilla. There is but one redoubtable fort detached from the city wall. This is at the western skirts of the town. It stands about 500 feet from the margin of the shore, at the corner of the wall. It is of a semicircular figure, its periphery bending towards the sea, and is mounted with 25 large pieces of thundering artillery. Besides this, there are several batteries which flank the harbour, both to the east and west.

The town, though not very large, and a great part in ruins, is, nevertheless populous, and contains nearly 70,000 inhabitants, of various nations, many of them are the fugitives from justice of other countries, consisting of Turks, Algerines, Moors, Tunisians, Egyptians, Arabs, Greeks, Jews, and Maltese.

The most of the Tripolitans are Mahometans; the Greek and Maltese Christians are but few; there are also about thirty Spaniards, who are but transient residents, chiefly carpenters and masons, and the Neapolitan slaves. The Jews are very numerous, and are held in the most abject slavery. On any emergent call for money, the Bashaw will dispatch his Mamelukes, who will enter the houses of the Jews, and wring from them their cash, their plate, or their wardrobe and jewelry, and if they but offer the least resistance, instant death, or a torturing bastinading, is their cruel lot.

Near the marine gate is a triumphal arch, said to have been dedicated to Augustus Cæsar, when the states of Barbary were under the Roman government, and in the zenith of their glory. Its form is quadrangular, from its base, till about 30 feet in height; it then terminates pyramidically, at about 45 feet. Each angle is about 25 feet. It is built of Italian marble, in squares of twelve feet by four, decorated with emblematic figures, in bass-relief, which the rude hand of Turkish barbarism has sacrilegiously mutilated, and very much defaced.

Not far from this are the ruins of an ancient castle, said to have been erected and possessed by a Carthagenian governor. The solitary walls bespeak decayed magnificence. Its numerous ventannas and other circumstances, prove it to have been built by other people than the Turks. One of its appertenant buildings is occupied by the Jews, as a distillery; the remainder, with the ramparts, are nearly dilapidated.

That part of the town inhabited by the Jews exhibits nothing but poverty, slavery, and wretchedness. The houses, mingling with mouldering ruins, are mere mud-wall huts; the streets, or rather alleys, are odiously filthy, swarming with meagre, tattered Bezonians,[4] and their naked, half-starved bantlings.

The Turks and Jews have each a flesh-market, without shelter or stalls, where the meat is both slaughtered and sold. Their beef, in general, is poor, but their mutton is super-excellent.

In the vicinage of Tripoli, there are a number of wells, over which stone arches are turned, from two white pillars, in the form of a gate-way, to which a tackle is affixed, and the water drawn from the wells in large leathern buckets, or bags, by means of a bullock, or cow. A sloping pit is dug, for the animal to descend, that it may raise the water with more facility. Large stone reservoirs receive the water, as it is drawn up, conducted from the bucket by a pipe. They will draw more than a barrel of water at a time, and very soon fill a receptacle twenty feet wide, and four feet deep. This, it must be understood, is built on the surface of the ground. From these reservoirs it is conducted by small aqueducts, to cheer the vegetable tribes, through different sections of the arid fields. At those places they also water their cattle and horses, and the citizens bring water for various uses. It is a little brackish.

From the ruins without the walls, it may be seen, that Tripoli has been much larger in circumference, than at present; as from history we may learn, that it was once the most populous, and flourishing town on the coast of Barbary.

About half a mile from the town, is a large cemetery, whither the women, in crouds, repair every morning, to mourn for their interred relations, performing genuflexion over their graves, and moistening the dust with their tears.

In a dark alley, in the castle, seated on a marble tomb, or coffin, within a grated cell, may be constantly seen, an old blind anchorite. He professed great friendship for the Americans, and would always grant us his benedictions, as we passed his cage, knowing us by our voices. The defunct, of whom he watches the returning spirit, was one of the Caramauli family, and had been an alcade of considerable eminence.

The mills in Tripoli are turned by camels, as our cider-mills are by horses. They have no bolts, and separate the bran from the flour by large sieves. They make excellent flour, for their wheat is of a superior quality. They tread out their grain according to the ancient custom, and cleanse it by winnowing.

Contiguous to, and in the vicinity of our prison, were a large number of weavers' shops, around which, every morning, you would see country people thronging, with yarn for sale. Their looms are much of the same construction as ours, and they weave much the same way as the Europeans, or Americans. Saddlers' and shoe-makers' shops are very thick, and the Jewish silver-smiths work in the street, in front of their little huts, with assiduous care, and are often robbed by the Turks, as they pass the streets. They have no signs to any of their shops or stores, nor any other public tokens of vendition. There are in the town, a French, English (so called), and Spanish hotel, with each a billiard-table, and tolerably well furnished with victuals and drink. Besides these, there are a number of cook-shops, where a person may get a pretty good dish of soup and meat, for one and a half buckamseen (six cents). There are not less than 50 grog-ships, kept by the Jews and Greeks, who pay pretty dear excise for their privileges, and are very often cheated and robbed by the Turks, their imperious masters. In these wretched cells, they retail aqua-deut, to the profligate Mahometans, who, notwithstanding the prohibitions of their religion, are frequently found beastly drunk. Near the centre of the town, is what we denominated a coffee-house, formed like a shed, through which the street passes. Here the indolent and wealthy resort, every morning, sitting on mats, spread on stone seats, about four feet from the ground, with pipes, six feet in length, smoking, drinking coffee, and playing at chess, until the zealous Marabewts proclaim from the steeples of the mosques, the hour of twelve, and warn the faithful to prayers. There is a bagnio,[5] near the Danish Consul's, and I do not know how many others. There are no printing-offices, post-offices, court-houses, banks, colleges, or academies, in Tripoli. They do not confine a person for debt, when he has nothing to pay, in which respect, their laws are more equitable than ours. Their criminals are never long confined, excepting some of the great men, on suspicion of conspiracy, or pretence of treasonable designs. Cells and dungeons, in the castle, are the places of confinement for state offenders.

About fourteen miles from this, is the old town of Tripoli, situated on the sea shore. This place was once populous and flourishing; but, at present, scarcely one hundred persons claim a residence among its ruins.

Derne is the next town of consequence, in the Bashaw's dominions. It is situated on the sea coast, in east longitude 22 degrees, 45 minutes, and in north latitude 30 degrees, and 55 minutes. It is built much after the same manner, and with the same materials as Tripoli, containing about 15,000 inhabitants. This place will ever be remembered as the theatre, on which that paragon of valour, the brave

General Eaton,[6] immortalized his name, and added new lustre to the stars of the American banners.

Braganza, lying on the sea coast, on the west side of the gulf of Sydra, the antiquated Syrtes, is also a place of considerable importance, but is sinking into ruins.

These are the only seaport towns, worth mentioning; but we were informed, by the inhabitants, that there are many interior villages, large, populous, and flourishing. Barca, the ancient Lybia, once famous for the temple of Ammon, is now truly a desert; scarce a town, or a cultivated spot of ground to be found in the whole country. Tolemata is its wretched capital.

In taking a perspective of Tripoli, we may observe a level country, either planted with beautiful groves of fruitful date-trees, and well cultivated gardens of lemons, oranges, olives, roots, and vegetables, or a totally barren, sandy desert, for about forty or fifty miles back from the sea, when lofty mountains variegate the landscape, till that of Atlas bounds the sight. There are many rivers which take their rise in Mount Atlas, and forming a confluence with those of Tunis, Algiers, and Morocco, pass on, and are annihilated in the vast Atlantic.

The climate of Tripoli is very hot, where a person is exposed to the sun, in the country back from the sea; but along the coast, being cooled by northern breezes, it is more temperate than could be expected from its situation; and that it is healthy, requires no further proof than what I have already mentioned, that among 307 Americans, being treated with every severity to endanger health, only six died during nineteen months, and two out of that number, owed their deaths to circumstances wholly adventitious. When the Syroc winds prevail, which are not frequent, nor long visitants, the morbid atmosphere seems impregnated with death, but the sea breezes on the coast, soon dissipate the contagion, and the lofty mountains on the south, barricade the interior against the stalking monster of disease. The rainy season usually commences in November, and continues, alternately, for five or six weeks. February and March are blustering neighbours, but they soon leave us, and the rest of the year is remarkably calm and serene. We never saw frost nor snow in Tripoli, for two winters.

We are told, that "under the Roman government, the states of Barbary were justly denominated the garden of the world, and to have a residence there, was considered as the highest state of luxury, and that Tripoli was then the most populous, opulent, and flourishing."[7] But whatever the soil may be, the town of Tripoli, at present, is greatly inferior, in every respect, to either Tunis or Algiers. The fertility of the soil cannot be controverted; for were it not extremely prolific, the exanimate inhabitants, oppressed by tyranny, and abandoned to indolence, could not possibly subsist. The country produced wheat, rye, barley, Indian-corn, oats, beans, peas, flax, hemp, honey, wax, olives, oil, plumbs, dates, figs, almonds, apples (but not in plenty,) pears, cherries, apricots, citrons, lemons, oranges, limes, pomegranates, with a great variety of roots and herbs, both esculent and medicinal. Pumpkins, squashes, cucumbers, and melons, in great plenty, and of an excellent flavour, and very cheap, are to be had in the markets.

The food of the lowest order of the Tripolitans, is black barley bread, oil, and vegetables. Salt is taken out of the cavities of rocks, along the shore, and of course, is very plenty, and cheap. Considerable quantities of saltpetre, is also found in Tripoli.

The deserts are peopled by the most terrific of the quadruped, and reptile species—lions, tygers, leopards, hyenas, and monstrous serpents, scorpions, and vipers. Their beasts of burthen are camels, dromedaries, asses, and a mongrel animal, generated between an ass and a cow, which is a very serviceable creature. The horses of Tripoli are said to be equal to those of Arabia, for speed and mettle. They never dock their horses, and their tails commonly sweep the ground. They are shod with a plate. Their cows are small, and without horns—in general they give but little milk. Their sheep have longer bodies, and shorter legs than ours. Their tails weigh from three to six pounds, and their wool is excellent. Swine they have none. Goats are plenty, large, and good. Bears, porcupines, foxes, apes, hares, rabbits, ferrets, weasels, moles, camelions, rats, mice, and almost all other reptiles exist in abundance. Eagles, quails, hawks, partridges, and all other kinds of wild fowl are to be found here in great plenty. The capsa sparrow is much celebrated for the beauty of its plumage, and for the exquisite melody of its unrivalled notes. Some of our men caught one, and presented it to the Danish Consul, who made them a very handsome remuneration. This bird is a rare patriot; it cannot live out of its own country.

The markets of Tripoli are well supplied with excellent fish. Their commerce and manufactures, compared with those of our own country, are very insignificant. An inland trafic is carried on with Arabia and Negroland. To Arabia, they send woolen manufactures, Morocco leather, indigo, cochineal, and ostrich feathers; for which they receive silks, muslins, sal-ammoniac, saffron, sugar, coffee, senna, cassia, and other drugs. To Negroland, they send salt, silk, and woolen manufactures, which they barter for gold dust, ivory, and Negroes. This trade is carried on by caravans. They exchange commodities with Tunis, and sometimes with Egypt. Their exports are Morocco leather, hides, wool, oil, ostrich feathers, barilla soap, wax, honey, cattle, horses, guns, figs, olives, dates, almonds, and various other fruits. They carry on a considerable traffic with Malta, chiefly in Maltese bottoms, and sell them a large number of cattle, sheep, goats, mules, and camels for which they receive European goods, and plank, for ship and boat building. Their principal manufactures, are blankets, and woolen cloths, leather, carpets, mats, saddles, tinsel cords, muskets, pistols, sabres, powder, soap, embroidered handkerchiefs, sword-knots, jewels, rings, &c. The arts and sciences are totally neglected.

The inhabitants, coming from various countries, are of various complexions, and of different statures. Those who are not attainted with the blood of the blacks, and who are not exposed to the sun, are as fair, and their skins are much smoother than the Americans, or Europeans, and, in general, they are of a larger size, strong, and bony. Notwithstanding the women in the town, who are kept from the weather, are very fair, delicate, and graceful, those of the country are, many of them, as tawny as the American squaws, and far more rustic and indelicate.

The supreme authority of Tripoli, is vested in a Bashaw, who is chosen by the Janizaries, and confirmed in his title every four years, by the Grand Seignior, without being re-elected. He has a council, or a divan, who wait upon him every morning, at ten o'clock. The Bashaw's herald, and two more officers, dressed in long scarlet robes, wrapped closely round them, and fastened by a sash, walk in a row to the castle, wait in a large square, and when the Bashaw makes his appearance, set up a hideous acclamation, proclaim his edicts, and his will, and then retire, undress themselves, and mix with the sycophantic croud.

Notwithstanding the Bashaw has a Divan, he is an absolute prince, and does, when he sees fit, take the lives or the property of his subjects, without the advice or consent of his council. In matters of state, relative to war or peace, he increases the number of his divan, and assembles all his experienced chiefs. Many of the people in Tripoli are much dissatisfied with his administration, and would fain have the Ex-Bashaw, his brother, restored to the throne. But there are no elections there but by the mob, in times of insurrections. The greater part of his revenue has hitherto consisted in the prizes he has taken, and the presents he has received from the Christian powers, who have made him the cat's-paw of their designs; and even the Americans have not disdained to purchase his forbearance by presents. The Jews pay heavy taxes. The dress of the Tripolitans is very multiform. Those of the poorer sort, in the country, wear nothing but a shirt, without collar or wristband, a blanket, a red cap and a pair of slippers. Those of the more opulent, in the city and country, wear a silk shirt, and embroidered waistcoat, a jacket with sleeves, broadcloth or fine muslin kilts, a handsome turban, a wampum belt, with a silver-mounted pair of pistols and sabre, boots or buskins, and a fine white silk and worsted cloak, with a head to it. The rich and mighty dress very superbly—a suit of clothes, such as the Mamelukes wear, full trimmed, would cost at least five hundred dollars. The most of the Mamelukes, and many others, shave their beards, leaving mustachios on their upper lips; but the greater part shave their heads only, and leave their beards for ornament, and having no collars to their shirts, vests, or coats, their necks are left bare. The dress of the women has been mentioned—it very nearly resembles that of the men. But when they walk the streets you cannot discover any thing of their apparel but a blanket, which completely envelopes them, all but one eye. The Jews and Greeks dress very much like the Turks, but they are distinguished by a black cap and blue turban.

CHAPTER XIII

Manners, Customs, &c. of the Tripolitans

THOUGH something of the manners, customs, &c. of the Tripolitans may be gathered from what has been already mentioned, yet much remains to be particularized. The Tripolitans, like the Moors, marry very young; many of their females not being more than twelve years old at their nuptials, so that they are sometimes grand-mothers at twenty-two, and are reckoned old at thirty. As Mahometans, it is well known, that their religion admits of poligamy to the extent of four wives, and as many concubines as they please; none but the opulent are able to indulge themselves in this privilege, and I believe very few even of the wealthy have more than one wife, as a plurality of wives subjects them to accumulated trouble and expence. In contracting marriage, we are told that the parents of both parties are the only agents, and the intended bride and bridegroom never see each other till the ceremony is performed. The marriage articles are made and signed before a cadi,[1] and then the friends of the bride produce her portion; or, if not, the husband agrees to settle a certain sum upon her, in case he should die, or divorce her on account of barrenness, or any other cause. The children of the wives have all an equal claim to the effects of the father and mother; but those of the concubines can only claim half a share. When the marriage is finally agreed upon, the bride is kept at home eight days to receive her female friends, who pay congratulatory visits every day. At the same time a talb[2] attends upon her to converse with her relative to the solemn engagements on which she is about to enter; on these occasions he generally accompanies his admonitions with singing a pious hymn, which is adapted to the solemnity. The bride, also, with her near relations, goes through the ceremony of being painted afresh. During this process, the bridegroom, on the other hand, receives visits from his male friends in the morning, and in the evening rides through the town accompanied by them, some playing on hautboys and drums, while others are employed in firing vollies of musketry. In the mean time, the women in the town collect in small companies, that is, such as are invited to the wedding, and at every corner of the streets set up a cry of *bu-bu-bu*. In all these festivities, the discharge of musketry forms a principal part of the entertainment. Contrary to the American or European mode, which particularly aims at firing with exactness, they discharge their pieces as irregular as possible, so as to have a continual succession of reports for a few minutes. On the day of marriage, the bride in the evening is put into a square or octagonal cage about twelve feet in circumference, which is covered with fine white linen, and sometimes with gauzes and silks of various colours. In this vehicle, which is placed on a mule, she is paraded round the streets, accompanied by her relations and friends, some carrying lighted torches, others playing on hautboys, and a third party again firing vollies of musketry. In this manner she is carried to the house of her intended husband, who returns about the same time from performing similar ceremonies. On her arrival she is placed in an apartment by herself, and her husband is introduced to her alone for the first time, who finds her sitting on a silk or velvet cushion, supposing her to be a person of consequence, with a small table before her on which are two wax candles lighted. Her shift, or more properly shirt, hangs down like a train behind her, and over it is a silk or velvet robe with close sleeves, which at the breast and waist is embroidered with gold. This dress reaches something lower than the calf of the leg. Round her head is tied a black silk scarf, which hangs behind as low as the ground. Thus attired, the bride sits with her hands over her eyes, when her husband appears and receives her as his wife, without any farther ceremony, for the agreement made up by the friends before the cadi is the only specific contract which is thought necessary. For some time after marriage, the family and friends are engaged in much feasting, and a variety of amusements, which last a longer or shorter time, according to the circumstances of the parties. It is often customary for the man to remain at home eight days, and the woman eight months after they are first married. If the husband should have any reason to suspect that his wife has not been strictly virtuous, he is at liberty to divorce her and take another; and the woman is at liberty to divorce herself from her husband; if she can prove that he does not provide for her a comfortable subsistance. If he curses her, the cadi imposes a fine in money for the first offence; for the second, a rich dress, and for the third time she may leave him entirely. He is then at liberty to marry again in two months. A woman convicted of adultery is punished with immediate death.

When a person dies, a number of women are hired for the purpose of lamentation; in the performance of which, nothing can be more grating to the ear, or more unpleasant than their frightful moans, or rather howlings: at the same time, these mercenary mourners beat their heads and breasts, and tear their cheeks with their nails. The bodies are usually buried a few hours after death. Previous to interment, the corpse is washed very clean, and sewed up in a shroud, with the right hand under the head, which is pointed towards Mecca: it is carried on a bier, supported upon men's shoulders, to the burying place, which is always, with great propriety, on the out side of the town; for they never bury their dead in the mosques, or within the bounds of an inhabited place, excepting now and then a saint or great personage. The coffin is not coloured, and a striped silk mantle is spread over it. The bier is accompanied by a number of people, two abreast, who walk a common gait, calling upon God and Mahomet, and singing hymns adapted to the occasion. The grave is made very wide at the bottom and narrow at the top, and the body is deposited without any other ceremony than singing and praying, in the same manner as on their way to the grave. Their graves are plastered over in the form of a ridge, sharp at the top, with the same conglutinating mortar as their roofs of houses, and they set up at each end of the grave a long smooth stone. It is frequently customary for the funeral friends of the departed to weep over their graves for several days after their funeral, taking neither food nor drink. When a woman loses her husband, she mourns four months and eight days, during which period she is to wear no silver or gold; and if she happens to be pregnant, she mourns till she is brought to bed. For the above time the relations of her late husband are obliged to support her. We do not learn that any mourning is due from the husband for the loss of his wife; but it is customary, particularly among the great people, for a son to mourn for the loss of his father, by not shaving his head or any part of his heard, and by not cutting his nails for a certain space of time.

Their method of expressing reverence, both to the Divine Being and to man, is by pulling off their slippers, which they always leave at the door of the house or mosque they enter; and when they attend their prince in the streets, they always follow him bare-footed. They never pull off their turbans, except when they sleep.

The manners of the well-bred Tripolitans are easy, natural and graceful, and their walk carelessly majestic. They seem never to be at a loss for words, and express themselves with remarkable fecundity. In general they are grave, decent and abstemious; but those who are addicted to licenciousness and inebriety, dive to the very depths of sensuality and shame. Their abdest[3] constitutes a very essential part of their religious ceremonies; for nothing is more conducive to health, in warm climates, than frequent bathings. They wash themselves every time they pray, every time they eat, and every time they attend the private calls of excremental necessity. They sleep on matrasses laid on stone platforms, raised about three feet above the surface of the ground, and always yield to drowsiness at any time of day. They have neither bedsteads, tables, chairs, benches, knives and forks, nor spoons, excepting wooden ones, to eat their soup. Their whole furniture consists of a carpet or mat, a looking-glass, bed, and a few cooking utensils. Their usual meals at noon are stewed fowls or mutton, and millet or rice. A number of them will gather round a large bowl, sitting flat on the ground, and lade in their victuals with their fingers with great dexterity and haste. The food is too warmly peppered to be agreeable to an American palate.

They have no wheel carriages, neither for pleasure nor use, excepting a couple of baggage waggons, left them by a part of Bonaparte's fleet on their way to Egypt; and though they have cattle, horses, camels, mules and asses in plenty, they never put any of them to their waggons, but made our people perform the part of draft animals.

Their manner of passing a slight salutation, is by laying the right hand on the breast and repeating Salam Alicum (the peace of God), but when they meet a beloved and long absent friend, they express their joy with the most enthusiastic emotions, falling on each other's neck and kissing with seeming raptures.

In the vicinity of Tripoli we saw a piece of ground prepared and sown with barley; it was first dug up with a kind of grubbing hoe, the seed was scattered and ploughed in with a single jack-ass and small wooden plough.

People who come any distance from the country with produce for market, instead of putting up at taverns as people do with us, encamp with their camels on the sand, without the gates. They wrap themselves in their blankets, which are their only clothing, and lie down beside their camels during the night. Tuesdays and Fridays are their market days, when they meet on the sands about a mile from town, where you will frequently see not less than ten thousand people in a morning. On such mornings there are no markets in town; the butchers, hucksters, &c. being at the fair to replenish their shops.

They go to their employments in general very early in the morning, and eat nothing till twelve o'clock. At four o'clock in the afternoon, let them be where they will, they quit their work, fall on their knees and call upon God and Mahomet. Every four hours the Marabewts sing out from the balconies of their mosques, announcing the hour of devotion, and proclaiming that God is great and Mahomet is his prophet, &c. They worship by kneeling, prostrating themselves on their faces, and beating their foreheads against the earth. The men and women never appear together in their mosques, or any other public places.

There are several schools in Tripoli, where may be seen an old grey bearded master sitting in the centre of the room, on a carpet, smoking his long pipe, surrounded by forty or fifty boys of different ages, seated on mats, each holding a square piece of board with a handle to it, on which is pasted his lesson written on paper. They all read loud at a time, and nothing is to be heard but a constant buz and confusion of sounds. Their learning extends no further than to read the Koran, to write a letter and cast accounts, in which many of them are great adepts. They write from the right to the left, and hold the paper in the left hand instead of laying it on the table.

Indolence seems to be the darling idol of the Tripolitans, for they place their whole bliss in ease. Sleeping, eating, drinking coffee, smoking and playing at chess, occupy nearly all the leisure hours of the wealthy, and the poor seem to have little recreation except basking in the sun. They will sometimes fight desperately when surrounded and compelled to it by self-preservation, but in general they are not courageous.

As to their religion, it is radically the same as all other Mahometans'; the ground of the whole faith is "that there has been from the beginning of the world but one true orthodox belief, which consists in acknowledging one true God only, and obeying the precepts of such ministers and prophets as he shall from time to time send into the world to reveal his will to mankind."[4] Upon this foundation,

Mahomet pretended to be a prophet sent into the world to reform the abuses crept into religion, and to reduce it to its original simplicity. He added, that as the endeavors of Moses and Christ were rendered abortive, God sent him as his last and greatest prophet, with a more ample commission than either Moses or Christ were entrusted with. Theirs were confined to persuasion only, but his extended to force. The sword was to effect what preaching and miracles had endeavored in vain. The divine law was to be propagated by force, and the throne of the faithful founded on the blood of unbelievers. The bounds of this kingdom were to be the same with those of the world, and all the nations of the world were to be governed by Mahomet. But as these conquests could not be made without danger, Mahomet promised that those who ventured their lives in establishing his kingdom, should enjoy the spoils and possessions of their enemies, as a reward in this life, and after death, a paradise of all sensual enjoyments, especially those of love. He added, that those who died in propagating the faith, would enjoy a distinguished place in paradise, experience pleasures peculiarly intense, and vastly superior to the rest of mankind. These particulars, together with the doctrine of predestination, and a prohibition of drinking spirituous liquors, formed the principal articles of Mahomet's creed, and were written by a monk, whom Mahomet employed, as himself could neither read nor write. Their commandments are five in number, viz. 1st. To pray five times a day. 2. To fast in the month Ramadam. 3d. To give alms, and perform works of charity. 4th. To go a pilgrimage to Mecca. 5th. To keep the body clean. Four other points are deemed of importance, though not absolutely necessary to salvation, viz. To keep Friday as sabbath; to be circumcised; to drink no wine, or other strong liquors, as before mentioned; and to abstain from swine's flesh, and from things strangled.

Although the general character of the Tripolitans is marked by an assemblage of the most degrading and atrocious vices, yet there may be found amongst them, men of liberal and charitable sentiments, fair and honorable characters, humane and generous dispositions, and real friends to mankind.

Tripoli is supposed to have been originally peopled from Egypt; but at what time, or who led the first colony thither, has never yet been developed. They were, however, an itinerant race, whose only objects were to find water and pasture for their numerous flocks and herds, which, with the spontaneous productions of the soil, were their only support. Like the wandering Arabs, they formed no settlements, built no houses, but dwelt in tents. About 891 years before the birth of Christ, Dido, sister to Pygmalion, King of Tyre, fled from her brother, at the head of a considerable colony, and built the celebrated city of Carthage, the ruins of which may be now seen, about 30 miles from Tunis. The Carthagenians, finding the states of Barbary divided into petty tribes and kingdoms, conquered and made them their tributary vassals. This government, which was called a republic, continued to be opulent and formidable; at once the envy and terror of the neighbouring nations, for about 700 years, during which time the city of Tripoli was built. The fortune of the Romans at length prevailed; the pride of Carthage was humbled in the dust, and Tripoli, as well as the other states of Barbary, was made a Roman province. The country still continued to flourish under the Romans; Barbary was esteemed one of the richest jewels in the imperial crown, and Tripoli the richest state in Barbary. The Christian religion was planted here in the time of the Apostles themselves, and flourishing until the fifth century, when the Vandals trampled on the Roman eagles, and reduced the whole of Barbary under their dominions. These fierce invaders of Africa did not, however, long possess the country they had conquered: The Greek emperors drove out the northern barbarians, and restored, in some measure, the arts and manufactures, against which, as well as religion, the ferocious Vandals had declared perpetual war. But this did not restore peace and tranquility to these parts of Africa: they were alternately ravaged by the Moors and Vandals, and at last totally conquered by the Caliphs of Bagdad, in the seventh century, and divided among their chiefs. The religion of Mahomet was now established in Barbary, and Tripoli soon began to decline.

Restless by nature, and instigated to conquest by the tenets of their religion, the Moors passed over into Europe, and reduced the greater part of Spain. But victory now began to forsake their standards. They were several times defeated, by the European armies, and at last, about the year 1492, totally driven out of Spain, by Ferdinand and Isabella. The only assylum open to the Mahometan fugitives, was Africa, where they settled among their friends and countrymen, on the Barbary coast. The expulsion of the Moors occasioned a perpetual war between them and the Spaniards, and finding themselves incapable of defence against the Christians, they had recourse to the Turks for assistance. Accordingly the two famous brothers, Barbarossa, admirals of the Turkish fleet, were sent to Barbary. Success attended the Turkish forces; the Spaniards, who had made themselves masters of great part of the country, were obligated to retire, and the Moors hoped to enjoy freedom and peace.

For some time they flattered themselves with a series of prosperity; but their hopes were soon rendered abortive; they found that they had only exchanged one master for another, and that the yoke of their deliverer was full as heavy as that of the Spaniards.

Ever since the attempts of Charles V, to reduce Algiers and Tunis, which would have been followed by a subjection of Tripoli and all the Barbary powers, they have continued to carry on the trade of piracy against the Christians, and have lately pretty much freed themselves from the Turkish yoke.

CHAPTER XIV

Public Transactions of the United States with the Regency of Tripoli;

INCLUDING GENERAL EATON'S EXPEDITION

To guard our commerce from predacious foes,
Repel their insults, and their fleets oppose;
Assert our right to navigate the main,
In spite of England, Barb'ry, France, or Spain;
To shew all pirates self-defence we meant,
Millions for *that*—for *tribute*—not a *cent;*[1]
For this our pines, proud monarchs of the wood,
Fell low to earth, and creeping, kiss'd the flood;
For this our oaks forsook their neighb'ring trees,
And hemp-grown canvas wing'd them o'er the seas;
For this our tars have quit their native shore,
Travell'd through death, and ferried streams of gore;
For this bold EATON, with his patriot band,
Scour'd the lone deserts of a barb'rous land,
And prov'd, those feats, Leonidas[2] of yore,
With his *three hundred Spartans;* with no more
Than 'leven Americans, our Eaton wrought
More lasting wonders, and more bravely fought.

IN giving the public transactions of the United States, &c. with the Regency of Tripoli, a lengthy and detailed account cannot be expected—I have, however, drawn from the Secretary of the Navy all the documents and information on the subject, (including many from the Secretary of State,) which he declares "can consistently be made public"; and also, from General Eaton himself, all which he deems necessary or important relative to his expedition. As far, therefore, as these are authentic, the following statements must be considered as correct.

I cannot well refrain from making the precursory remark—that what I have before asserted respecting the reprehensible conduct of many of our naval officers, will be fully substantiated, in the subsequent pages, by witnesses of the highest credibility, and from official documents—*not to be disputed.* Read the official delinquency of Commodore Morris—read his criminal abuse of David Valenzin, the unfortunate Jew—read the tardiness and pusillanimity of the voluptuous Commodore Barron—read the intriguing pacifications of Lear, sanctioned by Barron, in giving General Eaton orders to evacuate Derne five days previous to his sailing from Malta to enter on his negociations with Tripoli—read the report of the committee of Congress on the claim of the Ex-Bashaw, and also that of David Valenzin, where many highly interesting facts are developed—read ten thousand other corroborating testimonies, and then say whether I have been too severe in attaching a general, though not universal censure to our naval commanders, and their subordinate myrmidons.

I shall now proceed to give what information has fallen within the compass of my knowledge.

In the year 1796, the following treaty was entered into, between the two powers.

Treaty of Peace and Friendship, between the United States of America, and the Bey and Subjects of Tripoli of Barbary

Art. 1st. There is a firm and perpetual peace and friendship between the United States of America, and the Bey and subjects of Tripoli of Barbary, made by the free consent of both parties, and guaranteed by the Most Potent Dey[3] and Regency of Algiers.

Art. 2d. If any goods belonging to any nation with which either of the parties is at war, shall be loaded on board of vessels belonging to the other party, they shall pass free, and no attempt shall be made to take or detain them.

Art. 3d. If any citizen, subjects, or effects belonging to either party, shall be found on board a prize vessel, taken from an enemy, by the other party, such citizens or subjects shall be set at liberty, and the effects restored to the owners.

Art. 4th. Proper passports are to be given to all vessels of both parties, by which they are to be known. And considering the distance between the two countries, eighteen months from the date of this treaty, shall be allowed for procuring such passports. During this interval, the other papers belonging to such vessels shall be sufficient for their protection.

Art. 5th. A citizen or subject of either party, having bought a prize condemned by the party, or by any other nation, the certificate of condemnation, and bill of sale, shall be a sufficient passport for such vessel for one year; this being a reasonable time for her to procure a proper passport.

Art. 6th. Vessels of either party putting into the ports of the other, and having need of provisions or other supplies, they shall be furnished at the market price.

And if any such vessel shall so put in from a disaster at sea, and have occasion to repair, she shall be at liberty to land and reimbark her cargo, without paying any duties. But in no case shall she be compelled to land her cargo.

ART. 7th. Should a vessel of either party be cast on the shore of the other, all proper assistance shall be given to her and her people; no pillage shall be allowed, the property shall remain at the disposition of the owners, and the crew protected and succoured till they can be sent to their country.

ART. 8th. If a vessel of either party should be attacked by an enemy, within gun-shot of the forts of the other, she shall be defended as much as possible. If she be in port, she shall not be seized or attacked, when it is in the power of the other party to protect her; and when she proceeds to sea, no enemy shall be allowed to pursue her from the same port within twenty-four hours after her departure.

ART. 9th. The commerce between the United States and Tripoli, as a full and satisfactory consideration on his part, and on the part of his subjects, for this treaty of perpetual peace and friendship, are acknowledged to have been received by him previous to his signing the same, according to a receipt which is hereto annexed, except such part as is promised on the part of the United States to be delivered and paid them on the arrival of their Consul in Tripoli, of which part a note is likewise hereto annexed. And no pretence of any periodical tribute or further payment is ever to be made by either party.

ART. 11th. As the government of the United States of America is not, in any sense, founded on the Christian religion, as it has, in itself, no character of enmity against the laws, religion, or tranquility of Musselmen—and as the said States have never entered into any war or act of hostility against any Mahomedan nation, it is declared by the parties, that no pretext arising from religious opinions, shall ever produce an interruption of the harmony existing between the two countries.

ART. 12th. In case of any dispute, arising from a violation of any of the articles of this treaty, no appeal shall be made to arms, nor shall war be declared, on any pretext whatever. But if the Consul residing at the place where the dispute shall happen, shall not be able to settle the same, an amicable reference shall be made to the mutual friend of the parties, the Dey of Algiers, the parties hereby engaging to abide by his decision. And he, by virtue of his signature to this treaty, engages for himself and his successors, to declare the justice of the case, according to the true interpretation of the treaty, and to use all the means in his power, to enforce the observance of the same.

Signed and sealed at Tripoli of Barbary, the 3d day of Jumad, in the year of Hegira 1211, corresponding with the 4th day of November, 1796—by

(L.S.) JUSSUF BASHAW MAHOMET, Bey.
(L.S.) MAMET, Treasurer.
(L.S.) AMET, Minister of Marine.
(L.S.) AMET, Chamberlain.
(L.S.) ALLY, Chief of the Divan.

(L.S.) SOLIMAN KAYA.
(L.S.) GALIL, General of the Troops.
(L.S.) MAHOMET, Commandant of the City.
(L.S.) MAMET, Secretary.

Signed and sealed at Algiers, the 4th day of Argil, 1211, corresponding with the 3d day of January, 1797, by

(L.S.) HASSAN BASHAW, Dey.

And by the Agent Plenipotentiary of the United States of America.

(L.S.) JOEL BARLOW.

An alleged infraction of the 2d and 12th articles of this treaty, was the first pretext which the Bashaw of Tripoli made for evincing hostile intentions towards the United States, which was not long after the treaty, and as early as in the year 1799, which will be seen by the following.

On the 9th of February, 1799, Mr. Cathcart[4] and General Eaton arrived, from the United States, at Algiers, where Mr. O'Brian had been some months before them. Some days were consumed here in arranging a general settlement with Algiers, which being effected, they left that place on the 2d of March, and arrived at Tunis on the 15th. Mr. Cathcart soon after embarked for, and arrived at Tripoli. General Eaton remained at Tunis.

Mr. Cathcart's Letters

Extract of a letter from James Leander Cathcart, to the Secretary of State, dated

Tripoli, *April* 18, 1800.

In consequence of the decease of our political father,[5] I sent my drogoman to inform the Bashaw, that the next day I should hoist the banners of the United States half-mast, the only token of respect which I had in my power to pay to the manes of our much beloved patriot, intending to wait a proper opportunity to communicate to him your intimation. The Bashaw sent me a very polite message, expressing his concern for our loss, and requesting to know if the President had received his letter, which was forwarded by the Sophia. I answered in the affirmative, and ordered the drogoman to inform his excellency, that I would wait on him when he was at leisure.

In the evening he sent Farfara[6] to inform me, that he was indisposed, or would have been glad to see me, and requested, if I had any thing to impart, that I would communicate it to Farfara. I accordingly requested him to express to the Bashaw, his excellency the President's satisfaction with the arrangements that took place last year, and to assure him, that he had never considered him as dependent upon either of the other regencies; that he had always treated him as an independent prince, and the government of the United States would always consider him with as much respect, and treat him with the same friendship, that they did the heads of the other regencies. Farfara returned with the following answer.

"His excellency the Bashaw has desired me to request you to acquaint the President of the United States, that he is exceedingly pleased with his proffers of friendship; that the respect which he has shewn to his communication is really flattering; that had his protestations been accompanied with a frigate or brig of war, such as we had given the Algerines, he would be still more inclined to believe them genuine; that the compliments, although acceptable, were of very little value, and that the heads of the Barbary States knew their friends by the value of the presents that they received from them."

It being too late for any answer that evening, I made such comments on the Bashaw's message as might serve to eradicate from the mind of the Jew, the most distant expectation, that the President would ever make so great a sacrifice, which I informed him was entirely incompatible with the interests of the United States.

Considering it highly improper to delay giving a direct, explicit, and categorical answer to the Bashaw's insinuation, I sent my drogoman to the castle, to request an audience; I having previously formed a resolution, never to employ a third person, whenever the honour or interest of my country was concerned. The drogoman informed me, that his excellency had seen Farfara, and if I had any further communication to make, to employ him, as he was very much indisposed. Thus was I disappointed.

Farfara waited upon me in the afternoon, when I requested him to inform the Bashaw, that if he supposed that the cruisers which were sent by our government to Algiers, were given gratuitously, he had been misinformed; that during our negociation last year, I had acquainted him, that the frigate was given to that regency in lieu of cash, for the ransom of our citizens, which had been redeemed on credit, more than a year before her arrival; that the cruisers were built on commission, and paid for in cash, out of the public treasury, and were not the property of the Dey, as he supposed; that I had copies of their accounts by me, which he should peruse, if he thought proper, whereby he would be informed of the magnitude of his expectation, and the improbability of the United States having given them gratuitously; that I was sensible how disagreeable it would be, to disappoint expectations, when once formed; I therefore found it my duty to prevent any taking place, in order to avoid the chagrin attending a positive refusal, which, from the nature of the request, must naturally be expected from the President of the United States.

The Bashaw returned in answer, that he had concluded peace with the United States, for much less than he had received from other nations, and that he knew his friends by what he received from them.

I shall, by no means, broach this subject to the Bashaw again, as I have hindered him from having any ground for expectation, and shall continue to act in the same manner, should he ever make it a topic of conversation, as he can have no pretext to make a demand, and only insinuates, that he expects some mark of the President's friendship, more substantial than compliments. I imagine it will be best to take no further notice of it. The appearance of our frigates in the mediterranean will, I hope, eradicate any expectation that he may have flattered himself with, if any really exists, and, until that period, believe me, Sir, our commerce will never be upon a respectable footing in these seas.

Extract of a letter from the same to the same, dated

MAY 12, 1800.

GIVE me leave to inform you, in addition to mine of the 18th of April, a copy of which is enclosed with this dispatch, that on the 21st of said month a board of consuls were called by the Bashaw, relative to the affairs of Sweden, in order to facilitate, as much as possible, his depredations and unjust demands upon that nation. As I have already forwarded to you the particulars of their last arrangement, I at present refer you to the copy of the certificate herewith enclosed for the result. During the course of conversation the Bashaw observed, "that he never made reprisals on any nation, or declared war, but in consequence of their promises not being fulfilled, or for a want of due respect that was shewn to the Bashaws of Algiers and Tunis, but that some nations gave more to the officers in each of those regencies than they had given to him for their peace." The last remark was evidently pointed at the United States; but as it was made in general terms, I thought proper not to seem to understand it, especially as I could say very little more on the subject than what I had already communicated to him through the agency of Signior Farfara.

On the 2d of May a courier arrived from Tunis, which brought me the copies of your letters of the 15th of January, which arrived in the ship Hero. Before I had time to read them, Farfara came and informed me that the Bashaw wanted to see me immediately. I asked him if he knew what his excellency wanted; he said he did not; that he had received letters from Tunis, and seemed very much irritated. It being late in the evening I waited on him in dishabille, when the following conversation took place, which I have endeavoured to render verbatim.

"You have received letters from America: how were they brought to Tunis?"

In a vessel direct from America.

"What is her business at Tunis?"

She has brought the stores stipulated by treaty with that regency.

"What do they consist of?"

I do not know the particular articles which compose her cargo, but it chiefly consists of lumber and articles, such as were promised to your excellency when our peace took place.

"What do your letters from your government contain?"

They are merely copies of what I had already received, the contents of which your excellency was informed by Farfara.

This being a favourable opportunity to know whether our broker had acted with candor, I repeated what was contained in mine of the 18th of April, and found by the Bashaw's answers (which were exactly what Farfara had before informed me) that he had acted honestly.

The Bashaw observed that the United States had made liberal presents to Algiers and Tunis, that he was informed of the particulars of all our negociations, that he even had a list of the cargo which had arrived at Tunis, that it was worth a *treasure*. "Why do not the United States send me a voluntary present? They have acted with me as if they had done every thing against their will. First they solicited the interference of the Dey of Algiers, in consequence of which I concluded a peace with them for almost nothing, in comparison to what I have received from other nations, I having received many favours from Hassan Bashaw, during the continuance of the revolution in this kingdom. They next made me wait more than two years before they sent their consul, and then he came without the stipulated stores. Nevertheless, in order to convince them of my good and friendly intentions, I accepted of the small sum of eighteen thousand dollars in lieu thereof, not doubting but they would be grateful enough to make me some return for my civility; but I have the mortification to be informed that they have now sent a ship load of stores to Tunis, besides promising a present of jewels; and to me they have sent compliments. But I have cruisers as well as Tunis, and as good Raizes[7] and sailors. I am an independent prince as well as the Bashaw of Tunis, and I can hurt the commerce of any nation, as much as the Tunisians. Why then should so great a difference be made?"

From the tenor of the Bashaw's harangue, I perceived that his aim was to intimidate me, to say something that might hereafter be interpreted into a promise of a present, the value of which he would probably dictate himself. I therefore answered him as follows:—

"Whatever information your excellency has received relative to the value of the presents or stores which have been given to Tunis, it has been amazingly exaggerated. We have never made any but what were stipulated by treaty, nor can we ever make voluntary presents, it being incompatible with our form of government, the funds of the United States not being at the disposal of the President until an appropriation is made by an act of the legislature. The funds for carrying our treaty with Tripoli into effect are exhausted, and last year your excellency wrote to the President of the United States that you were contented with what you had already received. You, therefore, in justice, could not at present expect any thing from the United States, but a reciprocal tender of friendship. Had your excellency preferred the stores to cash, and waited with patience until they were forwarded, as the Bey of Tunis has done, I am convinced they would have arrived long ere now. But at present, as the United States have fulfilled the stipulations of the treaty, they are not in arrears to this regency, and any demands upon them must naturally be very unexpected." The Bashaw said he would converse with me on the subject at some other opportunity.

May 4th, the Siddi Mahomed Dagnize,[8] and Signior Farfara, came to the American house and informed me that the Bashaw had ordered them to ask me if I had taken any resolution in consequence of the conversation which I had with him on the 3d instant. I informed them that I had taken none whatever, and that it seemed unaccountable to me that his excellency should expect any other answer after what I had informed him in their presence; they stayed about an hour, during which time their conversation tended to persuade me that, considering the Bashaw's character, it was certainly the interest of the United States to make a sacrifice, that otherwise it would be impossible to remain long on good terms with him. I made use of the same arguments which I had done before. I, therefore, will not tire you with a repetition.

At 6, P.M. they returned, and informed that the Bashaw was very much displeased, and had ordered them to acquaint me that he was informed that the Sahibtappa,[9] at Tunis, had received more than forty thousand dollars from the United States, in cash, besides presents; that he had received very little more, and that he had never imagined the United States meant to put him on an equality with one of the Bey of Tunis's ministers.

I observed that the Bashaw was misinformed by his correspondent, who, in order to ingratiate himself in his favour, had informed him of things which had never taken place; that he was giving himself, as well as them and me, a great deal of trouble, without any hopes of reaping the least benefit therefrom; that I requested them to inform his excellency that I had not power to offer him a dollar, and that there were no funds in the United States appropriated for maintaining our peace with Tripoli, as we had carried our treaty into effect already; that he had wrote to the President of the United States, the Dey of Algiers, and the Bey of Tunis, that he had settled with the agent of the United States, and had received a cash payment in lieu, and in full of all demands, and that he was content; that only three years and an half had elapsed since our treaty commenced; that the first year he had received 40,000 dollars in cash, and the value of 8,000 in presents; that the second he had received 12,000 dollars, and that the last year he had received 18,000 and presents to the value of 4,000 more; that on the circumcision of his son, Siddi Aly, I had made him a present, superior to the presents which were made him by the consuls of other nations on the same occasion; that consequently the government of the United States were not deficient either in their respect to him, or tokens of friendship, as he had received, in the short period of three years and an half, cash and presents to the amount of 83,000 dollars, exclusive of 10,000 measures of grain which Hassan Bashaw had made him a present of, in consequence of his having concluded a treaty with the United States, which was worth at Tripoli near 20,000 dollars more; that I was persuaded that if his excellency would give himself the trouble to reflect on the circumstances which had taken place since the commencement of the treaty between the United States and this regency, that he would not hesitate a moment in acknowledging the justice and propriety of my observations.

In the evening the Bashaw's emissaries returned and informed me that they had encountered great difficulty in persuading the Bashaw to believe that the consul had not power to make him a present without an express order from his government. His excellency said that he had received many presents from the consuls of other nations, and that their conduct had afterwards been approved. They observed that the form of government of the United States was vastly different from the government of every other nation, with whom his excellency was at peace: that he had a recent example that the powers of a consul were limited, in the result of the Swedish consul's negociation, he having arranged the affairs of his nation without receiving orders from his court; that he knew the consequence—his bills were protested, he had received a severe reprimand from the King of Sweden, and was immediately suspended, and that his excellency might depend that the American consul would take care never to be reduced to a similar predicament, whatever might be the consequence of his non-compliance with his excellency's demand.

They further informed me that the Bashaw had ordered them to request me to write to my government, to inform them that when he had wrote to the President of the United States he was contented with what he had received; that he really was so, on a supposition that the presents to him bore some proportion to those that had been promised to Tunis; that at present he was informed to the contrary, and that he felt himself amazingly hurt when he considered that he had been treated with indifference, and that he never would be convinced that the friendship of the United States was sincere, until there was a greater equality observed in their donations between the two nations, or, in other words, until he received some further marks of the President's esteem, more substantial than mere compliments. They said that although the Bashaw was inclined to credit the impossibility of the consul's making him a present without orders from his court, that he likewise was sensible how much depended on the manner of his representation, that he believed he had treated him with every respect since his arrival at Tripoli, and he requested I would write in such terms as would insure him from the mortification of being disappointed, adding, this he expected from the consul as he values my future favour and a happy result to the objects of his mission. I replied that the object contemplated by the U. States in sending an agent the vast distance or near 6,000 miles, was to endeavour to maintain a friendly intercourse between the two nations on honourable and equitable terms, that as it had pleased God to employ me as the instrument to promote so desired an effect, he might rest assured I should take pleasure in representing *facts* for the consideration of government in as favourable a manner as the dignity annexed to my office would admit, that as it would be the height of presumption in me to dictate to the President of the United States what he ought to do in the present case, so on the other hand, I by no means consider it to be a part of my official duty in any means to oppose the liberal intentions of government, should they be found disposed to make him a present, but on the contrary, should I receive orders to that effect, I would take pleasure in executing them, but must again beg leave to repeat that the issue depended on them only. They retired, promised to make a faithful report to his excellency, protested they would use their influence in favour of the U. States, and request me not to close my letters until I heard farther from the Bashaw, either direct or thro' their agency.

May the 6th, I waited on the Bashaw to pay my compliments to him, in consequence of the festival; he treated me with great politeness, but I could easily discern that it was against his inclination; there was something in his countenance that indicated his smiles were not sincere, and ought not to be depended on.

May the 10th, Farfara came to the American house, and informed me that the Bashaw had concluded to write to the President of the United States himself, as he entertained some suspicion that I would not write to government with sufficient energy; that the Bashaw would send me his letter the first opportunity that should present, to forward it, which he hoped I had no objection to do. I replied, none in the least, and requested Farfara to procure me a copy, if possible, which he promised to do. Having waited until the date of this dispatch, without having heard any thing more on the subject, I hasten to get my dispatches in readiness to forward, by the first conveyance. Should any thing intervene, worthy of notice, before I receive the Bashaw's letter, it shall be the subject of another dispatch.

Extract of a letter from the same, to the Secretary of State, dated

MAY 27, 1800.

SINCE the date of the enclosed dispatch, I heard nothing from the Bashaw, until the evening of the 25th inst.[10] when Siddi Mahomed Daguize sent me the original in Arabic, of which the enclosed is a literal translation. The only conclusion which can be drawn from the Bashaw's proceedings, is, that he wants a present; and if he does not get one, he will forge pretences to commit depredations on the property of our fellow citizens. His letter to the President will be the means of keeping him quiet, until he receives an answer, provided no unnecessary delay is made, as he will expect to reap a benefit therefrom. Should government think proper to make him a present, it will have the desired effect, probably, for one year, but not longer. I therefore can see no alternative but to station some of our frigates in the Mediterranean, otherwise, we will be continually subject to the same insults which the Imperials, Danes, Swedes, and Ragusans[11] have already suffered, and will still continue to suffer.

Translated extract from a letter of the Bashaw of Tripoli,
to the President of the United States, dated

MAY 25th, 1800.

AFTER having cultivated the branches of our good will, and paved the way to a good understanding, and perfect friendship, which we wish may continue forever, we make known that the object and contents of this our present letter, is, that whereas, your consul who resides at our court in your service, has communicated to us, in your name, that you have written to him, informing him, that you regarded the regency of Tripoli, in the same point of view as the other regencies of Barbary, and to be upon the same footing of friendship and importance. In order to further strengthen the bonds of a good understanding, blessed be God, may he complete and grant to you his high protection. But, our sincere friend, we could wish that these your expressions were followed by deeds, and not by empty words. You will therefore endeavor to satisfy us by a good manner of proceeding. We, on our part, will correspond with you, with equal friendship, as well in words as deeds. But if only flattering words are meant, without performance, every one will act as he finds convenient. We beg a speedy answer, without neglect of time, as a delay on your part cannot but be prejudicial to your interests. In the mean time we wish you happiness.

Given in Tripoli, in Barbary, the 29th of the moon Hegia, the year of the Hegira 1214, *which corresponds with the 25th of May,* 1800.

THOMAS JEFFERSON, President of the United States of America.
To the illustrious and honourable Bey of Tripoli, of Barbary, whom God preserve.

GREAT AND RESPECTED FRIEND,

The assurances of friendship which our consul has given you, and of our sincere desire to cultivate peace and commerce with your subjects, are faithful expressions of our dispositions, and you will continue to find proofs of them in all those acts of respect and friendly intercourse, which are due between nations standing as we do in the relations of peace and amity with each other.

At the conclusion of our treaty with you, we endeavored to prove our respect for yourself, and satisfaction at that event, by such demonstrations as gave you, then, entire content; and we are disposed to believe, that in rendering into another language those expressions in your letter of the 25th of May last, which seem to imply purposes inconsistent with the faith of that transaction, your intentions have been misconstrued. On this supposition we renew to you sincerely, assurances of our constant friendship, and that our desire to cultivate peace and commerce with you remains firm and unabated.

We have found it expedient to detach a squadron of observation into the Mediterranean sea, to superintend the safety of our commerce there, and to exercise our seamen in nautical duties. We recommend them to your hospitality and good offices, should occasion require their resorting to your harbours. We hope their appearance will give umbrage to no power; for, while we mean to rest the safety of our commerce on the resources of our own strength and bravery, in every sea, we have yet given to this squadron in strict command to conduct themselves towards all friendly powers with the most perfect respect and good order: it being the first object of our solicitude to cherish peace and friendship with all nations with whom it can be held on terms of equality and reciprocity.

I pray God, very great and respected friend, to have you always in his holy keeping.

Written at the city of Washington, the twenty-first day of May, in the year of our Lord one thousand eight hundred and one.

(Signed) TH: JEFFERSON.

By the President,

(Signed) JAMES MADISON, *Secretary of State.*

Extract of a letter from Mr. Cathcart to the Secretary of State, dated

TRIPOLI, *October* 18, 1801.

ON the 16th I waited upon the Bashaw, in company with Captain Carpenter, to demand satisfaction for the insult our flag had suffered in having one of our vessels brought in here without any visible cause, her papers and passport being in perfect order; and likewise to demand restitution of property plundered from the brig.

The Bashaw answered, that he had not given orders to the Raize to bring in American vessels; that he had broke him, and dismissed him from his service, and then gave orders to the minister of marine to have every article that was plundered from the brig returned.

The Bashaw then commenced thus—"Consul, there is no nation I wish more to be at peace with than your's; but all nations pay me, and so must the Americans." I answered—"we have already paid you all we owe you, and are nothing in arrears." He answered—"that for the peace we had paid him, it was true; but to maintain the peace we had given him nothing." I observed—"that the terms of our treaty were to pay him the stipulated cash, stores, &c. in full of all demands forever"; and then repeated nearly to the same effect as is contained in my dispatch of the 12th of May, which, to avoid repetition, I forbear inserting. The Bashaw then observed, that we had given a great deal to Algiers and Tunis, and that the Portuguese captain informed him, that when he passed by Algiers about the middle of last month, that he had seen an American frigate in the bay, which he supposed had brought more presents to the Dey—"Why do they neglect me in their donations; let them give me a stipulated sum annually, and I will be reasonable as to the amount?"

In answer to the first, I replied, that it was true that one of our frigates was at Algiers, being one of a squadron of three 44 gun ships, and some smaller vessels, which were appointed to protect our commerce in the Mediterranean; but whether they had presents on board for the regency of Algiers, or not, I could not inform him; that some of them would have been at Tripoli before now, had I not informed them that they had better stay away until the spring, upon account of the badness of this road, which renders it very unsafe at this season. And in answer to his proposal of an annuity, I replied, with some warmth, exactly what I had requested Daguize to inform him of in my name yesterday evening. "Well then," replied the Bashaw, "let your government give me a sum of money, and I will be content; but paid I will be one way or other. I now desire you to inform your government, that I will wait six months for an answer to my letter to the President; that if it did not arrive in that period, and if it was not satisfactory, if it did arrive, that I will declare war in form against the United States; inform your government," said he, "how I have served the Swedes, who concluded their treaty since your's; let them know that the French, English and Spaniards, have always sent me presents from time to time to preserve their peace, and if they do not do the same, I will order my cruisers to bring their vessels in whenever they can find them." He then turned to Daguize and told him to explain to Capt. Carpenter what he had informed me (they both speaking French), and added, "that he did not wish to make it a private affair between the consul and him, and desired him to make it public, as he wished the whole world to know it; he then told Daguize to tell the captain that he hoped the United States would not neglect him, as six or eight vessels of the value of his would amount to a much larger sum than he ever expected to get from the United States for remaining at peace; besides, said he, I have a great desire to have some captains like you here to learn me to speak English."

I answered, that it was absolutely impossible for me to receive answers to the letters, which he desired me to write by Captain Carpenter, in six months, as it would be nearly that time before he would get home, upon account of the winter season; that I expected his excellency would wait until the answer arrived, let that be long or short; and observed, that none but those who held a correspondence with the Devil could determine whether he would be content with the President's answer, or not; as neither the President nor myself knew what would content him. I, therefore, requested him to inform me explicitly what was his expectations. To the first he answered——"I will not only wait for answers from your President, but I will now detain the brig and write to him again—but I expect when he sends his answers that they will be such as will empower you to conclude with me immediately—if they are not, I will capture your vessels; and as you have frequently informed me that your instructions do not authorize you to give me a dollar, I will, therefore, not inform you what I expect until you are empowered to negotiate with me; but you may inform your President, that if he is disposed to pay me for my friendship I will be moderate in my demands." The Bashaw then rose from his seat and went out of the room, leaving me to make what comment I thought proper upon his extraordinary conduct.

Extract of a letter from Mr. Cathcart to the Secretary of State, dated

TRIPOLI, *January* 4, 1801.

ON the 2d inst. in the evening, the banners of Sweden, by the Bashaw's request, were hoisted upon the Danish house, and a temporary flag-staff was prepared in order that the customary salute should be fired next day. When a peace takes place with any nation, it is customary for the different consuls to congratulate the Bashaw on the event; you may judge with what a grace I performed a ceremony so repugnant to my feelings—but it was necessary. I accordingly waited upon his excellency in company with the Danish consul, Swedish ex-consul, Mr. Bohrstrom, the present consul, and several others; after congratulation, perfumation, fumigation, and drinking of coffee and sherbet were over, commenced the following litigation:—"I have concluded a peace with the Swedes," commenced the Bashaw, "and I am certain that the king of Sweden is sensible that I was forced to declare war against his nation contrary to my inclination; for had my demands been satisfied in the first instance, I should not have captured their ships and enslaved their people; some nations," added he (meaning the U.S.), "have used me very ill; they look upon me as nothing; they have recourse to Algiers for all things; I should be glad to know which is thought most of at Constantinople?"[12] I could easily have solved that doubt, by saying that the Dey of Algiers had lately sent presents to the Grand Signior, to the amount of a million of dollars, which were powerful arguments in his favour; but as the conversation was general, I did not conceive it more incumbent on me to answer his prologue than any of the rest of the company; and, in fact, I could say nothing but what I have communicated already. The Bashaw observing my silence, directed his discourse to me, and asked me if I understood the Arabic and Turkish languages: I answered that I had a trifling knowledge of them, especially as his excellency and ministers all spoke Italian. "Pray," says the Bashaw, "what was the present Dey of Algiers in the reign of Mahomed Bashaw?" I answered that he was a person very much respected in consequence of his being the cousin of Hassan Bashaw, but had no post whatever. "And pray, what was Hassan Bashaw at that time?" First, he was *bik ilharche* of the marine, and afterwards was made prime minister and treasurer in Algiers, called the Hasnagi. The Bashaw turned up his nose with visible signs of contempt, and was going to proceed, when a person informed him that a piece of timber was not to be found in the whole regency large enough to make a flag-staff for the Swedes, unless they took one of the cruisers spars. "It is a difficult thing" says the son of Ali Bashaw, "to get a flag-staff put up when it once comes down; when the American flag-staff comes down, it will take a great deal of grease (meaning money), "to get it up again; the Danish flag-staff is broke, I hear, and wants mending with a new one." He smiled a ghastly *grin*, and said, "after all, what is twenty thousand dollars a year for a Christian nation to pay, that has such vast resources. Had I enough to live on, I would not trouble myself with cruisers, although my subjects always wish war, because it is to their advantage. How many Raizes," added he, "have I that know the way to the Great Sea?" Admiral Morad answered about twenty. There not being I believe one capable but himself, without his accompanying them, shews that the Bashaw and his officers pay no great regard to truth. "Well," replied his excellency, "I will find them vessels—in Tripoli, consul, we are all hungry, and if we are not provided for, we soon get sick and peevish." As the Bashaw spoke in metaphors, I answered him in the same manner, by saying, that when the chief physician prescribed the medicine, I should have no objection to administer the dose; but until then, I could say nothing on the subject. "Take care," answered the Bashaw, "that the medicine does not come too late; and if it comes in time, that it will be strong enough."

Extract of a letter from Mr. Cathcart, to the Secretary of State, dated

TRIPOLI IN BARBARY, *May* 16, 1801.

THIS evening (10th May) at 6, P.M. Hadgi Mahomude la Sore, the same that went to Algiers in the Hamdullah, came to the American house, and told me not to be alarmed, for the Bashaw had sent him to inform me, that he declared war against the United States, and would take down our flag-staff on Thursday the 14th instant; that if I pleased to remain at Tripoli, I should be treated with respect, but if I pleased I might go away. I sent my compliments to the Bashaw and informed him that it was my positive instructions not to remain an instant after a declaration of war took place, and that I should charter a vessel to-morrow if possible.

Thursday 14th, at 1, P.M. Hadgi Mahomude la Sore came to inform me that the Chavaux were coming to take our flag-staff down. I waited until the Baraskier arrived, and then sent said la Sore to offer him 10,000 dollars in addition to what I had already offered, which was rejected by the Bashaw, and orders given to cut away the flag-staff.

At a quarter past 2 they effected the grand achievement, and our flag-staff was chopped down six feet from the ground, and left reclining on the terrace. Thus ends the first act of this tragedy. I hope the catastrophe may be happy.

Extract of a letter from William Eaton, Esq. Consul of the United States at Tunis, to the Secretary of State, dated

TUNIS, *December* 8, 1800.

ON the 25th ult.[13] after having dispatched duplicates of my letter from the 1st to the 16th, it was intimated to me that there was an American ship in the road of Porto Farino. Instantly I sent off an express to enquire for facts. On the 27th, I received a note from Captain Coffin, of the Anna Maria, informing me that he had been ten days in the road, without being able to communicate with the shore, by reason of the weather, which was extremely bad. On the 28th, I asked a boat of the Bey, to board her, which he said should be ready on the 30th. Accordingly, on the 30th, I embarked at Tunis, in an open boat, and arrived on board, ten leagues, at eight in the evening of the same day. On the morning following, 1st Dec. I had the honour of receiving your letter of the 30th August, covering an invoice and bills of the ship's lading. Yesterday I returned to Tunis. Such part of the cargo as was between decks was chiefly discharged before I left the ship. The *quality* of the articles are acknowledged to be good; but it is objected that the *plank* and the *oars* are *too short*, and the government affect to be dissatisfied; that the keels, guns, and powder, are not come forward. I believe the fact to be, the government is dissatisfied that any thing is come forward. If this opinion requires evidence, I consider it sufficient to state, that the United States are the only nation which have, at this moment, a rich unguarded commerce in the Mediterranean, and that the Barbary regencies are *pirates*. I take to myself the merit of having once more, at least, suspended an expedition which was prepared for us—but we are yet deficient, and I am not without apprehension that this deficiency will be resorted to as a pretense for surprising our merchantmen; in which case they might do us incalculable mischief. These are considerations which, it is supposed, should compel exertions to fulfil our obligations with this regency.

The immense concessions he has received the summer past from Spain, Denmark, Sicily, Sweden, have so diminished the condition of our peace in his eye, that he says, *It is a trifle for so great a commercial nation, in consideration for the advantages of a free trade in this sea.*

To all whom it doth or may concern:

KNOW YE, by these presents, that I, James Leander Cathcart, agent and consul for the United States of America, in and for the city and regency of Tripoli in Barbary, finding just cause to complain of Jusef Bashaw, supreme commandant of said city and regency of Tripoli, and his ministers, towards the government and citizens of the United States of America, and conceiving it my duty to protect against said conduct: Now know ye, that I do hereby protest against the said Jusef Bashaw, supreme commandant of said city and regency, and against his ministers and counsellors, in behalf of the government of the United States of America, myself and fellow-citizens, for the following reasons, viz.

1st. BE IT KNOWN, that on the 17th of August, 1799, said Jusef Bashaw, supreme commandant of the regency of Tripoli, at the instigation of Morad Raiz, admiral of the cruisers of this regency, refused to receive the printed passports issued by the consul of the United States of America in this regency, in obedience to his orders from government, thereby claiming a superiority or preference to the regencies of Algiers and Tunis, he being duly informed that the said passports were accepted in the same form by the chiefs of said regencies, and in order as is my firm belief to have a pretext to send the merchant vessels belonging to the citizens of the United States, into this port for examination, said admiral Morad having publicly declared that he would go to sea with the vessels under his command, without a passport from this office, if they were not modified to his liking, and worded similar to the passports of the British; and the said Jusef Bashaw, on application being made by the said consul of the United States, refusing to exert his authority, is a clear and sufficient evidence, that he was accessary to the insolent demand of said Morad, or more properly speaking, that said Morad, acted, if not by his orders, at least with his tacit consent, thereby forcing the said consul of the United States to deviate from his instructions and to submit from imperious necessity to a humiliation incompatible with the honour and dignity of the nation he has the honour to represent.

2d. Be it known, that in the month of October, 1799, James Leander Cathcart, consul for the United States of America in this regency, having received several bales of cloth to dispose of, that said Jusef Bashaw sent the broker, Leon Farfara, to the consular house, requesting said consul to give him the preference in the sale of said cloth, promising to pay for the same like any other individual, and as cloths were sold of the same quality. I, knowing how he had served the late Venetian and Swedish consuls on a similar occasion, sent said Leon Farfara to inform him, that the cloth was not mine, and that I expected to be paid immediately, in order to be enabled to make a remittance to my correspondent, which he the said Bashaw promised to do; I, therefore, confiding in his promise, which I was taught to believe was sacred to all true Mussulmen, and more especially to a prince of the august family of Caramanly, did deliver unto him sundry pieces of cloth, to the value of five thousand seven hundred and eighty seven yuslicks, current coin of this regency, which at that time was worth Spanish dollars, two thousand three hundred and fourteen, and eighty cents, two yuslicks and one half being then equal to one dollar silver; but at present the coin of this regency having depreciated, owing to the great quantity of alloy mixed in the coinage, a dollar passes for three yuslicks, which makes a difference of one fifth part or 20 per cent. that I have repeatedly demanded the above sum, and have always been put off from time to time with promises, until the 22d day of September, 1800, when some oil belonging to said Bashaw being selling at public vendue, I sent my drogoman to purchase a barrel for the use of my house, value about eighteen dollars, which the hasnadar[14] refused to give unto him, unless I sent the money to pay for it first. I sent the drogoman immediately to the Bashaw to know the reason, who repeated the same words, saying the oil was not his, but belonged to the crew of the cruisers; that if I wanted oil I must first send the cash. I immediately sent for Farfara, who had acted as a broker in the sale of the cloth, and desired him to demand a positive answer from the Bashaw, whether he intended to pay me or not; that I was resolved to be kept no longer in suspense, and offered to take the money at the present value, which is only 1929 dollars, in full of all demands; the Bashaw sent the same answer which he had sent above fifty times before, that he would pay me, but at present it was not convenient, and desired Leon Farfara to inform me, that if I had a mind I might take one of the Swedish prizes for my money, which I declined. Knowing that he, having a quantity of prizes and other goods on hand for exportation, that he would probably force me to take a cargo of said goods to Leghorn or elsewhere, thereby exposing the United States to become responsible for said goods or their value, should any accident happen to said vessel, in the same manner as the claim originated upon Sweden, which was the first and principal cause of the present war, I therefore have deemed it more expedient to entirely lose the aforementioned sum, than to run a risque which might involve my country in a war.

And, as it appears from the above detail, that the said Bashaw never intends to pay me the above sum in cash, according to agreement, notwithstanding I have his receipt or promissory note, under the great seal of this regency, and I having waited above one year for the payment of the said sum without effect, I therefore debit the United States the said sum in my account current, leaving the government of the said United States to make the said claim a national claim; no individual being bound to be responsible to the United States for said sum, or any part thereof which may be recovered from said Jusef Bashaw hereafter.

3d. Be it known, that in the months of May, September, and October, 1800, the said Jusef Bashaw, supreme commandant of the said regency of Tripoli, having made certain demands upon the United States, in direct violation of the 10th article of the treaty existing between the United States of America and the regency of Tripoli, which the consul of the United States resident here found incompatible with the honour and interest of the nation he represents to comply with, that the said Jusef Bashaw, in direct violation of the 12th article of the said existing treaty, did publicly declare, that he would only wait until he receives answers from the President of the United States of America, which, if not satisfactory, that he would then declare war against said United States, as is more fully explained in my dispatches to government, copies of which were forwarded to our consuls at Algiers and Tunis. And whereas it is particularly specified in the 10th article of said treaty, that the money and presents demanded by the Bey or Bashaw of Tripoli, is a full and satisfactory consideration on his part, and on the part of his subjects, for said treaty of perpetual peace and friendship, and that no pretence of any periodical tribute or farther payment is ever to be made by either party; and said Bashaw of Tripoli having acknowledged the receipt of the money and presents stipulated by said treaty, I find myself justifiable both to God and my country in having refused to comply with the said Bashaw's unjust demands upon said United States of America.

And whereas, it is stipulated in the 12th article of the aforesaid treaty, that in case any dispute arises from a violation of any of the articles of said treaty, no appeal shall be made to arms, nor shall war be declared on any pretence whatever; but if the consul residing at the place where the dispute shall happen, shall not be able to settle the same, an amicable reference shall be made to the mutual friend of both parties, the Dey of Algiers; the parties thereby engaging to abide by his decision; and he, by virtue of his signature to the said treaty, having engaged for himself and his successors to declare the justice of the case according to the true interpretation of the said treaty, and use all the means in his power to enforce the observance of the same:—

Now, know all men by these presents, that I, James Leander Cathcart, consul for the United States of America, in said regency of Tripoli, do protest and declare, that the demands, made by the Bashaw of Tripoli upon the United States of America, are of such a nature, that I cannot settle the dispute arising therefrom; and that I conceive that I should not only be deviating from my official duty, but likewise acting as an accomplice and in conjunction with the said Bashaw of Tripoli, to treat our good friends, the Dey and Divan of Algiers, with indignity and disrespect, was I to refrain from making the aforesaid amicable reference. I, therefore, in virtue of these presents, do make the aforesaid amicable reference, transmitting the whole to the consul-general of the U.S. of America at Algiers, who is possessed of every information relative to the state of our affairs in this regency, having received duplicates of my dispatches for the government of the U. States; at the same time leaving it at the discretion of the consul-general of the United States at Algiers for the time being, to take such measures as he in his judgment may think most likely to promote the interests of the United States, and to maintain the peace of our country with this regency upon honourable and equitable terms.

4th. Be it known, That on the 25th of September, 1800, Raiz Amor Shelli, commander of a Tripoline cruiser of 15 guns, captured the American brig Catharine, James Carpenter, master, of and from New-York, and bound to Leghorn, valued at 50,000 dollars, or thereabouts; that said vessel was kept in possession of the subjects of Tripoli, until the 15th of October in the evening, and was then delivered up to the consul of the United States, in consequence of the Bashaw of Tripoli having wrote a letter to the President of the United States, the purport of which, being already known, needs no repetition; and that said vessel was exposed to much loss and peril, as appears by the master of said brig, his protest, already forwarded to our consul-general at Algiers; and that said brig was plundered of effects, valued by said master, James Carpenter, at 397 hard dollars, whereof was recovered to the value of 180 dollars, the value of 217 dollars being irrecoverably lost; notwithstanding the Bashaw had given positive orders to Hamet Raiz, or minister of marine, to cause every article that could be found to be restored to their lawful owner; yet said Raiz of the marine did not comply with the Bashaw's orders; (and he being the Bashaw's brother-in-law, it was out of my power to compel him) but, on the contrary, prevaricated from day to day, from the 16th to the 21st of October, with an intent, no doubt, to share the spoils with the aforesaid Raiz Amor Shelli, and on the night of the 21st inst. sent Ibram Farfara to inform me, that if the brig did not sail by day-light in the morning, that the port would be embargoed; and gave me to understand that if I did not promise to pay him anchorage for said brig, that she should be detained until the embargo should be taken off. This demand I absolutely refused to comply with. On the 22d, at day-light, I ordered the brig to get under way, and could not get the Pilot to go on board until said Ibram Farfara paid the Raiz of marine 5 dollars and 75 cents anchorage, which, not withstanding it being an unjust demand, complied with, sooner than have the brig detained one day longer.

I, therefore, for foresaid reasons, and for each of the aforementioned arbitrary acts, do protest against the foresaid Jusef Bashaw, supreme commandant of the regency of Tripoli in Barbary, and against his ministers and counsellors; but more especially against said Morad Raiz, admiral of the cruisers of this regency, for being the cause of my altering the national passports of the United States of America; and against said Hamet Raiz, or minister of marine, for the reasons before mentioned, as well as for falsely, insidiously, and slanderously asserting in my presence, and in the presence of Captain Carpenter, that the consul-general of the United States, Richard O'Brien, and the broker or banker of said United States,

Micaiah Cohen Bacri, had informed him, when he was last at Algiers, that the government of the United States had alone paid to the house of Bacri & Co. one hundred thousand dollars for their influence, thereby irritating the said Jusef Bashaw against the government and citizens of the United States of America; as the said Jusef Bashaw seemingly gave credit to the falsehood of said Hamet Raiz, and emphatically said that the government of the United States had treated an Algerine Jew better, and with more liberality, than they had the said Bashaw of Tripoli, notwithstanding I gave the direct lie without ceremony or hesitation to said Hamet, and told the Bashaw that I wondered how he could give credit to so barefaced a falsehood, for even had the United States given the abovementioned sum, the party concerned would be the last people in the world to divulge the same, it not comporting with their honour or interest, especially to Hamet Raiz, who was not only an enemy to the United States, but likewise to his excellency the Bashaw of Tripoli, he having by his false insinuations endeavored to persuade the Bashaw to annul the treaty of peace and amity at present subsisting between the said United States and this regency, to the prejudice of his character, honour, and dignity, whole word and signature I had always supposed to have been inviolably sacred; and that said Jusef Bashaw, in answer to the above, said, "you say that Hamet Raiz *lies*, and I say he tells truth"; thereby discrediting all I had said, and giving full credit to the imposition of said Hamet Raiz, or minister of marine.

Now KNOW ALL MEN, That for the reasons afore assigned, I, James Leander Cathcart, agent and consul for the United States of America, in the regency of Tripoli, having shewn sufficient cause to enter this protest against the said Jusef Bashaw, supreme commandant of the regency of Tripoli, his afore-mentioned ministers and counsellors, I do by these presents most solemnly protest against the conduct of said Jusef Bashaw, his ministers and counsellors, as being unjust and in direct violation of the 10th and 12th articles of the existing treaty between the United States and the said regency of Tripoli; and I, James Leander Cathcart, do further declare, that the dispute arising from the violation of said treaty, is of such a nature, that I cannot adjust the same before I receive express instructions from the President of the United States of America, or until our good friends, the Dey and Divan of Algiers shall decide upon the justice of the cause, according to the true interpretation of the existing treaty between the United States of America and this regency; and that I do hereby make an amicable reference to our good friends the Dey and Divan of the regency of Algiers, promising in the name of the United States of America, to abide by their decision agreeable to the true meaning of the stipulation contained in the 12th article of the treaty of peace and amity concluded between the United States of America and the regency of Tripoli, by the intervention of the late Hassan Bashaw, Dey of Algiers, and under the immediate guarantee of said regency, the said treaty having been duly ratified by the reigning Dey of Algiers, Mustapha Bashaw, whom God preserve.

Now I, James Leander Cathcart, agent and consul of the United States of America, conceiving it my duty so to do, do now transmit this said protest to the Chancery of the United States at Tunis, in order that it may be there duly registered, and from thence forwarded to the consul-general of the United States of America at Algiers, in order to prevent, as much as depends upon me, any appeal being made to arms, leaving the conducting of the whole affair entirely at the discretion of the consul-general of the United States of America for the time being, as before mentioned, not doubting but he will take such measures as he in his judgment may think more likely to promote the interests of the United States of America and maintain the peace of our country with this regency upon honourable and equitable terms.

In testimony of the above, I have hereunto subscribed my name and affixed (L.S.) the seal of my office, at the Chancery of the United States of America, in the city of Tripoli in Barbary, this 25th day of October, in the year of our Lord one thousand eight hundred; and in the 25th year of the independence of the United States of America.

(Signed) JAMES L. CATHCART.

In the Spring of 1801, the absolute threats of the Bashaw of Tripoli to commerce hostilities against the United States, induced our Executive to send a small squadron into the Mediterranean, under the command of Commodore Dale. The following were his orders.—

Extract of a letter from the Secretary of the Navy to Commodore Dale, dated

May 30, 1801.

Recent accounts received from the consul of the United States, employed near the regencies of Algiers, Tunis and Tripoli, give cause to fear, that they will attack our commerce, if unprotected, within the Mediterranean, but particularly such apprehension is justified by absolute threats on the part of the Bey of Tripoli.

Under such circumstance, it is thought probable, that a small squadron of well appointed frigates appearing before their ports, will have a tendency to prevent their breaking the peace which has been made, and which has subsisted for some years, between them and the United States. It is also thought, that such a squadron, commanded by some of our most gallant officers, known to be stationed in the Mediterranean, will give confidence to our merchants, and tend greatly to increase the commerce of the country, within those seas.

I am, therefore, instructed by the President to direct, that you proceed with all possible expedition, with the squadron under your command, to the Mediterranean. It will be proper for you to stop at Gibraltar and obtain permission from the governor for depositing provisions there, for the use of your squadron. It is not presumed there will be any refusal; but, should he deem it improper, you will then leave a letter with Mr. Gavino, the American consul, for the captain of the provision vessel that will be sent hereafter, directing him where to proceed.

On your arrival at Gibraltar, you will be able to ascertain whether all or any of the Barbary powers shall have declared war against the United States. In case all are tranquil, you will water your ships, proceed off the port of Algiers, and send to the consul, Mr. O'Brien, whom you will inform that you have arrived—that the views of your government are perfectly friendly—that you have a letter for him and the Dey—and that you request to see him; or that he send some person, in whom he can confide, for the letters—or that he send a permission for one of your officers to go to the city. You will have on board certain goods, which you will deliver on his requisition. They are for the biennial presents to the regency. The George Washington is preparing to carry timber and other stores for at least one year's annuity; and you have on board the President, thirty thousand dollars, which it is hoped and expected Mr. O'Brien will be able to induce the regency to receive for another year. The balance may go some time hence. But if Mr. O'Brien cannot induce the Dey to receive money instead of stores, you will retain the thirty thousand dollars, excepting 4 or 5,000 dollars, which, on Mr. O'Brien's requisition, may (if he should think it useful to commence with) be given him on your arrival, and which amount may be replaced if the Dey shall afterwards agree to receive the 30,000 dollars in full for one year's annuity, out of the 10,000 dollars hereafter mentioned as being intended for the Bey of Tripoli, and the stores will be sent as soon as possible.

When your business is arranged at Algiers, to your satisfaction, you will proceed to Tunis, and there cause the letter you carry to be delivered to Mr. Eaton, the consul. A ship is preparing and will sail as soon as possible, with stores, agreeable to treaty with that regency.

From thence you will proceed to Tripoli; on your arrival there send for Mr. Cathcart, American consul for that port, to whom deliver his letters, and either by him or one of your officers (which ever may be deemed most proper) send the President's letter to the Bey. You have on board ten thousand dollars, as a present from the President; the whole, or such part thereof as you may have on your arrival at Tripoli, and which Mr. Cathcart may conceive useful, will be given the Bey, provided he has conducted himself peaceably towards the United States.

You will be careful not to solicit the honour of a salute from any of those powers; if you do, they will exact a barrel of powder for every gun they fire.

You will enjoin upon your officers and men the propriety and utility of a proper conduct towards the subjects of all those powers. A good understanding with them being extremely desirable.

Should you find the conduct of the Bey of Tripoli such as you may confide in, you will then coast with your squadron the Egyptian and Syrian shores as far as Smyrna, and return by the mouth of the Adriatic—thence pay the Bey of Tripoli another visit; finding him tranquil, proceed to Tunis, and again shew your ships; and thence coast the Italian shore to Leghorn, where you may stay some days, and then proceed along the Genoese to Toulon, which port it will be instructive to your young men to visit. From thence proceed again to Algiers. If there should be no hostile appearance on the part of those powers, and you should be well assured that no danger is to be apprehended from either of them, you may on the 15th of October, commence your return home-wards; but if there should be any cause for apprehension from either of those powers, you must place your ships in a situation to chastise them, in case of their declaring war or committing hostilities, and not commence your return to the United States, until the 1st day of December.

On your return you will go into Hampton Road, and repair yourself to this place as soon as you can. Order the Philadelphia, if the season will permit; if not, let her go with the Essex to New-York—the Enterprize send to Baltimore.

But should you find, on your arrival at Gibraltar, that all the Barbary powers have declared war against the U. States, you will then distribute your force in such manner, as your judgment shall direct, so as best to protect our commerce and chastise their insolence—by sinking, burning, or destroying their ships and vessels wherever you shall find them. The better to enable you to form a just determination, you are herewith furnished with a correct state of the strength and situation of each of the Barbary powers. The principal strength, you will see, is that of Algiers. The force of Tunis and Tripoli is contemptible, and might be crushed with any one of the frigates under your command.

Should Algiers alone have declared war against the United States, you will cruize off that port so as effectually to prevent any thing from going in or coming out; and you will sink, burn, or otherwise destroy their ships and vessels wherever you find them.

Should the Bey of Tripoli have declared war, as he has threatened, against the United States, you will then proceed direct to that port, where you will lay your ship in such a position as effectually to prevent any of their vessels from going in or out. The Essex and Enterprize, by cruising well on towards Tunis, will have it in their power to intercept any vessels which they may have captured. By disguising your ships, it will be some weeks before they will know that the squadron is cruising in the Mediterranean, and give you a fair chance of punishing them.

If Tunis alone, or in concert with Tripoli, should have declared war against the United States, you will chastise them in like manner—by cruising with the squadron, from the small island of Maratimo, near the island of Sicily, to cape Blanco, on the Barbary shore; you may effectually prevent the corsairs of either from intercepting our commerce in material part of the Mediterranean sea, and may intercept any prizes they may have made.

Any prisoners you may take, you will treat with humanity and attention, and land them on any part of the Barbary shore most convenient to you. This mode will be humane, and will shew that we have no sort of fear, what such men can do. It will also tend to bring those powers back to a sense if justice which they owe to us. But you will be careful to select from them such Christians as may be on board, whom you will treat kindly, and land, when convenient, on some Christian shore. Should you have occasion, you may accept their services.

Extract of a letter from Commodore Dale, commanding the United States squadron in the Mediterranean, to the Secretary of the Navy, dated

GIBRALTAR-BAY, 2d *July*, 1801.

On my arrival here I found, lying at anchor, the High Admiral of Tripoli, in a ship mounting 26 guns, nine and six pounders, 260 men; and a brig of 16 guns, 160 men. He has been out 36 days, says he is not at war with America, nor has he taken any thing. He came in here for water, and is under quarantine at present. From every information I can get here, Tripoli is at war with America.

Extract of a letter from Commodore Dale to the Secretary of the Navy, dated

Tunis-Bay, *July* 18, 1801.

Mr. O'Brien informed me, "that the Dey of Algiers had been complaining very much of the United States in not making their annual payments good, and had gone so far as to say, that he would not put up with it much longer. He was now confident, he said, that the Dey would not speak so big, and had no doubt that the arrival of the President at Algiers had much more weight with the Dey, than if the Washington had arrived with stores. He did not think it a proper time to mention to the Dey, about receiving 30,000 dollars instead of stores." Mr. O'Brien took the cloth and linen on shore with him.

I arrived at Tunis-Bay the 17th instant, and sent a letter on shore to Mr. Eaton; the 18th he came on board. The Essex and the ship Grand Turk arrived the same day. From Mr. Eaton's information, this regency has been much in the same way as Algiers, and the appearance of our ships will have the same effect on the great and mighty Bey of Tunis.

Extract of a letter from Commodore Dale, to the Secretary of the Navy, dated

Malta Harbour, *August* 18, 1801.

I arrived off Tripoli the 24th ult. the 25th, I received a letter from Mr. Nissen, consul for Denmark, at Tripoli; he was requested by Mr. Cathcart to act for him in his absence, should there be a necessity for it. The letter was wrote at the request of the Bey, to know if my intentions in coming off Tripoli, were to make peace or war. I wrote him that my intentions in the first instance were friendly, but the act of his excellency in declaring war against the United States, had put that disposition out of my power, and that I was determined to take his vessels of every description, and his subjects wherever I could find them; but at the same time I should be glad to know his reasons for declaring war, and on what principles he expected to make peace. That on those points I wished information as soon as possible, that I might inform the President of the United States, and ascertain his determination respecting the business. The next day the Bey sent off a Jew to negociate for a peace or truce. I informed him, that his excellency had not answered my letter; that I was not empowered to make a new treaty, but if the Bey would answer my letter, and send off one of his officers, and was serious in the business, I would then treat with him about a truce. The Jew went on shore. I have not heard from him since. The Bey wrote me previous to this, that he had good reasons for declaring war against the United States, but if I would come on shore, he was very certain we should be able to make a peace. He said he did not like the 1st and 12th articles in the old treaty, and did not wish to have any thing to do with the Dey of Algiers.

I am happy to inform you that the Enterprize, on the 1st inst. on her passage to this place, fell in with a polacre ship, mounting 14 guns and 80 men, a corsair belonging to Tripoli. The enclosed is a copy of Mr. Sterrett's letter to me, which will give you an account of the action and the result of it. Mr. Sterrett is a very good officer, and deserves well of his country. After being 18 days off Tripoli, and seeing nothing in that time but two small vessels, Tunisians, one bound in and the other out, and receiving information that the Bey had boats stationed along the coast, both to the eastward and westward; on the 11th inst. I determined to run along the coast, to the westward, as far as the island of Pidussa, from Pidussa to this place for water. I arrived here the 16th inst. saw nothing on my passage.

Copy of a letter from Lieutenant Andrew Sterrett, to Commodore Dale, dated on board the United States schooner Enterprize,

AT SEA, *August* 6, 1801.

SIR,

I HAVE the honour to inform you, that on the 1st August, I fell in with a Tripolitan ship of war, called the Tripoli, mounting 14 guns, commanded by Raiz Mahomet Sous. An action immediately commenced within pistol shot, which continued three hours, incessant firing. She then struck her colours. The carnage on board was dreadful, she having 20 men killed and 30 wounded; among the latter was the Captain and first Lieutenant. Her mizen mast went over the side. Agreeable to your orders, I dismantled her of every thing but an old sail and spar. With heart-felt pleasure I add, that the officers and men throughout the vessel, behaved in the most spirited and determined manner, obeying every command with promptitude and alertness. We had not a man wounded, and sustained no material damage in our hull or rigging.

I remain your most obedient servant,

ANDREW STERRETT.

Extract of a letter from Commodore Dale, to the Secretary of the Navy, dated

GIBRALTAR BAY, *October* 4, 1801.

HAVING completed my water on the 21st of August, I sailed again. On the 30th I brought to a Greek ship, from Constantinople and Smyrna, bound into Tripoli, loaded with beans and merchandize, and having on board one Tripolitan officer, 20 soldiers, 14 merchants, 5 women, 4 of them black, and one white child, all Tripolitans: I took them all on board. I thought this a favourable opportunity to try to bring about, and settle an exchange of prisoners with the Bey, should his corsairs take any Americans, (I say God forbid.) I accordingly sent three of the Tripolitans on shore in a small boat, with a letter to Mr. Nissen, the Danish consul, requesting him to make known the contents of it to the Bey. The next day, Mr. Nissen came off at the Bey's request, to know if I would make a truce. Mr. Nissen informed me, that he had told the Bey, before he came off, that he could not say any thing to me on that subject, until he had answered my letters on that point. The Bey told him to go off and try, and if I would, he would then talk to me about the exchange of prisoners, and a peace. My mind was made up on that subject, knowing I had no orders to make a truce, little was said on that subject. Mr. Nissen told me that the Bey said, that he would not give one American for all the soldiers, and that only eight of the merchants, were his subjects. He cared very little about any of them. At length, the Bey agreed to give three Americans for twenty-one soldiers, and three for the eight merchants. Circumstanced as I was, I was under the necessity to act as I did, namely, to put them all on board the Greek ship again, and permit them to go into port. I wrote to Mr. Nissen to inform the Bey, that I agreed to the exchange of three Americans for the soldiers, but I did not consider the merchants as prisoners, nor could I fix on any thing respecting them, until I knew the determination of my government, and that the present transaction was not to be a precedent in any future negociation. This transaction took place on the 3d of September, the ship's company then very sickly, 94 men on the doctor's list, and a number more complaining, not knowing to what extent the sickness might go, and not having more than one month's provision on board, at eight P.M. I was under the necessity of coming to a determination to give up the blockade of Tripoli, and proceed for Gibraltar.

Mr. Gavino informed me about a month ago, that the Tripolitan Admiral had laid up his two corsairs here, and took his passage, with eight of his officers, on board of an English ship bound to Malta; leaving the captain of the brig and 20 men, to take care of the two vessels, and bring the ship home, if he had an opportunity; sent the remainder of his men over to Tetuan in boats.

I think it necessary that two frigates should remain in those seas all the winter, under the present circumstance. The Philadelphia to rendezvous at Sarragosa, the south-east end of the Island of Sicily. I shall give Capt. Barron orders to shew himself off Tripoli and Tunis, every now and then, to let those fellows know and see, that we are on the watch for them. The Essex to rendezvous at Gibraltar and Algeziras, as may be most convenient, to keep a good look out, and know what is going on in this quarter.

DURING this summer, Mr. Cathcart and General Eaton conceived the project of co-operating with the exiled Bashaw of Tripoli, who had been driven from his throne by his brother. Gen. Eaton says—

ABOUT this time (28th June) I received a letter from Mr. Cathcart, dated at Leghorn, June 15th, which suggested to me the plan of using Hamet Bashaw, the legitimate sovereign of Tripoli, then an exile in Tunis, as an instrument, in favour of the United States, to chastise the perfidy of our enemy, his younger brother, who had treasonably usurped the government. I did not then enter decidedly into the measure; doubting whether any construction of my original instructions from government, would authorise the discretion.

But, on the 17th July following, Commodore Dale arrived with his squadron, at Portoforine, forty miles from Tunis; and on the 18th, on his board, he put into my hands the letter from the department of state, dated 20th May, preceding; which, by his discretionary instructions, removed that obstacle. This discretion was highly proper at that time, and on that station. For Tunis may be said, by a figure, to be a scite on the on the enemy's flank, from which his whole camp may be reconnoitred without his having the means of preventing it; and from which he may be annoyed in his operations without the capacity of resistance. I soon entered into convention with Hamet Bashaw, conditioned, on his part, that, on his being restored to his dominion, he should place the usurper and family into our hands as hostages of a perpetual peace. And I sketched the project to the department of state, in my report of 5th September following.

The moment of the appearance of a force on the Barbary coast, was peculiarly favourable, both as it affected Tunis and Tripoli. It checked, for a moment, the arrogance of the former; and it gave a paralytic shock to the latter. The enemy was securely calculating on the booty he expected from American captures—he had no apprehensions of a force so near him; and was consequently unprepared to counteract its operations. His best corsairs, comprising his chief naval force, and the chosen strength of his Turkish soldiery, were either blockaded at Gibraltar, or were at sea, not in a capacity to return immediately to his succour. He had but a few guns, badly mounted, on his castle batteries; not soldiers to man them; and scarcely a centinal on their ramparts. His interior was agitated by dissentions, and his capital distressed by famine. Of this last circumstance, however, I was not informed till after the departure of the Commodore for his station. It had been carefully concealed from me until the alarmed commerce of Tunis betrayed it in a demand of the Bey for my passports of safe conduct to his merchantmen bound to that port with provisions. At once to seize the advantages which the occasion offered, and to silence the Bey's demand for passports, which, if granted, would, according to Barbary's exclusive privileges, have covered the property at all events, I announced Tripoli in a state of blockade, and dispatched an express vessel to the commodore he with the information. He confirmed the blockade, pledged himself for its support. Nine days afterwards appeared in the road of Tunis, on his way to Gibraltar, having quitted the enemy's coast by reason of sickness in his ship. He left with me, however, a letter of instructions to keep up the idea of a blockade. On the eleventh, having sprung a mast, he appeared again in the bay with a signal to speak the consul—I went on board. He then stated to me that he, in fact, had no orders which would authorize him to act offensively—nor yet to hold a prisoner he might take—that he had consequently released the crew of the corsair captured by Lt. Sterrett, as well as sundry considerable merchants of Tripoli, who had fallen into his hands coming from Smyrna, on the Bashaw's promise to give up seven Americans in exchange, when taken. That he expected fresh instructions at Gibraltar; believing that the information of the war had seasonably reached the United States; when he should return to Tripoli—he enjoined on me, at the same time, to keep up the colour of a blockade—I never saw the commodore afterwards; though I kept the enemy three months in a state of blockade when we had not a ship of war within three hundred leagues of his port; his chief commerce and whole supplies of provisions depending on Tunis, and my passports being still withheld.

The statement General Eaton here makes of the force and situation of Tripoli, I believe to be perfectly correct—for it was not much better defended at the time we were captured. The General further adds—

Being myself in a very imperfect state of health, from the convalescence of a fever, which had reduced me very low the preceding summer, my physician advised me to take a sea voyage. Accordingly I embarked in the United States transport, the George Washington, and proceeded to Leghorn. The Bey of Tunis, immediately after my departure, demanded passports of my charge des affairs—who wrote me and received my answer.

On my arrival at Leghorn, the President's answer to the Bey's demand for forty 24 pound battery guns, came to hand, unsealed. It conveyed, in pretty explicit language, a resolution *no longer to owe to humiliating concessions our right to navigate the seas freely.*

This Mr. Cathcart and myself construed as assurance of the approbation of government to our measures; and as an encouragement to perseverance.

Being informed from Tunis, that overtures of reconciliation had been made by the ruling Bashaw of Tripoli to his exiled brother, it was resolved that I should return immediately to Tunis, in order to defeat his designs.

We now viewed the project with Hamet Bashaw more essential to the object of effecting a peace than ever before. It was thought a very unfortunate circumstance that a construction of the constitution should have prohibited Commodore Dale from receiving discretionary orders on leaving the U. States for the expedition: the consequence certainly was, that the fair prospects which presented themselves on his first arrival on the enemy's coast, failed in execution—and that the expedition of 1801 effected nothing essential to the issue of the war. The measure of setting the Tripolitan prisoners at liberty, which was calculated by benevolent experiment to move the gratitude of the Barbarian, operated, in effect, a quite different sentiment on his mind; for he attributed to fear those acts of generosity which a civilized enemy would have acknowledged proofs of magnanimity. His corsairs escaped the vigilance of our ships and got safe home. About one hundred Swedish captives were employed making gun-carriages on the castles, and in repairing their platforms and parapets. He had found means to procure supplies of ammunition and a competence of provision—and was now in a pretty good situation of defence. If he succeeded in getting possession of his rival brother, it would relieve him from apprehensions of an internal revolt, and would tend to render the terms of peace with the United States much more exorbitant; or the war, on his part, more active, and pernicious to our commerce. There being no direct passage to Tunis to be procured, it was thought advisable, both on account of dispatch and safety, to embark in my own armed ship Gloria—which I accordingly did, on the 28th February, and arrived March 12th. She was a new, well built Danish ship, of about 800 tons, captured by the Bey of Tunis, and finally abandoned by the Danish negociator, which I had purchased; but for which I was refused a Mediterranean passport on a construction of our law—in consequence of which I was mounted upon her deck fourteen 12 and 6 pounders, and on her forecastle and quarter six smaller guns. On my arrival at Tunis I found Hamet Bashaw actually on the point of departing for the kingdom of Tripoli, under the escort of forty armed Turks, sent by the ruling Bashaw for his *protection!* Despairing of the aids he had anticipated from the Americans—and refused further supplies of provisions by the Bey of Tunis, he was compelled to embark in a Russian ship for his passage. The Bey of Tunis now demanded my passports for him and his retinue; and renewed his demand for passports for his merchantmen to Tripoli. I refused to grant either one or the other. He became outrageous—threatened the nation with war, and myself with chains. I began to be apprehensive of real danger, and was desirous of communicating this state of things to the commanding officer on the coast. There was no American vessel of war near, and it would be improper and unsafe to confide this information to accidental conveyance.

There were then with me, at the American house, Doctor William Turner, and Mr. Charles Wadsworth, of the navy; and Captains George G. Coffin, and Joseph Bounds, American masters of merchantmen, whom I consulted, and, with their advice, dispatched the Gloria to the commanding officer, with a detail of facts; and suggested to him the exertions I thought requisite to prevent the friendly Bashaw falling into the enemy's hands, as well as to seize the Tripolitan soldiers who guarded him; and at the same time I requested he would give the Gloria a warrant to act under my orders till *the arrival of the commodore.*

The Gloria fell in with Capt. M'Niel, the only commander on the coast, three days after leaving port, who approved of my measures; sent back the ship with his warrant to act under my orders, offensively against the Tripolitans, until the arrival of the commodore; and went himself in search of the Bashaw.

Mean time I had wrought upon the Bey's minister to countenance and aid my project, in consideration of my promise to give him ten thousand dollars on condition of *his fidelity, and in case of its success.* I thought it good policy to secure the minister; not so much for the service he would render, as to check the mischief which seemed impending. He confessed it was the intention of the enemy Bashaw, by this illusive overture, to get possession of the rival brother, in order to destroy him; and he permitted my drogoman, under an injunction of secrecy, to communicate the design to Hamet Bashaw. This determined him to go to Malta under a pretext to his people of evading the Swedish and American cruisers. He arrived safely—dismissed his escort, and reported himself to me.

Having now gained what I considered the most important point in our plan, the security of the friendly Bashaw, I immediately dispatched the Gloria to convey the intelligence to our commodore and to the government.

The ship arrived seasonably at Gibraltar; but what was my astonishment to learn that, instead of meeting there a squadron, prepared to seize this advantageous position, to find a solitary captain of a frigate, just from his counting-house, ready to stamp defeat, and pass censure on a measure, the ground of which he could not have surveyed! Captain Murray discarded this project, and dismissed my ship in a manner most injurious and most disgraceful to me; but proceeded himself to Tunis, where he arrived early in June, and tarried six days with me without intimating any thing of his proceeding at Gibraltar, though he expressed his dissent to the plan concerted with Hamet Bashaw. The Gloria arrived a day or two after the Constellation's departure. But a general discontentment prevailed among the crew. Two of them had been taken off by Captain Murray at Gibraltar; two or three others deserted after arrival at Tunis; and all were unwilling to go to sea, it being known that sundry cruisers of the enemy were out.

During these transactions, it appears, the Sapatapa had betrayed to the ruling Bashaw the plot of his brother with the Swedes and Americans to dethrone him. The Swedish admiral had embraced the project, and entered into some arrangements with Captain M'Niel to give it effect; but waited the arrival of the American squadron—for as an offensive and defensive alliance was understood to exist between the Swedish court and government of the United States, so far as related to Tripoli—that admiral had orders to act with the advice and concurrence of the American Commodore.

The alarm excited in the apprehensions of the usurper by these manoevers induced him to come forward with propositions of peace; first through the mediation of Tunis, then of Algiers; and to call to the defence of his city as many of his Moorish and Arabic subjects as were still in submission.

On the 17th of July, 1802, the brig Franklin, Capt. A. Morris, of Philadelphia, was sent into Bizerte, a port in the kingdom of Tunis, sixty miles from the capital, by sea—and the next day vessel and cargo were put up at public auction in Tunis.

On the 11th, I wrote the advice, which Captain Murray answered, August eighteen. In consequence of which I took the depositions. They day after its date I received the advice from Captain Murray. Notwithstanding the engagements he had entered into with Hamet Bashaw, as appears by his letter of 18th August, he abandoned the enemy's coast the 28th of same month—and from that day, till some time in April or May of the year 1803, no American ship nor vessel of war appeared in sight of Tripoli.

The capture of the Franklin, and the safe arrival to Tripoli of the captives, in sight of the Constellation, gave the court of Tunis a contemptible opinion of the vigilance and enterprize of our frigates. The deserters from the Gloria at Tunis had promulgated the transactions which took place at Gibraltar, respecting this ship, in such a manner that they became known to the Sapatapa. It was a matter of exultation at that piratical court, that the "*American Consul was abandoned by his countrymen.*" And the occasion was seized to "*humble his pride!*"

The ship intended for a cruiser, and part cargo commissioned for by the Sapatapa as part payment for his cargo of oil, had arrived the 13th January, 1802; but were rejected by the minister because I would not furnish passports to his coasters for Tripoli; and by the event of peace, they sunk more than cent. per cent. in value. My project with Hamet Bashaw was considered as blown out. The expense of the Gloria had continued from the 1st of March without produce; and I saw so immediate prospect of relief from this expense; for I could obtain no information from the commodore—though I knew he had arrived at Gibraltar 25th May—and thought he must have been informed of the arrangements made to terminate the war—as the dispatches, conveying the intelligence, arrived at Gibraltar a little before him, and were copied in the consular office there—and as he lay seventy-seven days in that port between the 24th May and 19th August, he must have had ample time to read them.

It was at this juncture of affairs, that the Sapatapa required immediate settlement.

Besides bringing forward the privateer ship and merchandize above mentioned for the minister, I had made him very considerable remittances in cash on the score of the Anna Maria's cargo, and other matters. On presenting my accounts, he struck out the sum before stated, as conditionally engaged for his *secret service.* Against this, I remonstrated; alledging that he had forfeited right to the gratuity on account of having shifted his ground; offered himself as the mediator of peace in behalf of the enemy; and, as I had good reasons to believe, had betrayed to him the whole affair. At any rate, the condition was in no sense fulfilled; and of course no obligation on my part towards him. He affected not to understand any thing about this subject; but insisted on the deduction as an *error!* We had frequently before compared accounts, and agreed. The case went before the Bey. I demanded that the Sapatapa should produce his books in evidence—he said he kept none—he *was not a trader*—but he swore by the head of his master that his statement was honest—his master, of course gave judgment against me—there is no appeal from that decision. Nor could I obtain forbearance. The minister, when retired from the hall of justice, said, with a sarcastic cant, "*we know how to keep Consuls to their promises!*"

It was in this dilemma that I found myself compelled to apply to the commercial agent of the Bey for a loan of 34,000 dollars, on a credit of six months, 2,000 dollars of which were discounted by him for use.

Mr. Cathcart having been made acquainted with the conduct of Capt. Murray, wrote, on the 25th August, a letter to the Department of State. This document will do something to establish what I am desirous of shewing, that our project with Hamet Bashaw was the result of deliberation—and that I acted in concurrence with an agent who held the highest confidence of government.

Thus stood affairs with me until the 8th September, when the Bey of Tunis, as if sedulously calculating to harass my feelings, conceived the project of sending the Gloria to America, with a letter to the President of the U. States, demanding a frigate of thirty-six guns—the letter was accompanied to me with his passport to the ship as a protection against Tripolitans,* and his peremptory order to dispatch her without delay. I availed myself of this protection, at the risque of the Bey's resentment, to send the ship to Leghorn, and ordered the crew discharged—the discussion of the Bey's renewed demand for a frigate, with his minister, and his letter to the President may, at least, add one more proof of the arrogance and exorbitance of his disposition towards the United States as communicated.

Though our ships of war had now all left the coast, I still kept up a correspondence with Hamet Bashaw; till at length he proceeded to Derne, and was affectionately received by his subjects; who renewed their allegiance to him. He now sent two agents to me; one of his generals and his secretary, to bring this intelligence; who arrived about the 1st of December. The Bashaw was soon after joined by a nephew, who had been banished to Cairo, at the head of a multitude of mountain Arabs: so that he found himself with a force sufficient to act against the usurper; and only waited the arrival of our squadron to block him by sea when he should move and invest him by land. His agent had been with me about sixty days, incog. when Commodore Morris appeared, for the first time, February 22d, 1803, in the road of the Golette, for the purpose of contesting the Bey's claim to property, belonging to his subjects, taken upon the Impirial Polacca, the Paulina. The Commodore went on shore under the pledge of the Bey's honour that he should be treated with the same distinctions as officers of the same rank of other friendly powers. After some discussions, he satisfied the Bey's claim, as was supposed; and entered into some engagments with the agents of Hamet Bashaw, for which he held the express sanction of the government. These agents renewed to the United States, in the name of their Sovereign, the condition to deliver the usurper, his family, and admiral into our hands as hostages of peace; and, they assured us, that it only required a force to prevent their escape by sea, to ensure the success of the project; for the subjects of Tripoli were very universally attached to the legitimate Bashaw, and incensed against the usurper for his barbarities. They said the object could be carried without the squadron's firing a gun! The Commodore promised to be before Tripoli in June following, for this purpose. The agents urged more expedition, and wept to urge in vain!

*Those Beys reciprocally respect each other's passports, even an enemy's ship—and as they always give a passport for a year prize vessels when sold, it very much helps the sale of their prizes. [Ray's note]

While with me, I had exhibited to the Commodore a view of my affairs; mentioned to him what I supposed would be the balance, which was 22,000 dollars, due on my note to the Bey's agent, and the cause in which it originated—read to him my letter of 9th November, 1802, to the Department of State, wherein it was stated that I should have need of twenty-three thousand dollars for defraying expences incident to my measures with Hamet Bashaw. He expressed his entire satisfaction with my transactions; and his opinion that government would indemnify me; especially for the amount which the Bey's minister had fraudulently extorted from me, as he had repeatedly heard the commercial agent confess was the case. He was requested, on going to pay his visit of congé to the Bey, to say something to the minister (to whom it appeared the cash was going) to engage his forbearance until I could receive relief from America. This he said he would do. And every thing seemed to have resumed a tranquil appearance at Tunis. But the next morning the Bey's agent came forward with additional claims on the score of the prize; some trifling articles of no great value. A contest of words, contradictions and reproaches ensued on the subject. The parties became incensed against each other. The Commodore left the American house; and, instead of going to take leave of the Bey, as is always customary, and for which carriages were waiting, shaped his course for the marine to embark. It was at this moment of irritation and distrust, that the agent followed after; refused him a passage in his sandals to the Golette, and demanded payment of the balance of my note.

The next day, at the palace, I remonstrated with the Bey against this violation of faith and outrage offered to the dignity of my nation, mingling on the occasion something of those feelings which a sense of the personal indignities I had suffered at his court could not but excite in my own breast, with such plainness as to produce my expulsion from his kingdom. This may, indeed, have been a premeditated matter; for I am conscious that I had rendered myself politically obnoxious both to his and to the resentment of his minister, by having uniformly resisted to their exorbitant exactions. During more than four years agency at that court, I never yielded a concession incompatible with the dignity and interest of my country. This was to them an unprecedented ground to be assumed by a tributary Consul! If, in any instance, I may have made a sacrifice, it has been to parry a certain danger; and chiefly occasioned by the delays of the United States in forwarding their peace stipulations; or to some incident in which I had no volition. Even the Bey himself, notwithstanding his decision in favour of his minister against me, in the case before stated, bore testimony in presence of every American present, to the zeal and integrity of my conduct as an agent, and even expressed his personal respect for me as an honest man; but alledged that my *head was too obstinate*; and said he *must have a consul with a disposition more congenial to the Barbary interests!*

Though I felt no regret in leaving the country, the manner in which I was hurried out of it, left many of my individual concerns unsettled, vastly to my injury. The prohibitions to which I had been previously subjected by the government, in consequence of my adherence to positions relative to the commerce of this regency with the enemy, which duty compelled me to hold, had operated also greatly to my disadvantage; for which there is no remedy.

Having gone through this statement of events, which produced the items of my claim now before this honourable House; and brought into view the most considerable transactions of my agency; both as they relate to my exertions to keep the peace at Tunis, and to assist the operations of the war against Tripoli, I beg it may be considered, that so far as respects the latter, I have been but the chief acting agent of a measure which was recommended and urged by not only Mr. Cathcart, an agent of the government, best acquainted with the probabilities of its success, but by every other agent and citizen of the United States with whom I could consult, and who were entitled to my confidence—a measure ultimately adopted by every commanding officer who has appeared on that station since it took shape, and approved by the Executive. That I have taken no steps in the measure but what resulted from the position on which I was placed, and the nature of my duty; and but what met the concurrence of Mr. Cathcart and such other officers of the government as were on the ground: that so far as my agency had any influence on the measure it succeeded: and that, if we have not experienced all the benefits calculated to result from its full effect, it ought to be attributed to the *inertia* of a commander, or commanders, over whose conduct I had no controul: that it was not apprehended any expences as should be incident to its prosecution would be defrayed out of its success; and that it would be a public saving both of life and property; as would eventually have been the case, if it had been prosecuted with suitable energy.

It may not be improper to recite, that my ship Gloria was to be employed *on this emergency* only till *the arrival of a commodore on the coast*. But it was impossible to imagine his arrival would be delayed eleven months after the plan was mature for execution—or that, on his arrival and finding it in that stage, he should make no effort to give it effect. He was entreated to send only one of his ships with the agents, to the friendly Bashaw, in order to encourage his perseverence until he could bring the whole squadron to co-operate with him. This he refused, on a pretext that the ships were on short rations, and must all accompany him to Gibraltar to provision.

This may have been the case; but it is nevertheless true that the whole squadron lay nine days, after arriving at that port, without taking in even a biscuit or a bucket of water: the commodore was occupied with *His Royal Highness*, the Duke of Kent, soliciting a court of admiralty to adjudicate upon David Valenzin, the Jew, whom he picked out of an Imperial vessel, near Malta. It is true that the first appearance of this commodore before Tripoli, was not till the 22d of May, 1803. It is true, that during this term of a year, from his first arrival on the station, he never burnt an ounce of powder, except at a royal salute fired at Gibraltar, in celebration of the birth day of *His Britannic Majesty*, or on similar occasions. And it is equally true, that during the period of seventeen months he commanded the whole force of the U. States in the Mediterranean, he was only nineteen days before the enemy's port!

I certainly feel no inclination to act the informer: nor would I state these facts were it not that those delinquencies have most deeply affected me, rifled me of my honour, and, for ought I know, reduced me to extreme poverty. Whereas, had I been supported with that energy, nay, with that integrity, which was due to the confidence of the government in the Commander in Chief of the expedition, I should have saved both my honour and my property. I should at least have saved myself the mortification of this appeal to the equity and sensibility of the national legislature. And, it is confidently believed, my country would have experience lasting benefits from my exertions.

It is presumed the project with Hamet Bashaw is still feasible. The very circumstance of his *existence* is evidence of his holding a position formidable to the enemy; for it is well known, a Turkish despot never lets a rival exist whom he can destroy. And, I must be permitted still to adhere to the opinion, which has actuated my conduct in this affair, that it is the most eligible way of securing a permanent peace with that regency; for there is *no faith in treaties with the ruling Bashaw!*

Besides the impression to be made on the world by this species of chastisement, it would have a beneficial influence on the other Barbary regencies. To them the precedent would be dreadful; for it would be no very difficult matter, in case of war, to start a rival in either of those regencies, the government of Algiers being military elective, and the Beylique of Tunis, though hereditary, now held by usurpation. This may account, perhaps, for the Sapatapa having, after deliberation, seceded from his engagements with me in favour of re-establishing the legitimate Bashaw of Tripoli.

But whether the project be yet practicable or not, it is believed, sufficient evidence has been produced to convince the understanding of every one, who is willing to be convinced, that the object which that enterprize aimed to secure, was worth an experiment. With the discretionary instructions I held, I should have thought myself chargeable with a criminal omission, had I not used every effort to secure it: for if a prominent occasion offers which might place the life and dominion of the enemy into our hands, would it not have been treacherous to have neglected it?

It may be asserted, without vanity or exaggeration, that my arrangements with the rival Bashaw did more to harrass the enemy, in 1802, than the entire operations of our squadron. Yet the force sent into the Mediterranean that season, was adequate to all the purposes of war, and, with the favourable positions which had been secured, might have put an end to it in sixty days after arriving at the port, had the arrival been seasonable. This is not my solitary opinion. The Bey of Tunis himself, when hearing of the plan concerted between the Americans and the rival Bashaw, exclaimed—"Seid Joseph is ruined!" meaning the ruling Bashaw of Tripoli. But it is now pretended the enterprize was abandoned on the score of *economy!* Oliver Cromwell *searched the Lord* whenever he had occasion to veil his sinister views from *men! Economy* seems to be the mask of the day with us to disguise the most palpable and inexcusable neglects of duty; for it is hackneyed by every hypocrite whose baseness wants a shield for delinquency; or whose jealousy seeks to blast the merit of that vigilance and energy which cannot but upbraid his remissness. Hence the very commander, who recoils at the prodigality of seeing a single ship employed in the prosecution of a measure which might have decided the fate of the enemy, and at a moment when no alternative existed, seems wholly unconcerned at having employed the whole operative naval force of the United States an entire year, in the Mediterranean, attending the *travels of a woman!*

Let it not be inferred from these strictures, that your petitioner is an infidel to the doctrine of the economy! On the contrary—*he believes*—but not in a misapplication of the term, nor a perversion of the principle. Without the arrogance of believing himself capable of advising—may he not be permitted to ask—if this kind of concern for the public weal should have influence to circumscribe the provisions which the necessary operations of the present moment require on the Barbary coast, will it not betray us into degradations and sacrifices which will be felt by the latest generations of posterity? Can there be a doubt that the regencies are all covertly leagued in the war? Is not the question at issue between them and us, whether we will yield ourselves *tributary*, and subscribe to conditional *articles of slavery*; or take an attitude more analogous to our national glory and interest? Is there a citizen in America who would not rather contribute something extraordinary for an effectual resistance to the pretensions of these Beys, than by an illusive calculation of gaining by withholding those contributions, take the yoke of a Barbary pirate; subscribe to voluntary chains; and leave the blush of ages embalmed on our tombs!

Let my fellow-citizens be persuaded, that there is no bourn to the avarice of the Barbary princes—like the insatiate grave, they can never have enough. Consign them the revenue of the United States as the price of peace, they would still tax our labours for more *veritable expressions of our friendship*. But it is a humiliating consideration to the industrious citizen, the sweat of whose brow supports him with bread, that a tythe from his hard earnings must go to purchase oil of roses to perfume a pirate's beard!

It would be indeed something astonishing that those pitiful hordes of sea-robbers should have acquired such an ascendendency over the small and even considerable states of Christendom, were it not easily accounted for upon commercial principles. It is true, that Denmark and Sweden (and even the United States, following the example) gratuitously furnish almost all their materials for ship-building and munitions of war; besides the valuable jewels and large sums of money we are continually paying into their hands for their forbearance, and for the occasional ransom of captives. Holland and Spain bring them cash, naval constructors, engineers, and workmen, in their dock-yards. Without these resources they would soon sink under their own ignorance and want of means to become mischievous. Why this humiliation! Why furnish them the means to cut our own throats! It is from a degrading counting-house policy in the cabinets of the more powerful nations of Europe, to keep these marauders in existence as a check upon the commercial enterprize of their weak neighbours—and from a principle of a commercial rivalship among the tributaries, which aims to supplant each other in the friendship of these chiefs by the preponderence of bribes: a principle, however, which ultimately defeats its own object—for the Beys, like apostate lawyers, take fees on both sides, and by a rule of intervention, turn their arguments against the client who has the heaviest purse.

But what good reason is there why the United States should follow in the train of those tributaries? We have not chosen to accept the right of free navigation, nor any other of the appendages of liberty as the grant of an European power—and shall we humiliate ourselves to accept them as the fief of a Barbary pirate, because the circumscribed powers of Denmark and Sweden, economical Holland and dormant Spain, afford us precedents? Or because it would be convenient to England and France? I don't know what need we have of Europe any more than that quarter has of us. It is an acknowledged fact, that during the late war, there was a period when the produce of the United States supported the existence of England. If we find her interfering in our foreign relations to the annoyance of our commerce, can we not retaliate the injury by starving her in her own Island? France is, perhaps, more invulnerable; but France has vulnerable points. She may recollect that Achilles perished of a wound in his heel. As for the other nations of Europe, have we not as little to fear as to hope from them? Why not then once more leave the beaten tract of European policy and bad example; and once more demonstrate to the world that we have the means and the enterprize to defend and protect our national rights!

Is the inveteracy of habits an argument against this experiment? What hinders the government of the United States from saying to those piratical descendants from the Isle of Lesbos, as the Romans to a Grecian pirate of antiquity, "Tuta! we can, by our arms, force you to reform the abuses of your bad government?" The enterprize and intrepidity of a Rogers,[15] a Preble, and a Sterrett, have proved to us, that those Mussulmen are no more impregnable to a manly front than other savages.

In addition to the ordinary inducements of the Barbary states to commit piracies on our commerce, there is another incentive equally powerful, which may have escaped the notice of the people of the United States, and yet which affects only us. We are the rivals of Algiers and Tunis, in one principal article of commerce in the Mediterranean; which is bread corn. Immense quantities of that essential life article, are annually shipped from both those regencies to the ports of Spain and Italy; and occasionally to other ports of Christiandom in that sea. This article of commerce at Algiers, as well as all others, is farmed by the Jew house of Bocri and Busnah; who are well known to have a preponderating influence in all the affairs of that government.

At Tunis, the government itself monopolises the entire commerce of the kingdom. In both regencies that rivalship cannot but excite a spirit of hostility to our commerce; more particularly so, as this is the chief article of exportation in both countries; from which the governments receive their principal revenue; and an article which always commands ready sale and cash payment, or advantageous barter.

In case of a rupture with either, or both those regencies, a plentiful supply of this article to those ports in the Mediterranean, and a close blockade of the enemy's ports, might bring them to their senses. It would be next to an invasion of their country, the most wounding blow which could be inflicted. It would convince them that they have as much need of our friendship as we have of theirs. Are not such the principles of reciprocity we should wish to establish?

On the 15th of April, in this year, the Bashaw of Tunis wrote to the President of the United States, for forty pieces of cannon, 24 pounders, &c.

As has been observed, the expedition of Commodore Dale was attended with little or no success. He left the station, and was succeeded by Commodore Morris, in the spring of 1802. The reprehensible conduct of this delatory commodore, is sufficiently exposed in the preceding remarks of Gen. Eaton. It was in April or May when he arrived on the station, and we hear nothing of his making his appearance on the Barbary coast until the February following. These circumstances of his delinquency, and his treatment of Valenzin, the Jew, ought to stamp his character with eternal infamy!

On the 15th of June, the brig Franklin, Captain Morris, from Philadelphia, was captured by a Tripolitan corsair, adjacent to Carthagena; and another American brig, which was in company, got off. On the 26th she was carried into Algiers—of the crew there were eight—they were all loaded with chains.

Extract of a letter from Andrew Morris, Captain of the brig Franklin, to James Leander Cathcart, Esq. Consul of the United States, &c. &c. dated

Tripoli, *July* 22, 1802.

I take this early opportunity to inform you of my capture. I sailed with the brig Franklin, belonging to Messrs. Summerl & Brown, of Philadelphia, from Marseilles, with an assorted cargo for the West-Indies, on the 8th ultimo; and on the night of the 17th following, then off Cape Palos, was boarded by one of three Tripoline corsairs, mounting four carriage and four swivel guns, that sailed from this place on or about the 20th May. I shall pass over the occurrences of that night, as you are well acquainted with the conduct of these barbarians towards the unfortunate that fall into their hands. They proceeded with the prize to Algiers, where we arrived the 26th, and, as I conjecture by the representations of Mr. O'Brien, they were obliged to make a hasty retreat on the 27th following; but not without giving me an additional load of chains. What with calms and contrary winds, we did not reach Biserta, in the neighbourhood of Tunis, until the 7th inst. where, after a tarry of five days, we departed, leaving the brig there in charge of their agent, and arrived here on the 19th inst. Through the interference of Mr. Nissen, his Danish majesty's consul here, I have the liberty of the town, and by a lucky event, a Mr. Bn. M'Donough has claimed my two officers and one seaman, and has obtained their release as British subjects: two more, that were foreigners, which I reported as passengers, have likewise been liberated; so that they have only myself and three seamen captives. You will readily agree with me, that this will lessen the value of the capture to the Bey.

The three galliotts are now all in port; they are to sail immediately; it is said Murad Ruiz, alias Lisle, is to go in one of them, or in a small Italian Polacre, of 12 guns.

THIS year was distinguished by no other events than what have been mentioned; and it would puzzle the most scrutinizing enquirer to find out, what our mighty commodore and his squadron were doing through the whole season: for, as Gen. Eaton says, during the term of a year from his first arrival on the station, he never burnt an ounce of powder, except at a royal salute, fired at Gibraltar, in celebration of the birthday of his Britannic mejesty; and that during the period of 17 months, he commanded the whole force of the United States in the Mediterranean, he was only *nineteen days* before the enemy's port!

On the 22d May, 1803, Commodore Morris, for the first time, made his appearance off Tripoli! And what did he achieve? Nothing: after tarrying 19 days, he returned to his usual employment, and was succeeded in his command by Commodore Preble. During, or in the course of this summer, Capt. Rogers destroyed a Tripolitan corvette, and took a number of prisoners. It was on the 5th of October, when Commodore Preble arrived at Tangier Bay, and I should have mentioned that Capt. Rogers had the command of the squadron from the time Commodore Morris left it, until Preble arrived. His operations off Tripoli, the fate of the Philadelphia, &c. have all been related, and need not a recapitulation.

CHAPTER XV

Sketch of General Eaton's Expedition

Lines Addressed to Gen. Eaton,

On reading the Congressional debate respecting his Golden Medal. Written on board the U. States frigate Essex.

And was it, then, a subject of debate,
With those wise *Solons*, in the house of state,
Whether should *Derne's* conqu'rer stand or fall,
Or matchless bravery meet reward at all?
Whether should Eaton, *unexampled* brave,
Who fought to rescue, and who bled to save
Three hundred captive souls from chains and death,
Whose lives hung, trembling, on a murd'rer's breath,
Whether his name descend to future days,
On the bright *Medal* of a nation's praise?
Or, should his trophies be by all forgot,
Mix with the rubbish of the times, and rot?
"Small was his force, half naked were his foes,
"And, tho' so num'rous, easy to oppose."
Thus argu'd *Randolph; Clay*[1] the same avows,
And fain would pluck the laurel from his brows—
The sword of vict'ry from his hand would wrest,
And tear the badge of valor from his breast;
But, thank them not, though justice still is found,
And grateful honours wreath his temples round.
And was it nought those burning sands t' explore,
Where feet of Christians never trod before?
Where freedom's banners ne'er had been unfurl'd,
Since the bold Romans flourish'd o'er the world?

'Midst fierce Barbarians, whom no laws can bind,
Wild as the waves, and treach'rous as the wind,
To rear that standard and so long defend,
With less than *twelve* on whom he might depend?
To storm a citadel of tenfold might,
And hold that fortress, till the flag of white
Woo'd him to yield it, on the terms of peace—
Who gave his captive countrymen release?
For EATON's boldness first appall'd the foe,
Who, forc'd like Pharaoh, let the people go.
When the blest shade of WASHINGTON, above,
Saw the bold chief thro' Lybian deserts move,
The sword of vengeance waving in the sky,
Resolv'd to free his brethren, or to die,
Those patriot *'lev'n*, attending on his way,
His visage beam'd a more celestial ray;
To WARREN and MONTGOM'RY[2] shew'd the sight,
Then sunk in glory, and absorb'd in light.
Oh! did he live! did *Vernon*'s boast again
Shine in our fields, or in our councils reign,
His voice from Eaton never would withhold,
Altho' with pearls enrich'd, the burnish'd gold;
But by his hand would ardently be prest,
The conscious symbol to his dauntless breast.
Then let mean envy *Randolph*'s spire betray,
And dart thine arrows, impious hand of *Clay!*
The hand of heav'n—for heav'n rewards the brave,
Will bless thee, Eaton, e'en beyond the grave.
While gratitude shall warm Columbia's breast,
Thy name shall live, thy merits stand confest;
Thy deeds shall brighten on th' historic page,
Year after year, and age succeeding age—
Wreaths of thy fame, transferr'd by bards sublime,
Shall bloom forever mid the wrecks of time.

SOME circumstances relative to the origin of this expedition have been already mentioned. The disinterested patriotism, the enterprize, the activity and the intrepidity of this second Laonidas, cannot be too highly appreciated, or too much extolled. Had he not been basely deserted by Com. Barron, who had promised to aid his exertions, he would unavoidably have marched triumphantly to Tripoli, and saved the United States 60,000 dollars, besides a large amount of national honour. The following letter will exhibit a brief statement of the General's co-operations with the Ex-Bashaw, and of his conquest of Derne.

I LEFT the United States in the squadron, in persuance of this project, July 4, 1804. On the 15th November following sailed from Syracuse for Alexandria, Egypt—arrived 28th, proceeded to Grand Cairo; with much difficulty drew Hamet Bashaw from the Mameluke army. In February, formed a camp on the left of Alexandria, consisting of twelve different nations; chiefly Arabs. On the 6th March, entered the desert of Lybia (modern Barca), were fifty days passing to the rear of Derne; during which time we suffered every privation—were twenty-five days without meat, and fifteen without bread, subsisting on half a pint of rice per man. Three days we were without any thing; supporting existence by roots dug in the sand, and by a species of wild fennel and sorrel, which we sometimes found in the ravines. On the 26th April, I summoned the garrison of Derne to surrender; the governor, a Turkish general, laconically answered—"My head, or your's!" On the 27th, I carried the city by assault; early in the charge, in which we turned the flank of, and routed eight hundred Turks with only seventy Christians, I received a ball through my left wrist. At 4, P.M. we were in complete possession of the city; and at 5, my wound was dressed by a surgeon from the brig Argus. On the 13th May, the enemy's army, which had long been preparing for the expedition, attacked us in quarters, and were defeated with great loss and shame; being driven quite to their fortified camp. These events undoubtedly produced the solicitude in Joseph Bashaw for peace with the United States. Though a negociation was opened about the middle of May, no armistice was provided for us on the coast; consequently we continued our hostilities till the 10th of June, every day skirmishing, when the enemy were totally defeated before the walls of Derne; and the next day took flight to the desert, for Upper Egypt. We now received intelligence of peace and ransom; and consequently abandoned the coast, and the unfortunate too credulous friends we had created there. Our object was to have overthrown the usurper at Tripoli, forced a peace with the regency, and to have marched our fellow-citizens in slavery triumphantly from their cells to our fleet. We should have succeeded if we had been fairly seconded. The number of Americans, through the desert and in the assault of the 27th April, was only *eleven*. I had one company of Greeks, recruited in Alexandria; and one company of French artillery, found in the same place. Lieutenant O'Brannon, of the marine corps, and Lieutenant Mann, of the navy, who accompanied me, merit honourable mention.

The vessels employed before Derne were the brig Argus, Captain Hull: the schooner Nautilus, Captain Dent; and the sloop Hornet, Lieutenant Evans—all of whom behaved with distinguished courage and good conduct. Lieutenant Evans, laid his sloop, of six brass sixes only, within pistol shot of a water battery, of nine long nine pounders, and silenced it with grape in three quarters of an hour. During the conflict, a shot from the enemy's battery carried away his ensign halliards. Lieutenant Blodget seized the flag, went up the shrouds, and, amidst an incessant shower of musketry, nailed it to the mast head, without receiving any injury; though, in the transaction, a musket ball lodged in his watch while in his fob—which miracle saved his life.

Those of us who did duty on shore, and had passed the desert, were ninety-five days and nights without undressing, except to change linen.

I am, Sir, very truly,

Your friend and well wisher,

WILLIAM EATON.

Washington, February 22, 1807.

GEN. EATON had entered into stipulations with the Ex-Bashaw to restore him to his throne and his family; and Com. Barron, after having favoured his views and applauded his conduct—after having pledged his faith both to Eaton and the Ex-Bashaw, to give them all the aid which they required, at the moment when they put their designs in execution—at the moment when success attended their first efforts, and their yet immature project, a dishonourable peace is concluded, under the auspices of Barron, who pronounces it a "moment highly favourable to treat of peace," when he had not been in sight of Tripoli for eight months—some of his frigates had not ever been nearer it than Malta; seldom, if ever, more than two of them cruizing off the port, and generally not but one; his squadron had never been displayed to the enemy's view, nor a shot exchanged with the batteries of Tripoli since Com. Preble left the coast, except *en passant;* and what is a truth, equally demonstrable, no visible preparations were making at head-quarters for the investment of the ensuing summer, which could give the enemy any uneasiness.

A concise statement of these facts may be seen in the report of the committee of Congress to whom was referred the petition of Hamet Caramanli, Ex-Bashaw of Tripoli.

Report of the committee to whom was referred the application of
HAMET CARAMANLI, *Ex-Bashaw of Tripoli.*

THE Ex-Bashaw founds his claim on the justice of the U. States, from his services and sufferings in their cause, and from his having been deceived and amused with the prospect of being placed on his throne, as legitimate sovereign of Tripoli, and frequently drawn from eligible situations for the purpose of being made the dupe and instrument of policy, and finally sacrificed to misfortune and wretchedness. The committee, from a full investigation of the documents which have been laid before Congress, with other evidence that has come within their knowledge, are enabled to lay before the Senate a brief statement of facts in relation to the Ex-Bashaw, and the result of their deliberations thereon.

This unfortunate prince, by the treason and perfidy of his brother, the reigning Bashaw, was driven from his throne, an exile to the regency of Tunis; where the agents of the United States in the Mediterranean, found him; and as early as August, eighteen hundred and one, entered into a convention to co-operate with him, the object of which was to obtain a permanent peace with Tripoli, to place the Ex-Bashaw on his throne, and procure indemnification for all expences in accomplishing the same. This agreement was renewed in November following, with encouragement that the United States would persevere, until they had effected the object; and in eighteen hundred and two, when the reigning Bashaw had made overtures to the Ex-Bashaw, to settle on him the two provinces of Derne and Bengazi, and when the Ex-Bashaw was on the point of leaving Tunis, under an escort furnished him by the reigning Bashaw, the agents of the United States prevailed on him to abandon the offer, with assurance that the United States would effectually co-operate and place him on the throne of Tripoli.

The same engagements were renewed in eighteen hundred and three, and the plan of co-operation so arranged, that the Ex-Bashaw, by his own exertions and force, took possession of the province of Derne; but the American squadron, at that time under the command of Commodore Morris, instead of improving that favourable moment, to co-operate with the Ex-Bashaw, and to put an end to the war, unfortunately abandon the Barbary coast, and left the Ex-Bashaw to contend solely with all the force of the reigning Bashaw, and who in consequence was obliged, in the fore part of the year eighteen hundred and four, to give up his conquest of Derne, and fly from the fury of the usurper into Egypt. These transactions were from time to time, not only communicated by our agents to government, but were laid before Congress in February, eighteen hundred and four, in the documents accompanying the report of the committee claims on the petition of Mr. Eaton, late consul at Tunis, which committee expressed their decided approbation of his official conduct, and to which report the committee beg leave to refer.

In full possession of the knowledge of these facts, the government of the United States, in June, eighteen hundred and four, dispatched Commodore Barron with a squadron into the Mediterranean, and in his instructions, submitted to his entire discretion, the subject of availing himself of the co-operation of the Ex-Bashaw, and referring him to Mr. Eaton, as an agent sent out by govornment for that purpose.

After Commodore Barron had arrived on the station in September, eighteen hundred and four, he dispatched Mr. Eaton and Capt. Hull into Egypt to find the Ex-Bashaw, with instructions to assure him that the commodore would take the most effectual measures with the forces under his command, to co-operate with him against the usurper, his brother, and to establish him in the regency of Tripoli. After encountering many difficulties and dangers, the Ex-Bashaw was found in Upper Egypt with the Mamelukes, and commanding the Arabs; the same assurances were again made to him, and a convention was reduced to writing; the stipulations of which had the same objects in view; the United States to obtain a permanent peace and their prisoners; the Ex-Bashaw to obtain his throne. Under these impressions, and with the fullest confidence in the assurances he had received from agents of the United States, and even from Commodore Barron himself, by one of his (the Bashaw's) secretaries, whom he had sent to wait on the Commodore for that purpose, he gave up his prospects in Egypt—abandoned his property in that country, constituted Mr. Eaton General and commander in chief of his forces, and with such an army as he was able to raise and support, marched through the Lybian desert, suffering every hardship incident to such a perilous undertaking; and with his army, commanded by Gen. Eaton, aided by O'Brannon and Mann, three American officers, who shared with him the dangers and hardships of the campaign, and whose names their country will forever record with honour, attacked the city of Derne in the regency of Tripoli, on the twenty-seventh day of April, one thousand eight hundred and five, and after a well fought battle, took the same; and for the first time, planted the American colours on the ramparts of a Tripolitan fort. And in several battles afterwards, one of which he fought without the aid of the Americans, (they having been restrained by orders, not warranted by any policy, issued as appears by Mr. Lear, the American consul,) defeated the army of the usurper, with great slaughter, maintained his conquest, and without the hazard of a repulse, would have marched to the throne of Tripoli, had he been supported by the co-operation of the American squadron, which in honour and good faith he had a right to expect. The committee would here explicitly declare, that in their opinion, no blame ought to attach to Commodore Barron; a wasting sickness, and consequent mental as well as bodily debility, had rendered him totally unable to exercise the duties of commanding the squadron, previous to this momentous crisis, and from which he has never recovered; and to this cause alone may be attributed the final failure of the plan of co-operation, which appears to have been wisely concerted by the government, and hitherto bravely executed by its officers.

But, however unpleasant the task, the committee are compelled by the obligations of truth and duty, to state further, that Mr. Lear, to whom was entrusted the power of negociating the peace, appears to have gained a complete ascendency over the Commodore, thus debilitated by sickness; or rather having assumed the command in the name of the Commodore,* to have dictated every measure to have paralized every military operation by sea and land; and finally, without displaying the fleet or squadron before Tripoli, without consulting even the safety of the Ex-Bashaw or his army, against the opinion of all the officers of the fleet, so far as the committee have been able to obtain the same, and of Commodore Rogers (as appears from Mr. Lear's letter† to the secretary of state, dated Syracuse harbour,

**Extract of a letter from Capt. Dent*—"It was generally believed by the officers in the Mediterranean, that Mr. Lear had a great ascendency over the commodore in all his measures relative to the squadron, and from frequent observations of Mr. Lear's intimacy with the commodore during his debilitated state, I am of the same opinion." [Ray's note]

†"I must here pay a tribute of justice to Commodor Rogers, whose conduct during the negociation on board, was mixed with that manly firmness, and evident wish to continue the war, if it could be done with propriety, while he displayed the magnanimity of an American, in declaring that we fought not for conquest, but to maintain our just rights and national dignity, as fully convinced the negotiators, that we did not ask but grant peace.

"You will pardon me if I here introduce a circumstance evincive of the spirit of our countrymen. At breakfeast this morning Commodore Rogers observed, that if the Bashaw would

July 5th, 1805,) to have entered into a convention with the reigning Bashaw, by which, contrary to his instructions, he stipulated to pay him sixty thousand dollars, to abandon the Ex-Bashaw, and to withdraw all aid and assistance from his army. And although a stipulation was made that the wife and children of the Ex-Bashaw should be delivered to him on his withdrawing from the territories of Tripoli, yet that stipulation has not been carried into execution, and it is highly probable was never intended to be. The committee forbear to make any comment on the impropriety of the order issued to Gen. Eaton to evacuate Derne, five days previous to Mr. Lear's sailing from Malta, for Tripoli, to enter on his negociation; nor will the committee condescend to enter into a consideration of pretended reasons, assigned by Mr. Lear, to palliate his management of the affairs of the negotiation; such as *the danger of the American prisoners in Tripoli, the unfitness of the ships for service, and the want of means to prosecute the war;* they appear, to the committee, to have no foundation in fact, and are used rather as a veil to cover an inglorious deed, than solid reasons to justify the negociator's conduct. The committee are free to say, that in their opinion, it was in the power of the United States, with the force then employed, and at a small portion of the sixty thousand dollars, thus improperly expended, to have placed Hamet Caramanli, the rightful sovereign of Tripoli, on his throne; to have obtained their prisoners in perfect safety,[‡] without the payment of a cent, with assurance, and probable certainty of eventual remuneration for all expence; and to have established a peace with the Barbary powers, that would have been secure and permanent, and which would have dignified the name and character of the American people.

Whatever Hamet, the Ex-Bashaw, may have said in his letter of June 29th, 1805, to palliate the conduct which first abandoned and then ruined him, the Senate cannot fail to discern that he was then at Syracuse, in a country of strangers to his merits, and hostile to his nation and religion, and where every circumstance conspired to depress him; which, together with the fear of starving, left him scarcely a moral agent.

Upon these facts, and to carry into effect the principles of duty arising out of them, the only remuneration now left in the power of the United States to make, the committee here-with present a bill for the consideration of the Senate. The committee are confident that the legislature of a free and Christian country, can never leave it in the power of a Mohometan to say, *that they violate their faith, or*

---

consent to deliver up our countrymen without making peace, he would engage to give him two hundred thousand instead of sixty thousand dollars, and raise the difference between the two sums from the officers of the navy, who he was perfectly assured, would contribute to it with the highest satisfaction." [Ray's note]

‡ *Extract from a letter of Commodore Rogers.*—"I never thought the prisoners were in danger." *Extract from a letter of Lieutenant Wormely, then a prisoner in Tripoli.*—"I do not believe that there was any danger to be apprehended for our lives, even if Gen. Eaton and Hamet Bashaw had have marched under the walls of Tripoli." [Ray's note]

withhold the operations of justice from one who has fallen a victim to his unbounded confidence in their integrity and honour.

THUS betrayed and abandoned by the idle squadron, which had nothing else to do but yield him the promised assistance, the brave General Eaton was obliged to fly from Derne, and the Ex-Bashaw and his army, to escape for their lives. But the universal plaudits bestowed on the General, on his arrival in America, and the approbation of government, are sufficient testimonials of the high sense of merit which the Americans entertain of his services, and must be a great alleviation of the mortifying chagrin which he felt at being so ungenerously deserted in the very extremity of a perilous enterprize. Notwithstanding General Eaton was the chief cause of what they call bringing the Bashaw to *terms*, yet he was never consulted in the negociations of peace; but when the names of Barron, of Morris, and of Lear are lost in oblivion, that of Eaton will shine still more conspicuous on the catalogue of American heroes.

TREATY

Of peace and amity between the United States of America, and the Bashaw, Bey and subjects of Tripoli in Barbary.

ARTICLE 1. There shall be, from the conclusion of this treaty, a firm, inviolable and universal peace and a sincere friendship between the President and citizens of the United States of America, on the one part, and the Bashaw, Bey and subjects of the regency of Tripoli in Barbary, on the other, made by the free consent of both parties, and on the terms of the most favoured nation. And if either party shall hereafter grant to any other nation, any particular favour, or privilege, in navigation or commerce, it shall immediately become common for the other party, freely, where it is freely granted to such other nation; but where the grant is conditional, it shall be at the option of the contracting parties to accept, alter or reject such conditions in such manner as shall be most conducive to their respective interests.

Art. 2. The Bashaw of Tripoli shall deliver up to the American squadron now off Tripoli, all the Americans in his possession; and all the subjects of the Bashaw of Tripoli, now in the power of the United States of America, shall be delivered up to him; and as the number of Americans in possession of the Bashaw of Tripoli, amount to three hundred persons, more or less, and the number of Tripoline subjects in the power of the Americas, to about one hundred, more or less, the Bashaw of Tripoli shall receive from the United States of America, the sum of sixty thousand dollars, as a payment for the difference between the prisoners herein mentioned.

Art. 3. All the forces of the United States, which have been, or may be in hostility against the Bashaw of Tripoli, in the province of Derne, or elsewhere within the dominions of the said Bashaw, shall be withdrawn therefrom, and no supplies shall be given by, or in behalf of the said United States, during the continuance of this peace, to any of the subjects of the said Bashaw, who may be in hostility against him, in any part of his dominions; and the Americans will use all means in their power to persuade the brother of the said Bashaw, who co-operated with them at Derne, &c. to withdraw from the territory of the said Bashaw of Tripoli; but will not use any force or improper means to effect that object; and in case he should withdraw himself as aforesaid, the Bashaw engages to deliver up to him his wife and children now in his power.

Art. 4. If any goods belonging to any nation, with which either of the parties are at war, should be loaded on board vessels, belonging to the other part, they shall pass free and unmolested, and no attempts shall be made to take or detain them.

Art. 5. If any citizens or subjects, with their effects, belonging to either party, shall be found on board a prize vessel, taken from an enemy by the other party, such citizens or subjects shall be liberated immediately, and their effects so captured shall be restored to their lawful owners, or their agents.

Art. 6. Proper passports shall immediately be given to the vessels of both the contracting parties on condition, that the vessels of war belonging to the regency of Tripoli, on meeting with merchant vessels, belonging to citizens of the United States of America, shall not be permitted to visit them with more than two persons at a time, besides the rowers; these two only shall be permitted to go on board, without first obtaining leave from the commander of said vessel, who shall compare the passport and immediately permit said vessel to proceed on her voyage; and should any of the said subjects of Tripoli insult or molest the commander or any other person on board a vessel so visited, or plunder and of the property contained in her, on complaint being made by the consul of the United States of America resident at Tripoli, and on his producing sufficient proof to substantiate the fact, the commander or rais of said Tripoline ship or vessel of war, as well as the offenders, shall be punished in the most exemplary manner. All vessels of war belonging to the United States of America on meeting with a cruiser belonging to the regency of Tripoli, on having seen her passport and certificate from the consul of the United States of America residing in the regency, shall permit her to proceed on her cruize unmolested, and without detention. No passport shall be granted by either party to any vessels, but such as are absolutely the property of citizens or subjects of said contracting parties, on any pretence whatever.

Art. 7. A citizen or subject of either of the contracting parties, having bought a prize vessel, condemned by the other party, or by any other nation, the certificate of condemnation and bill of sale, shall be a sufficient passport for such vessel for two years, which, considering the distance between the two countries, is no more than a reasonable time for her to procure proper passports.

Art. 8. Vessels of either party, putting into the ports of the other, and having need of provisions or other supplies, they shall be furnished at the market price; and if any such vessel should so put in, from a disaster at sea, and have occasion to repair, she shall be at liberty to land and re-embark her cargo, without paying any duties; but in no case shall be compelled to land her cargo.

Art. 9. Should a vessel of either party be cast on the shore of the other, all proper assistance shall be given to her and her crew. No pillage shall be allowed, the property shall remain at the disposition of the owners, and the crew protected and succoured, till they can be sent to their country.

Art. 10. If a vessel of either party shall be attacked by an enemy within gun shot of the forts of the other, she shall be defended as much as possible. If she be in port, she shall not be seized or attacked when it is in the power of the other party to protect her; and when she proceeds to sea, no enemy shall be allowed to persue her from the same port, within twenty-four hours after her departure.

Art. 11. The commerce between the United States of America and the regency of Tripoli; the protection to be given to merchants, masters of vessels and seamen; the reciprocal right of establishing consuls in each country, and the privileges, immunities and jurisdictions, to be enjoyed by such consuls, are declared to be on the same footing with the most favoured nations respectively.

Art. 12. The consul of the United States of America shall not be answerable for debts contracted by citizens of his own nation, unless he previously gives a written obligation so to do.

Art. 13. On a vessel of war, belonging to the United States of America, anchoring before the city of Tripoli, the consul is to inform the Bashaw of her arrival, and she shall be saluted with twenty-one guns, which she is to return in the same quantity or number.

Art. 14. As the government of the United States of America has, in itself, no character of enmity against the laws, religion or tranquility of Mussulmen, and as the said states never have entered into any voluntary war or act of hostility against any Mahometan nation, except in the defence of their just rights to freely navigate the high seas, it is declared by the contracting parties, that no pretext arising from religious opinions shall ever produce an interruption of the harmony existing between the two nations. And the consuls and agents of both nations respectively, shall have the liberty to exercise his religion in his own house. All slaves of the same religion shall not be impeded in going to said consul's house, at hours of prayer. The consuls shall have liberty and personal security given them, to travel within the territories of each other, both by land and sea, and shall not be prevented from going on board any vessel that they may think proper to visit. They shall have likewise the liberty to appoint their own drogoman and brokers.

Art. 15. In case of any dispute arising from the violation of any of the articles of this treaty, no appeal shall be made to arms; nor shall war be declared on any pretext whatever; but if the consul residing at the place where the dispute shall happen, shall not be able to settle the same, the government of that country shall state their grievances in writing, and transmit it to the government of the other; and the period of the twelve calender months shall be allowed for answers to be returned, during which time no act of hostility shall be permitted by either party; in case the grievances are not redressed, and a war should be the event, the consuls and citizens, or subjects of both parties reciprocally, shall be permitted to embark with their effects unmolested, on board of what vessel or vessels they shall think proper.

Art. 16. If in the fluctuation of human events, a war should break out between the two nations, the prisoners captured by either party shall not be made slaves, but shall be exchanged rank for rank. And if there should be a deficiency on either side, it shall be made up by the payment of five hundred Spanish dollars for each captain, three hundred dollars for each mate and supercargo, and one hundred Spanish dollars for each seaman so wanting. And it is agreed that prisoners shall be exchanged in twelve months from the time of their capture; and that the exchange may be effected by any private individual legally authorised by either of the parties.

Art. 17. If any of the Barbary states, or other powers, at war with the United States of America, shall capture any American vessel, and send her into any of the ports of the regency of Tripoli, they shall not be permitted to sell her, but shall be obliged to depart the port, on procuring the requisite supplies of provisions; and no duty shall be exacted on the sale of prizes, captured by the vessels sailing under the flag of the United States of America, when brought into any port of the regency of Tripoli.

Art. 18. If any of the citizens of the United States, or any persons under their protection, shall have any disputes with each other, the consul shall decide between the parties, and whenever the consul shall require any aid or assistance from the government of Tripoli to enforce his decisions, it shall immediately be granted to him; and if any dispute shall arise between any citizen of the United States and the citizens or subjects of any other nation, having a consul or agent in Tripoli, such disputes shall be settled by the consuls or agents of the respective nations.

Art. 19. If a citizen of the United States should kill or wound a Tripoline; or, on the contrary, if a Tripoline shall kill or wound a citizen of the United States, the law of the country shall take place, and equal justice be rendered, the consul assisting at the trial. And if any delinquent shall make his escape, the consul shall not be answerable for him in any manner whatever.

Art. 20. Should any of the citizens of the United States of America, die within the limits of the regency of Tripoli, the Bashaw and his subjects shall not interfere with the property of the deceased, but it shall be under the immediate directions of the consul, unless otherwise disposed of by will. Should there be no consul, the effects shall be deposited in the hands of some person worthy of trust, until the party shall appear who has a right to demand them, when they shall render an account of the property. Neither shall the Bashaw or his subjects give hindrance in the execution of any will that may appear.

[*Signed with the names of both the contracting parties.*]

List of the Naval Force

Which might have been employed before Tripoli, by the middle of July, actually at rendezvous at Syracuse, the fourth and eleventh.—

Frigates—	
1 President,	44 guns.
2 Constitution,	44
3 Congress,	36 guns.
4 Constellation,	36
5 Essex,	32
6 John Adams,	32
Brigs.—	
1 Argus,	18
2 Syren,	18
3 Vixen,	14
4 Franklin,	8
Schooners.—	
1 Enterprize,	14
2 Nautilus,	14
Sloop.—	
1 Hornet,	8

Carrying in all 318 guns & mortars

Gun-Boats from the United States.—

No. 1 not sail'd.

Nos. 2, 3, 4, 5, 6.

7 not arrived.

Nos. 8, 9.

Gun-boats from Tripoli—two.

Gun-boats from the Adriatic—six.

Total number of guns, including 33 belonging to the gun-boats, 351.

Commodore Preble attacked Tripoli successfully with less than one third this force; and with no collateral circumstances in his favour.

This force, in co-operation with Eaton and the Ex-Bashaw, would undoubtedly have coerced the tyrant of Tripoli in a very short time.

The size of this volume will not admit of my mentioning much more of the public transactions of the United States with Tripoli; but as the case of David Valenzin, the Jew, has been hinted at, I shall here insert the report of the committee of claims, to whom was referred the petition of the said David Valenzin; by which it will be seen, that it was the evident intention of Commodore Morris, and some other gentlemen of the navy, to have defrauded him of his cash, as they had of his liberty—that he was suffered to languish in painful suspense for a long time, destitute of food and clothing, when in fact he had two thousand sixty-four dollars and eleven cents in the bank of discount and deposit, in the place where he was; and that this cruel treatment was the cause of his death.

Report

Of the Committee of Claims, to whom was referred the petition of David Valenzin.

Under the particular circumstances of this case, your committee feel it is a duty they owe to the House and to themselves, not only to present the facts which have governed their opinion, but also to state minutely the whole progress of the enquiry.

The petition was referred to the committee on the 10th day of November, 1804. It was accompanied by no evidence whatever. Neither the petitioner, nor any person in his behalf, appeared to exhibit proof in support of the claim, or to point out the source from which it might be obtained. It was not even known to any member of the committee by whom the petition was presented. On the 15th November, the committee thought proper to transmit the petition to the Secretary of the Navy, with a request that he would furnish whatever evidence might exist in his department, respecting the transactions complained of by the petitioner. The answer of the Secretary was necessarily delayed until Commodore Morris, who was then in the Potomac, and hourly expected, should arrive in this city. On the 30th November, the committee received from the Secretary the documents which accompanied their former report. The only information derived from these documents, which could reflect any light upon the subject, was a declaration subscribed by Commodore Morris, in which it was stated that on the 17th January, 1803, Lieut. Sterrett, by his order, captured and brought in for trial the Imperial polacca Paulina, Lucca Radish, master, bound from Malta to Tripoli, having on board Tripoline subjects, among whom was David Valenzin, the petitioner, who appeared principal in the charter-party and claimant of the greater part of the cargo; that the commodore attempted to procure an adjudication of the prize at Malta, but was refused by the governor of that island; that he then proceeded to Gibraltar, in the hope of trying the validity of the capture at that place, but the Duke of Kent, then governor of Gibraltar, declined taking cognizance of the affair; that he was compelled in consequence to send the papers with the Tripolitan to America; that David Valenzin was, at the time of the capture, a subject of the Bey of Tripoli, the papers which had been secreted by him, clearly proving to him to be such; and that he was declared to be so both by Mr. Cathcart and his own servant.

From this reputation alone the committee did not feel themselves justified in recommending any relief for the petitioners; at the same time apprehensive that other facts might exist material in the case, they delayed their report until the 12th December, when, no further evidence appearing, the report, with the papers received from the navy department, was presented to the House. Upon the suggestion of a member in his place, that the petitioner had expressed to him a desire to be heard before the committee, and that evidence would be adduced to establish the claim, the report and petition were ordered to be recommitted. The committee convened the next morning, and the petitioner appeared, attended by a stranger, who being acquainted with the petitioner's language, had kindly offered to assist him as an interpreter. The petitioner then declared himself a Jew, born at Venice; that his mother dying when he was sixteen years old, his father removed to Tripoli, where he established himself as a merchant; that his brother and himself arriving to years of maturity, left their father and commenced business at Rosetta, in Egypt, from whence, for many years past, they had carried on a circuitous Traffic with Tripoli, through Smyrna and Malta; that in one of these voyages he was captured by the American squadron, divested of all his property and papers, and sent a prisoner to this country, where he had long expected a trial; that he had been offered his liberty, by the Secretary of the Navy, and a passage to the Mediterranean, in a public vessel, which he had declined until the legality of his capture should be determined; that he knew not what disposition had been made of his effects, nor in what way to obtain his papers.

After hearing the petitioner, the committee the same morning addressed a letter to the Secretary of the navy, requesting further information in the case, if in his power to furnish it; particularly, what disposition had been made of the polacca? For what purpose Valenzin had been brought a prisoner to the United States? And in whose possession were his papers, if any were found upon him at the time of his capture? The answer, which is said to furnish the only official information, relative to the case, existing in that department, contained a letter from Daniel C. Heath, prize-master on board the polacca. This letter, the writer of which, it is understood, immediately left the city on a furlough, barely states that the prize, by order of Commodore Morris, had been delivered up to Lucca Radish, her commander; that he knew not why Valenzin was brought hither as a prisoner; and that his papers were committed to the care of Lieut. Sterrett. As no notice was taken in this letter of the petitioner's property, the committee were left to conclude that it had passed with the polacca into the hands of her captain, nor were they undeceived in this respect until some time afterwards. They also remained ignorant in whose hands the papers were deposited until the morning of the 27th December, when, by accident, they learned that the marshal of the district of Maryland had them in his custody. The committee made no delay in communicating this fact to the House. A resolution was instantly adopted, empowering the committee to send for such persons and papers as might be necessary to the investigation of the claim. They availed themselves of this authority by issuing their warrant and dispatching a messenger to Baltimore the next day. He returned on the 30th with all the papers and documents said to have been found on board the polacca at the time she was captured.

These were numerous, written partly in Arabic, partly in a corrupt dialect of the Italian, spoken on the coast of Barbary, and wholly unintelligible to every member of the committee. By the aid, however, of two gentlemen in the House acquainted with the Italian language, they were enabled to make some progress in translating a few of what appeared the most important documents. Whilst the committee were thus employed, Commodore Morris, who had taken his departure shortly after his communication already mentioned, returned to this city, and at the request of the committee, immediately appeared before them. He repeated the statement he had before given, and seemed confident that the petitioner was a Tripolitan, rightfully captured, and his property lawful prize; that he had two complete setts of papers, the one clearly shewing him to be a subject of Tripoli; the other, of a more recent date, fraudulently calculated to prove him a subject of the Emperor of Germany; the latter being readily produced by him at the time of his capture, whilst the former were found concealed in the bottom of a cask. He added, that as the polacca was not in a condition to cross the Atlantic, he had ordered her to be delivered to Lucca Radish, the master; and *as the property taken from the petitioner was of a perishable nature, he had directed it to be sold at Malta, for the benefit of the captors.* The committee being thus, for the first time, informed of the sale of the petitioner's property, were particular in their enquiries as to its amount, and the manner and proceeds of the sale. To these enquiries the commodore made no other answer than by referring the committee to Mr. Heath, the prize-master, who, he made no doubt, would furnish all the necessary information on the subject. Mr. Heath, it appeared, had left Washington the 20th December, the day on which his letter to the Secretary of the Navy was delivered to the committee, nor could it be ascertained by the most diligent enquiries, in what direction he had gone. This circumstance, added to the extreme difficulty of decyphering the petitioner's papers; the doubtful evidence which resulted even from such as could be translated, and the reserve, manifested by those who possessed originally the means of information, served to produce a delay which the committee deeply regretted, but which, by their utmost efforts, they could not avoid. Being informed that William Eaton, Esq. late consul at Tunis, was daily expected in Washington; that he had seen the petitioner in the Mediterranean, and was well acquainted with his language, the committee indulged a hope that from him, at least, some useful information might at length be derived.

Meanwhile it was perceived that the petitioner's apparel was not such as to render him comfortable during the inclemency of the season; believing the government bound to provide him with necessary food and clothing until the proper measures were taken for his liberation, the committee on the 5th January, addressed a letter to the Secretary of the Navy, in which they freely communicated to him the embarrassments they experienced in the investigation—the further delay which must inevitably attend it—the destitute condition of the petitioner—and requesting to be informed whether, as the head of a department, he did not consider it compatible with his duty to make some temporary provision for the petitioner's relief. To this letter an answer was received the 17th of the same month.

On that day Mr. Eaton, who had just arrived, attended the committee. He assisted them in further translating the Italian, but was unable to interpret the Arabic originals, the import of which is still undiscovered. From an attentive examination of the papers, one circumstance appeared strongly marked. In such as bore date prior to the commencement of hostilities between the United States and Tripoli, wherever the petitioner's name occurred, he was uniformly denominated *a subject of Tripoli.* In those dated subsequent to that event that he was uniformly styled an *Austrian* or *Imperial subject.* The former are those which were said to be secreted at the time of his capture. Amongst the latter is a passport, purporting to be signed by the Imperial Consul at Rosetta. The unfavourable presumption which naturally arose from conduct so equivocal, was in some measure removed by the remarks of Mr. Eaton; who declared it as his opinion, that *Jews,* (and the petitioner was evidently of the number) throughout the coasts of the Mediterranean, were not considered as the proper subjects of any nation: particularly that none of the Barbary powers would, in any case, recognise them as such—unless for some special or mercenary purpose; and finally, that the petitioner appeared to him one of those *sea-pedlars* (such was his expression), who are frequently found in that part of the world, but whose residence is never known.

At this stage of the enquiry your committee did not deem it so essential to decide the propriety of the original capture, as to discover whether the captors had conformed to the requirements of law, in relation to the prisoner or the prize. No certain evidence had yet been obtained of the amount and value of the property taken—nor indeed of its actual sale.

Accidentally hearing, on the 17th January, that the account of sales had been returned to the navy department, and the proceeds deposited in the bank, the committee immediately wrote a letter to the Secretary of the Navy, desiring information on these points. His answer, of the next day, did not communicate the information desired, inasmuch as no returns, it seemed, had been made to that department. The secretary, however, mentions that he had heard, informally, a sum of money had been deposited in the bank by the prize-master, which was said to have proceeded from the sale of Valenzin's property.

The presence of Mr. Heath now appeared to your committee indispensable. A suggestion that he might be at Havre-de-Grace, or at Dover, had induced them to write him as early as the 11th January, directed to both those places, but without success. On the 19th the committee made out their warrant, and sent a messenger in pursuit of him. On the morning of the next day, it is understood, the unfortunate petitioner, in a moment of insanity, put a period to his own existence!

Notwithstanding this melancholy catastrophe, your committee have thought it their duty to complete, as far as might be in their power, the enquiry they had thus far pursued; and as the messenger returned with Mr. Heath on Sunday last, they have since proceeded to take his examination, which is subjoined, and which appears to be a free disclosure of all the circumstances attending his management of the prize. He testifies, after explaining the time and manner of the capture, that

David Valenzin, and several other prisoners, were put on board the Enterprize, and sent to Tunis; from which place he received the order of Commodore Morris, to deliver to the Bey of Tunis, or his order, the greater part of the cargo. The residue being the property of David Valenzin, and but a small proportion of it in a perishing condition, was sold by order of the commodore, and the sales completed by the 8th June, 1803. The gross amount of sales was $2,665 70—the nett proceeds, after deducting five doubloons paid to Commodore Morris, leaving a balance of 2,064 dollars 11 cts. was by him deposited, with the approbation of the Secretary of the Navy, in the bank of discount and deposit in this city, on the 17th December, 1803. On which day also he left his papers relative to the disposal of the cargo with Mr. Goldsborough, clerk in the navy department.

From the whole evidence, thus collected, your committee are clearly of opinion, that in whatever light the original capture is to be viewed, the disposition of the prize was irregular and illegal. If it was the intention of the captors to consummate their right to the property captured, it was obviously their duty to transmit the same, accompanied by the necessary papers, without delay, to the United States, for adjudication. Even admitting the propriety of selling such of the prize goods as were in a perishing condition, still the residue, with the proceeds of such as were necessarily sold, might and ought to have been thus transmitted at the time the prisoner was sent to the United States. By the sale of the property under the attending circumstances, it is worthy of consideration, whether a serious, if not an insurmountable obstacle may not have been created to a trial of the validity of the capture in a court of maritime jurisdiction. To subject the claimant or claimants to the inconvenience and expence of seeking redress from the ordinary courts of law in a case so situated, can be neither right nor reasonable. Justice, therefore, evidently requires that provision be made by the legislature for their indemnification.

Your committee are also of opinion, that until David Valenzin was duly liberated from his imprisonment, an obligation rested upon the government of the United States to provide for his decent support; and that of course, the individuals who have generously contributed to his necessities, and who have defrayed the expence of his interment, ought to be remunerated. With these impressions, your committee respectfully offer to the House the following resolutions, viz.

Resolved, That provision ought to be made by law for restoring to the legal representatives of David Valenzin, the value of the property captured from him in the Mediterranean, by the American squadron, in the month of January, 1803.

Resolved, That provision ought to be made by law for indemnifying the individuals who, during the imprisonment of the said David Valenzin, contributed to his support—and who have defrayed the expences of his interment.

CHAPTER XVI

Return Home

I HAVE before mentioned, that on the 5th of June, 1805, I entered on board the United States frigate Essex, of which Capt. Cox was then commander. The next morning we sailed for Syracuse, and arrived there a few days after. There were a great number sick on board the ship, and two of the Philadelphia's crew, James Ingalson and John Garrabant, soon after died. This place was the rendezvous of our squadron. There we lay till about the middle of July. While here I went ashore, and meeting a Mr. Irving, we proposed visiting the cave of Dionysius. We hired a boy to conduct us thither for a quarter of a dollar; it is about two miles from town. We passed through several very pleasant gardens, groves of orange trees, and beautiful vineyards. When we came to the entrance of the cave, he struck fire and lighted a torch. We entered it by a gradual descent. It is hewn out of a solid rock. I do not exactly know the dimensions of it; but should suppose it to be about 100 feet in length, 40 in breadth and 30 in height. At the top it is quite narrow, and at the farthermost end of it is a winding communication to the palace of the tyrant, where he used to sit and sate his infernal ears with the groans of his subjects. This communication, from its ingenious construction, is called Dionysius' ear. It is formed in such a winding manner as to convey a low whisper, to the apartment above, in distinct accents. Our guide fired off a pistol, which made a report louder than a 24 pounder in the open air. Here are to be seen the staples and rings in the sides of the wall, where the wretched victims of a despot's cruelty were often fastened, to groan out their lives in tortures, merely for the amusement of their tormentor. They were placed in an erect posture against the wall—an iron ring around their necks—their arms extended and pinned to the wall, and their feet chained to the floor. In this situation many a hapless wretch, without the least shadow of a crime, has wasted his life in fruitless lamentations and excruciating agonies. Just released from Turkish slavery, the reflections and sensations, which a sight like this inspired, are to be conceived, but not described.

Contiguous to the cave is a spacious amphitheatre, cut out of the like stone. It is covered with moss, and very much decayed.

On our return we visited the catacombs. Their entrance is through a Church, where we found a grey old Italian, who lighted a torch, and conducted us into this subterraneous repository of the dead. It is partitioned into vaults—about twelve feet wide, arched, and between seven and eight feet in height.

From the time I was liberated from Tripoli, until my arrival in America, I was considered as, and did the duty of captain's clerk. As I contemplate publishing a pamphlet, supplementary to this volume, I must beg to be excused for an absent conclusion.

Poetry,

PUBLISHED IN
The Albany Register,
DURING THE SUMMER OF 1807

WILLIAM RAY

Independence

Tune—"*Anacreon in Heaven.*"[1]

More free than the Mohawk that glides thro' our plains,
 Republicans! meet round this joyous libation;
From freedom-blest millions resound the bold strains—
 From earth-tilling peasants, the lords of our nation,
  Loud echoes to fame,
  The day shall proclaim,
  That gave Independence her blood-written name,
And own'd Nature's equal eternal decree—
Heav'n ne'er form'd you slaves—man was born to live free.

While Jefferson o'er us sublimely sits head,
 No treason the league-union'd states can dissever;
Of freedom the guardian—of tyrants the dread.
 His name will grow dearer and dearer forever;
  When world cannot save—
  Green garlands shall wave,
  And Liberty blossom o'er Jefferson's grave,
To prove nature's equal eternal decree—
Heav'n ne'er form'd us slaves—man was born to live free.

From no haughty lordlings our tenures we hold,
 From natives we bought the rich soil we inherit,
Our great and our mighty—the wise and the bold,
 The badge of their pow'r is the pledge of their merit;
  If, traitors, they yield
  The blood-purchas'd field
  No wealth shall avail them—no dignity shield;
They curse Nature's equal eternal decree—
Heav'n ne'er form'd us slaves—man was born to live free.

Where late yell'd the savage, and wolves howl'd for prey,
 Gay villages rise and the arts flourish round us;
And science forth beams like the dawning of day,
 Nor earth holds our commerce, nor ocean can bound us;
  Lo! India's vast shore
  Our seamen explore!
  See Lybia's wild deserts an Eaton march o'er!
To prove Nature's equal eternal decree—
Heav'n ne'er form'd us slaves—man was born to live free.

Those heav'n-belov'd heroes, who fought, bled and died,
To give us our wisdom-built free constitution,
Stars mounting, the ruins of time shall outride—
Their virtues out-blazon the earth's dissolution!
Through death's darkest gloom
Fresh laurels shall bloom,
And youth spring immortal from Washington's tomb
To prove Nature's final eternal decree—
Heav'n ne'er form'd us slaves—man was born to live free.

Then free as yon Mohawk that glides through the plains,
Republicans! meet round this joyous libation;
From freedom-blest millions resound the bold strains—
From earth-tilling peasants, the lords of our nation,
Loud echoes to fame,
The day shall proclaim,
That gave Independence her blood-written name,
And own'd Nature's equal eternal decree—
Heav'n ne'er form'd us slaves—man was born to live free.

Amsterdam, July 4, 1807.

War; or a Prospect of It,

From recent instances of British outrage.

Vot'ries of Freedom, arm!
The British Lion roars!
Legions of valor, take th' alarm—
Rush, rush to guard our shores!

Behold the horrid deed—
Your brethren gasping lie!
Beneath a tyrant's hand they bleed—
They groan—they faint—they die.

Vet'rans of seventy-six,
Awake the slumb'ring sword!
Hearts of your murd'rous foes transfix—
'Tis vengeance gives the word.

Remember Lexington,
And Bunker's tragic hill;
The same who spilt your blood thereon,
Your blood again would spill.

Ye who have seen your wives,
Your children, and your sires,
To British ruffians yield their lives,
And roast in savage fires;

Our cities lost in flames—
Your mothers captive led—
Rise and avenge their injur'd names,
Ye kindred of the dead.

But not Revenge alone,
Should urge you to the field!
Let Duty lead you firmly on,
And Justice be your shield.

Sure as we sail to join
And crush our impious foes,
War, fire and sword, and death combine,
And woes succeed to woes.

Behold, with blushes red,
    The sea like blood appears;
Our streams are bridg'd with fancied dead,
    And brim'd with orphans' tears;

But union can perform
    The wonders of a host—
Avert the danger, quell the storm,
    And drive them from our coast.

Unite, and side by side
    Meet vict'ry or your graves;
That moment we in War divide,
    That moment we are slaves.

July 20, 1807.

Cash

Wise moralists in vain have told
How sordid is the love of gold,
    Which they call filthy trash;
Thou stranger of these eyes of mine,
Ten thousand virtues still are thine,
    Thou all-sufficient cash!

Though they intrinsic worth be small,
Yet, money, thou art all in all—
    Though transient as a flash,
In passing just from hand to hand,
The earth is at thy sole command—
    It gravitates to cash.

Possess'd of thee, we may defy
Not death itself—but very nigh,
    For when the tyrant's lash
Is felt (and ah! 'twas felt by me)
It *did*—it *will* the vassal free—
    Then who despises cash?

By nature void of ev'ry grace,
If thou hast (reader! view thy face)
    But this cosmetic wash;
'Twill whiten and improve the skin,
Thy monkey-nose, thy cheeks, thy chin,
    Are beautified by cash.

And though your mental pow'rs be weak,
(To you who money have I speak)
    Ne'er fear to cut a dash;
For men of genius and of sense,
If *poor*, will make a *poor* defence
    Against the man of cash.

Or, should you for the basest crimes,
Become indicted fifty times,
    This settles all the hash;
For bills which leave the poor no hope
T' escape the dungeon, or the rope,
    Are cancell'd, all, by cash.

Nay, 'twill be found that money can
The grovelling beast transform to man,
    Though diff'rent natures clash;
For 'tis a fact beyond dispute,
The miser's far beneath the brute—
    A lump of living CASH.

And yet what crowds around him wait—
Behold him cloth'd in pow'r and state—
    The garter, star and sash;
Fools fly before the potent nod
Of him whose flesh, whose soul, whose God,
    Whose heav'n itself is CASH.

But, sons of Plutus, lest you go
To those infernal *mines* below,
    Where teeth are said to gnash,
Give to the needy—bribe the grave—
O, if you wish your souls to save,
    Be gen'rous of your CASH.

Triumph of Principles

In the election of Governor T*OMPKINS*.—Quidism deprecated.

CALL'D to the governmental chair,
By half a million's voice;
A character so bright, so fair,
Is worthy of the choice.

A name, expiring envy owns,
Has robb'd her of her breath;
And fell detraction vents her groans,
As in the pangs of death.

And malice casts a dying glance,
And bites her serpent-tongue—
For all she ever could advance,
Was—"*Tompkins is too young!*"

And youth is an atrocious crime,
—Devoid of sense or wit—
So Walpole, on a certain time,
Declar'd to William Pitt.

When William, saucy youth, replied,
Though vast your life appears,
Your crimes, your follies and your pride,
Are equal to your years.

No matter whether *young* or *old*—
Where born, of *whom* or *when;*
For true republicans all hold
To *principles*—not *men*.

And now, while war impending low'rs,
And threatens to descend;
From discord, O ye gracious pow'rs,
Our citizens defend.

From governors, though grey with age,
Who base apostates' prove,
And sacrifice to party rage
Their patriotic love:

From senators who strive to bribe
The councils of the state,
And all the treason—sav'ring tribe,
However *would-be* great:

From demagogues of ev'ry name,
Who all their arts employ,
The people's passions to enflame—
The people to destroy.

The monarchist, we often find,
Is loyal to his king;
The hog acts after his own kind,
The scorpion hath his sting:

Some fed'ralists are men of *worth*,
Some virtues have, though hid;
But, of all animals on earth,
O save us from the *Quid!*

To the Memory of Commodore Preble

While war, fierce monster, stain'd with guiltless blood,
Roars, threats, and rages round th' infuriate flood;
While hostile Britons murd'ring fleets employ
T' infest our harbours and our ships destroy—
Impress our tars in their inglorious cause,
In base defiance of all nations' laws;
When each bold vet'ran, in his country's name,
Is call'd to save her freedom and her fame;
When few whose brav'ry and whose nautic skill
Can duly execute her sovereign will;
What sighs of sorrow waft from shore to shore,
With these sad tidings—"*Preble is no more!*"

Erst when mad Tripoli, in prowess vain,
With her rapacious corsairs block'd the main;
Pour'd round our ships in predatory swarms,
With purple banners and audacious arms—
Our neutral cargoes plunder'd on the waves,
And made our free-born citizens her slaves;
When our late frigate groan'd upon the shoals,
So deeply freighted with three hundred souls,
Who sigh'd in durance till yon lamp of night
Full twenty changes had renew'd its light,
'Twas *Preble* first that dauntless squadron led,
Where *Somers* perish'd, and *Decatur* bled;
Where *Wadsworth, Israel,* met in death their fate,
With kindred martyrs equally as great;
'Twas *Preble* first those barb'rous pirates show'd—
Justice *was all the tribute that we ow'd,*
And prov'd that when Columbia vengeance bears,
'Tis nought but *merry* that the victim spares.

Let British bards, in mercenary lays,
Chaunt forth elegiac strains to Nelson's praise;
Though oft victorious, and though madly brave,
He fought that tyranny might crush the slave;
He fought that tyrants o'er the world might rule,
And died a mad-man, as he liv'd a fool.

But *Preble*'s cause e'en heav'n itself might own,
In heav'n 'tis cherish'd, and through earth 'tis known!
In heav'n 'tis warbled from enraptured choirs,
It charms their numbers, and it tunes their lyres—

The cause of FREEDOM—dear to him who knows
The adverse horrors, and the poignant woes
Of slav'ry, dungeons, hunger, stripes and chains,
With dismal prospects of augmented pains!
To free the captive, noble, gen'rous deed,
Who would not swear to fight, or sigh to bleed?
To free the captive, *Preble* wing'd his aid,
And greater valor never was display'd.
When round our prison's solitary walls
Burst the dread meteor-bomb-shells—rain'd the balls!
Our hearts for liberty or death beat high,
And who for freedom would not wish to die?
To him we look'd, on him our hopes relied—
The friend of seamen, and the seamen's pride;
To him we look'd, and righteous heav'n implor'd
To speed the vengeance of his slaught'ring sword;
Nor is he now, though vain his efforts prov'd,
The less lamented or the less belov'd;
But each late captive, year succeeding year,
Will bless his mem'ry, and his name revere.

Yes, gallant chief! though virtuous, just and brave,
Thine is the lot of man—the dreary grave!
With heroes sainted, who have gone before,
Like them we prized thee, and like them deplore!
And though thine arm, of Barb'ry once the dread,
Lies cold and wither'd 'midst the unconcious dead,
Unfading laurels at thy name shall bloom,
Spring from thy dust, and flourish round thy tomb!

Lamented chief! though death be calmly past,
Our Navy trembled when he breath'd his last!
Our Navy mourns him, but it mourns in vain,
A *Preble* ne'er will live—ne'er die again!
Yet hope desponding, at the thought revives,
A second *Preble!*—a *Decatur* lives!
His worth, *his* merit, *well* are understood,
His hand is skilful and his heart is good;
Bold shall he chase yon demons of the wave,
For all who know him—know him to be brave.

To him Columbia casts her streaming eyes,
Wipes their free torrent, and suspends her sighs.

September 7th, 1807.

Spring

[*Published in the* Northern *Budget*—Troy, May 3, 1806]

How pleasing, now, to range the fields,
When nature all her fragrance yields,
And when she deigns to bring,
Of vernal joys, the green-rob'd train,
Who dance, enraptur'd, o'er the plain,
Led by the charmer, SPRING.

The lambs their sprightly gambols play,
The birds awake the matin lay,
And mount upon the wing—
Convene, and, forming dulcet choirs,
Sate their chaste, innocent desires,
And hail the smiling SPRING.

Not the sweet voices of the *Nine*,[2]
Should *Orpheus* and *Apollo* join,
And each attune the string,
Could half the music yield, for me,
As, warbling from yon bush and tree,
The melody of SPRING.

Though, naked and forlorn, the trees
(Like sailors shipwreck'd on the seas)
Late felt the Winter's sting,
'Tis thine to clothe them, and to warm,
To feed them——to repel the storm—
So beautiful is SPRING.

Though modern bards, and those of yore,
Have sung thy praises o'er and o'er,
Again the Muse shall sing
Of all thy virtues, and thy pow'r
To charm the bud into a flow'r,
Thou soul-enliv'ning SPRING.

Confin'd to cities' noisy sports,
Whether in Congress, or in courts,
'Tis but a joyless thing;
Midst the dull round of pleasures stale,
The cit but seldom can inhale
The balmy breath of SPRING.

While tumults craze the heads of state,
The rich, voluptuous and the great,
    Or President, or King;
The peasant, in his homely fare,
Devoid of titles, wealth or care,
    Tastes all the sweets of SPRING.

But since the fairest flow'r must fade—
Must meet destruction all that's made,
    When death his dart shall fling,
Let us enjoy the passing hour,
Till we arrive where ev'ry flow'r
    Blooms in eternal SPRING.

FINIS.

Explanatory Notes

TITLE PAGE

1. Ray is drawing from at two least sources. The second line is taken from Samuel Foote's play *The Devil upon Two Sticks* (1778). The third line, and possibly the first, is somewhat misquoted from Laurence Sterne, *A Sentimental Journey* (1768); the original line in Sterne's account is "Disguise thyself as thou wilt, still, slavery, said I, still thou art a bitter draught."

EXORDIUM

1. At the outset of the French and Indian War in 1754, Windham, Connecticut, residents were terrified by screams in the night, which were taken for attackers. Morning revealed that the sounds had been made by an unexplained, catastrophic die-off of frogs in the local pond.

2. A journalist and editor of the Lichtfield, Connecticut, newspaper *Witness*, jailed for defaulting—out of principle—on a libel payment.

3. An early American form of bankruptcy law.

4. Ray's term for the Pasha (a political rank in the Ottoman Empire), ruler of Tripoli. In *Horrors of Slavery* "the Bashaw" refers to Yusef Qaramanli, also called Jusef or Joseph Caramanly. The "Ex-Bashaw" Ray refers to later in the narrative is Yusef's deposed brother, Hamet Qaramanli.

5. Conspirators; after the first century BCE Roman politician Lucius Sergius Catilina.

6. The word *Turk* was used beginning in the fifteenth century to describe Muslims in North Africa, referring to the Ottoman Empire's long occupation of the region.

CHAPTER I — INTRODUCTORY REMARKS

1. From Jefferson's fifth State of the Nation address, 1805; spoken in reference to the liberation of the captives in Tripoli.

2. Jonathan Cowdery was ship's doctor aboard the *Philadelphia*; his short narrative, *American Captives in Tripoli; or, Dr. Cowdery's Journal in Miniature; Kept During His Late Captivity in Tripoli*, was published in 1806.

CHAPTER II — COMMENCEMENT OF SERVICE

1. Spoken by Cassius in an Act 4, Scene 3, confrontation with Brutus in Shakespeare's *Julius Caesar*.

2. Robert Treat Paine, Jr., "Song. To Arms, Columbia!"; Paine (no relation to Thomas) was an early nineteenth-century poet and editor whose father was a signer of the Declaration of Independence.

3. Forcibly recruited into British naval service.
4. Alexander Pope, *Essay on Man*, Epistle IV.
5. A member of a press-gang, especially one using trickery.

CHAPTER III — A SKETCH OF BIOGRAPHY

1. Pope, *Essay on Man*, Epistle IV.
2. John Hancock, "Oration on the Anniversary of the Boston Massacre of 1770."
3. Aaron Burr, vice president under Jefferson (1801–1805). Ray refers here to Burr's treason trial in 1807 for conspiracy to seize western Spanish and U.S. lands; he was acquitted. One of the witnesses testifying against Burr in his conspiracy trial was General William Eaton, whose successful march on Derna would become a key event in the closing months of the Tripolitan War.
4. Thomas Chatterton was a mid-eighteenth-century English poet who committed suicide at age seventeen.
5. Jonathan Swift, the eminent Irish satirist.
6. A shrewish wife, after Xanthippe, wife of Socrates.
7. Cat o' nine tails, a whip with multiple tails for inflicting maximum injury.

CHAPTER V — EMBARKATION—CELEBRATION OF INDEPENDENCE—EXEMPLARY PUNISHMENT, &C.

1. John Hancock, "Oration on the Boston Massacre," 1774.
2. Greek mythological creature with one hundred arms and fifty hands.
3. Early American political party advocating a strong central government; George Washington and John Adams were Federalists. William Ray was a Republican, or Democratic-Republican, the party of Thomas Jefferson and James Madison.

CHAPTER VI — A VOYAGE

1. Daniel Mendoza, an English Jew who was a champion boxer in the eighteenth century.
2. Religious hermit.
3. Probably a reference to David Porter, lieutenant on the *Philadelphia*. Ray calls him "Lt. P." later in the narrative; Porter went on to become a naval hero in the War of 1812.
4. Edward Preble, commodore of the U.S. Mediterranean squadron, 1803–1804.
5. Lieutenant Stephen Decatur, who would set fire to the captured *Philadelphia*, thus preventing the Tripolitans from recommissioning the ship; a hero of the Tripolitan War.
6. William Bainbridge, captain of the *Philadelphia*.
7. Ray paraphrases Cicero's oration against Verres, substituting "American" for the original "Roman"; a speech common to early American schoolbooks and oratory anthologies.

CHAPTER VII — EXERCISING SHIP

1. Richard Morris, commodore of the U.S. Mediterranean squadron, 1802–1803; he would be attacked by Ray (and by General William Eaton) for his lack of aggression.
2. A common, pidgin language spoken throughout the Mediterranean; used for trade, it incorporated elements of French, Arabic, Italian, Greek, and Spanish.

CHAPTER VIII — REMARKS ON DR. COWDERY'S JOURNAL

1. Peter Lyle, also called Lysle, a Scotsman and former captive who had converted to Islam to serve the Bashaw. His Muslim name was Morad Raiz, or Admiral Morad.
2. A form of torture by which the victim was strung up by the ankles and whipped on the soles of the feet.
3. A reference to the Bashaw, who had deposed his brother Hamet.

4. John Wilson, the first American captive to "turn Turk." As an overseer, he treated his former shipmates harshly.
5. Assistant to the ship's doctor.
6. Assistant or servant.

CHAPTER IX — A PETITION

1. Drinking alcohol.
2. Ray had been granted an exemption by the Bashaw at the urging of the Danish consul Nicholas Nissen, whom Ray assisted as a copyist.

CHAPTER X — COMMODORE PREBLE'S ENGAGEMENT WITH THE TRIPOLITANS

1. Thomas Truxtun or Truxton; an American naval hero of the Revolutionary War and the Quasi-War with France.
2. Samuel Barron, commodore of the U.S. Mediterranean squadron, 1804–1805; he had difficulty fulfilling his duties as commodore due to a liver disease.
3. Brother of Stephen Decatur.

CHAPTER XI — ELEGY

1. From "I'd Rather Stay with You," a song by Charles Dibdin, popular composer of sea chanteys.
2. Turkish term for a military or political leader.
3. Tobias Lear, consul general to Tripoli, who orchestrated the treaty that ended the Tripolitan War. He was vilified by Ray and others for this settlement, which seemed to waste Eaton's efforts in Derna.
4. From Pope's "The Temple of Fame."
5. A member of a third-party coalition of Democratic-Republicans and Federalists; Ray condemned Quidism in his later newspaper writing.

CHAPTER XII — DESCRIPTION OF THE PLACE

1. Benedict Arnold, known for his treasonous actions during the Revolutionary War.
2. Dr. Joseph Warren, head of the Massachusetts revolutionary government, who died at the Battle of Bunker Hill while volunteering as a private.
3. Ottoman term for the ruler of Tunis.
4. Beggars.
5. Prison.
6. William Eaton, former consul and U.S. Army captain, whose actions during the Tripolitan War are described (and defended) by Ray in Chapters XIV and XV. Eaton marched with eleven Americans and four hundred mercenaries across five hundred miles of desert to take the city of Derna, east of Tripoli. He was later outraged that the United States reneged on its promise to reinstate Hamet Qaramanli as Tripolitan Bashaw; Eaton clashed with Jefferson and others after his return to America.
7. From Thomas Shaw, *Travels, Or Observations, Relating to Several Parts of Barbary and the Levant* (1738).

CHAPTER XIII — MANNERS, CUSTOMS, &C. OF THE TRIPOLITANS

1. An Islamic judge; also spelled "qadi."
2. A scholar.
3. Ritual bathing.
4. Adapted from the Quran.

CHAPTER XIV — PUBLIC TRANSACTIONS OF THE UNITED STATES WITH THE REGENCY OF TRIPOLI; INCLUDING GENERAL EATON'S EXPEDITION

1. A reference to the rallying call "millions for defense, not one cent for tribute!"; coined by Jefferson during the XYZ affair, it was used during the Barbary crises as well.
2. Spartan king who defeated a far superior Persian force with only three hundred men.
3. Ottoman term for the ruler of Algiers.
4. James Leander Cathcart, eleven years a captive in Algiers in the late eighteenth century, became consul to the region after his redemption.
5. George Washington died December 14, 1799.
6. Leon Farfara, Jewish financial agent to the Bashaw.
7. The Arabic word for sea captain.
8. One of the Bashaw's officials.
9. Tunisian court official.
10. Abbreviation for *instant*, in or of the present month.
11. Modern-day Croatians.
12. Capital of the Ottoman Empire, which had nominal rule over North Africa.
13. Abbreviation for *ultimo*, in or of the past month.
14. Treasurer.
15. Captain John Rodgers replaced Barron as commodore of the U.S. squadron, 1805–1806.

CHAPTER XV — SKETCH OF GENERAL EATON'S EXPEDITION

1. Senators John Randolph and Henry Clay questioned whether Eaton's victory in Derna was sufficient cause to award him a Congressional Medal of Honor.
2. Likely references to Joseph Warren and Richard Montgomery, Revolutionary War heroes.

POETRY

1. Theme song of the Anacreontic Club of London, a social society; the song, written by John Stafford Smith with lyrics by Ralph Tomlinson, was popular in America.
2. The Muses.

Further Reading

WILLIAM RAY'S PUBLISHED WORKS

The American Tars in Tripolitan Slavery. In *The Magazine of History with Notes and Queries. Extra Numbers—No. 13–16*. New York: William Abbatt, 1911. 255–550.

Horrors of Slavery; or, The American Tars in Tripoli. Containing an Account of the Loss and Capture of the United States Frigate Philadelphia; Treatment and Sufferings of the Prisoners; Description of the Place; Manners, Customs, &c. of the Tripolitans; Public Transactions of the United States with That Regency, Including Gen. Eaton's Expedition; Interspersed with Interesting Remarks, Anecdotes, and Poetry, on Various Subjects. / Written During Upwards of Nineteen Months' Imprisonment and Vassalage among the Turks. Troy: Oliver Lyon, 1808.

Poems, on Various Subjects, Religious, Moral, Sentimental and Humorous. To which is added, a brief sketch of the author's life, and of his captivity and sufferings among the Turks and barbarians of Tripoli, on the coast of Africa—written by himself. Auburn, N.Y.: U. F. Doubleday, 1821.

Poems, on Various Subjects, Religious, Moral, Sentimental and Humorous. To which is added, a brief sketch of the author's life, and of his captivity and sufferings among the Turks and barbarians of Tripoli, with a description of the country, and the manners and customs of the inhabitants. New York: Printed for the author, 1826.

[Walpole, Walter, Esq.; attributed to William Ray] *Sophia; or, The Girl of the Pine Woods: A Tale, Founded Principally on Fact. To which are added, a few select poems, by William Ray.* Geneva, N.Y.: H. Leavenworth, 1823.

[Attributed to William Ray]. *Sophia, or The Girl of the Pine Woods. To which is added Lafitte, or The Barratarian chief: an American tale.* Dansville, N.Y.: A. Stevens, 1838.

[Attributed to William Ray]. *Sophia, or The Girl of the Pine Woods; and The Golden Eagle.* Paterson, N.J.: David Burnett, 1834.

The Trials, Wonderful Escapes, and Final Deliverance of Miss Sophia Thompson: Founded on facts. [Boston]: Evan's Power Press, 1836.

BARBARY NARRATIVES

Adams, Robert, and S. Cock. *The Narrative of Robert Adams, an American Sailor, Who Was Wrecked on the Western Coast of Africa, in the Year 1810, Was Detained Three Years in*

Slavery by the Arabs of the Great Desert, and Resided Several Months in the City of Tombuctoo. With a Map, Notes and an Appendix. Boston: Wells and Lilly, 1817.

"American." *Humanity in Algiers, or, the Story of Azem.* Troy: R. Moffit, 1801.

Carey, Mathew. *A Short Account of Algiers, and of Its Several Wars against Spain, France, England, Holland, Venice, and Other Powers of Europe, from the Usurpation of Barbarossa and the Invasion of the Emperor Charles V to the Present Time. With a Concise View of the Origin of the Rupture between Algiers and the United States. To Which Is Added, a Copious Appendix, Containing Letters from Captains Penrose, M'shane, and Sundry Other American Captives, with a Description of the Treatment Those Prisoners Experience.* 2nd ed. Philadelphia: Carey, 1794.

Cathcart, James L., and Jane Bancker Newkirk. *Tripoli. First War with the United States.* LaPorte, Ind.: Herald Print, 1901.

Cathcart, James Leander. *The Captives: Eleven Years a Prisoner in Algiers.* La Porte, Ind.: Herald, 1899.

Cochelet, Charles, and R. Phillips. *Narrative of the Shipwreck of the Sophia on the 30th of May, 1819, on the Western Coast of Africa, and of the Captivity of a Part of the Crew in the Desert of Sahara with Engravings.* London: Sir Richard Phillips, 1822.

Cowdery, Dr. [Jonathan]. *American Captives in Tripoli; or, Dr. Cowdery's Journal in Miniature; Kept During His Late Captivity in Tripoli.* Boston: Belcher & Armstrong, 1806.

Foss, John. *A Journal of the Captivity and Sufferings of John Foss; Several Years a Prisoner at Algiers: Together with Some Account of the Treatment of Christian Slaves When Sick:—and Observations on the Manners and Customs of the Algerines.* Newburyport, Mass.: Angier March, 1798.

Paddock, Judah. *A Narrative of the Shipwreck of the Ship Oswego, on the Coast of South Barbary, and of the Sufferings of the Master and the Crew While in Bondage among the Arabs; Interspersed with Numerous Remarks Upon the Country and Its Inhabitants, and Concerning the Peculiar Perils of That Coast.* New York: Collins & Co., 1818.

Pitts, Joseph. *Narrative of the Captivity of Joseph Pitts, among the Algerines, and of His Fortunate Escape from the Mahometans.* Frederick-Town: Hardt and Cross, 1815.

Riley, James. *An Authentic Narrative of the Loss of the American Brig Commerce, Wrecked on the Western Coast of Africa, in the Month of August, 1815. With an Account of the Sufferings of Her Surviving Officers and Crew, Who Were Enslaved by the Wandering Arabs on the Great African Desert, or Zahahrah; and Observations Historical, Geographical, &C. Made During the Travels of the Author, While a Slave to the Arabs, and in the Empire of Morocco.* New York: Collins & Co., 1818.

Robbins, Archibald. *A Journal, Comprising an Account of the Loss of the Brig Commerce,: of Hartford, (Con.) James Riley, master, upon the western coast of Africa, August 28th, 1815; also of the slavery and sufferings of the author and the rest of the crew, upon the desert of Zahara, in the years 1815, 1816, 1817; with accounts of the manners, customs, and habits of the wandering Arabs; also, a brief historical and geographical view of the continent of Africa.* Hartford: F. D. Bolles, 1817.

Rowson, Susanna. *Slaves in Algiers; or, A Struggle for Freedom. A Play, Interspersed with Songs, in Three Acts.* Philadelphia: Wrigley and Berriman, 1794.

Sumner, Charles. *White Slavery in the Barbary States.* Boston: J. P. Jewett and Company, 1853.

Tyler, Royall. *The Algerine Captive; or, The Life and Adventures of Doctor Updike Underhill, Six Years a Prisoner among the Algerines.* Walpole, N.H., 1797.

About the Editor

Hester Blum is an assistant professor of English at the Pennsylvania State University. She is the author of *The View from the Masthead: Maritime Imagination and Antebellum American Sea Narratives* (University of North Carolina Press, 2008).

www.ingramcontent.com/pod-product-compliance
Lightning Source LLC
LaVergne TN
LVHW050427260826
846286LV00001B/27
* 9 7 8 0 8 1 3 5 4 4 1 3 7 *